Alaska Railroad:
History Through the Miles

Barton Jennings

Alaska Railroad: History Through the Miles
Copyright © 2017 by Barton Jennings

All rights reserved. This book may not be duplicated or transmitted in any way, or stored in an information retrieval system, without the express written consent of the publisher, except in the form of brief excerpts or quotations for the purpose of review. Making copies of this book, or any portion, for any purpose other than your own, is a violation of United States copyright laws. "Alaska Railroad" and "ARR" are trademarks of the Alaska Railroad Corporation and are used with permission.

Publisher's Cataloging-in-Publication Data
Jennings, Barton

Alaska Railroad: History Through the Miles
284p.; 21cm.
ISBN: 978-0-9849866-6-8

Library of Congress Control Number: 2017900719

First Edition
135798642

Front cover photo by Barton Jennings
Back cover photo by Sarah Jennings

Please send corrections or comments to sarah@techscribes.com

TechScribes, Inc.
PO Box 620
Avon, IL 61415
www.techscribes.com

Printed in the United States of America

for Sarah, my ever-patient wife

Photo by Sarah Jennings.

Contents

Preface 7
Acknowledgments 9

Part 1 – Route Guides for the Alaska Railroad 11
The Route Guides 13
Anchorage to Seward *Coastal Classic* & *Glacier Discovery* 15
Anchorage to Fairbanks *Denali Star* & *Hurricane Turn* 55
Palmer Branch (A Branch) 139
Suntrana Branch (D Branch) 147
Whittier Division (F Branch) 151
Eielson Branch (G Branch) 165
Fairbanks International Airport Branch (H Branch) 179
Anchorage International Airport Branch (J Branch) 183
Valdez Spur 187

Part 2 – Other Information on Alaska and the ARR 189
Alaska – The Basics 191
Alaska Gold Rushes 195
History of the Alaska Railroad 197
Railroad Operations 203
Proposed Railroad Changes and Expansion in Alaska 217
Alaska Railroad Anchorage Terminal 223
Railfanning Anchorage, Alaska 229
Railfanning Fairbanks, Alaska 233
Other Alaska Railroads 237
Fairbanks Pioneer Park 247
Tanana Valley Railroad Museum 255
Museum of Alaska Transportation and Industry 261
Engine 557 Restoration Company 265
The Wildlife of Alaska 269
For More Information 281
About the Author 283

Map courtesy of Alaska Tour & Travel. Used with permission.

Preface

Each year, hundreds of thousands of visitors head to Alaska, and many of them plan to include the Alaska Railroad in their journeys. This guide is not designed to be a complete history of the Alaska Railroad (ARR), but instead provide a great deal of information for those who like to ask "where are we and what once happened here?" Additionally, information is provided about the railroad's equipment, future plans, and some of the related activities that a rail enthusiast might find interesting.

This material was created from years of research and notes taken while riding the passenger trains of the Alaska Railroad. Each ride over the railroad unveils something new, so there is no way that this book can include everything. However, for most people interested in the railroad, it is hoped that something new will be presented. For those riding the trains for their first time, it is hoped that this book will answer the many questions that often come up.

For more than 100 years, the Alaska Railroad and its predecessors have been operating passenger trains in Alaska. With the physical completion of the railroad in 1923, when the Mears bridge over the Tanana River at Nenana was completed in February, passenger service began from the coast at Seward up through Anchorage and on to Fairbanks. The railroad expanded further in World War II with the construction of the lines to Whittier, and from Fairbanks to Eielson Air Force Base. The passenger trains operated by the Alaska Railroad cover almost the entire railroad, providing passengers some of the greatest views available anywhere. Each year almost 500,000 people ride one of these trains to enjoy the views or to simply travel between communities.

The railroad is not just a passenger carrier. In 2015, the Alaska Railroad moved 4.29 million tons of freight, 22,000 cargo-filled trailers and containers, and 37,500 hopper and tank cars. This means that any journey across the railroad will also in-

Alaska Railroad: History Through the Miles

clude a glimpse of the company's freight business. Much of this business is also noted in this book, especially when the freight business directly impacts the railroad's operations.

This book is organized into two parts. Part 1 contains the Route Guides, which provide commentary on and background information about the passing scenery. Part 2 contains other information that may be of interest to passengers in general and railfans in particular. I hope that you enjoy your visit.

Acknowledgments

Many employees of the railroad have shared their stories, and local rail enthusiasts have also provided hints about the history of the line. The website *John's Alaska Railroad* is one of the premier sources of historic information and should be the first stop for anyone wanting to explore the history and current changes of the railroad. Additionally, many unique sources of information about the railroad's route are available to researchers. Documents of the Geographic Names Information System of the United States Geological Survey, and the *Dictionary of Alaska Place Names* by Donald J. Orth (a free Google e-book), are great resources about the many names of communities, streams, and places found along the railroad. Another source is *Geology of the Alaska Railroad Region* by Stephen Reid Capps. This book is also a free Google e-book, although copies of the 1940 book from the U.S. Government Printing Office can still be found.

An exceptional source of information about the building of the Alaska Railroad is the *Alaska Railroad Record*. An "Official Publication of the Alaskan Engineering Commission," the weekly reports describe in detail what was happening as the railroad was being built, including changes in operating patterns and the completion of major projects. As the documents state: "The purpose of the *Alaska Railroad Record* is to furnish each week in a concise form current information concerning the operation and construction of the Government railway system in Alaska." Copies are very hard to find, but some volumes are available free through Google.

There are numerous other sources available, including modern books and historical reports. It is hoped that this book, or some of these sources, are able to answer any of the questions that you might have.

A big thanks also goes out to the managers and employees of the Alaska Railroad. Over the years, the railroad has been an excellent host to my many visits, and everyone there has been

Alaska Railroad: History Through the Miles

more than willing to share what they know. The same can be said for many residents along the line who have also shared their stories, often over a delicious cinnamon roll.

Thanks go to all of these people and more who made this book possible.

Part 1

Route Guides for the Alaska Railroad

ARR 4324 at Denali. Photo by Barton Jennings.

The Route Guides

Because the Alaska Railroad operates passenger trains over almost its entire system, this book will provide information about all routes that the railroad owns. This includes the major passenger train routes, as well as the branches and routes which seldom, if ever, see a passenger train.

All of the route guides start at Anchorage, the origin of all regular Alaska Railroad passenger service, except for the Fairbanks to Anchorage *Denali Star*, and the *Hurricane Turn* operated out of Talkeetna. Both of these trains cover the route of the Anchorage to Fairbanks *Denali Star*, so this route guide will provide information about what a passenger will see from the train.

It should be noted that this guide is not designed to be a complete history of the railroad, but instead it provides a great deal of information for those who like to ask "where are we and what once happened here?" Because of this, the guide includes information about current as well as former station locations, historic towns, and major stream crossings along the line.

Directions on this railroad will be based upon the railroad's own terminology. A train heading from Anchorage to Seward is heading south, so to the left is railroad-east, and to the right is railroad-west. Trains heading from Anchorage to Fairbanks are heading north. Because of the change in direction, and the fact that some passengers may be sitting backwards, the east and west direction will generally be used for the direction to look from the train.

Note that every station and bridge location is identified by a milepost location, shown as a number in the left-hand column of the following route guides. Railroads identify locations along their routes by mileposts, much like highways do. For the Alaska Railroad, the mileposts date back to the construction of the railroad, and their distance is from the former passenger station at Seward. There are signs every mile along the railroad that identify this distance, so watch for them if you wish.

Alaska Railroad: History Through the Miles

Photo by Sarah Jennings.

Photo by Barton Jennings.

Alaska Division –
Anchorage to Seward
Coastal Classic & *Glacier Discovery*

114.3   ANCHORAGE – The name Anchorage comes from Knik Anchorage located just offshore. The town has had a number of names before Anchorage, including Alaska City, Brownville, Ship Creek, Port Woodrow, and Woodrow.

Perched on the Knik Arm of the Cook Inlet and framed by the Chugach Mountain Range, Anchorage began as a railroad construction base in 1913, saw a post office open in 1914, and saw boom times through both World War I and II as a military staging city. Anchorage has grown into Alaska's center for finance and industry. It is the state's largest city with more than 275,000 people. *Reader's Digest* recently named Anchorage one of "The Best Places to Raise a Family" in the U.S. Because it is protected by the Kenai Mountains, Anchorage is relatively dry, receiving only 15.9 inches of precipitation and 69 inches of snow yearly. Normally, snow is on the ground in Anchorage from October until April. The record high temperature in Anchorage is 86°F, set during June 1953. The coldest was set in February 1947 at -38°F.

Anchorage is an important community in world freight movements. Approximately 90 percent of the consumer goods for Alaska flow through either the port or the airport. The Ted Stevens Anchorage International Airport is the third busiest freight airport in the United States (behind FedEx in Memphis and UPS in Louisville) and among the top ten in the world. It has long been a refueling and freight consolidation center for flights from around the world. For passengers, there are more than 280 flights daily, handling more than 5 million passengers yearly.

For the rail enthusiast, there are plenty of interesting and historic sites around the Anchorage station. Just to the northeast of the Anchorage station is a small park with a number of historical markers. A visit here is a must for anyone interested in learning more about the development of the Ship Creek area, including the many railroad facilities. There is also a pedestrian bridge that you might want to walk across. The Ship Creek Pedestrian Bridge was originally built in 1916 as a 196-foot railroad bridge comprised of fourteen 14-foot spans. It was rebuilt in 1938 and 1956. Bridge 114.6 was removed from train service in 1987, when it was converted to pedestrian use only.

The current Anchorage station was built in 1942 for $261,000, and had the two-story wings added on in 1948. To the east of the station is the former freight house. Built in 1941, the 349-foot wood frame building was extended in 1948. The three-bay engine repair shop (230' x 320'), visible to the north, has a very interesting history, starting near Denver, Colorado. It was originally part of the Kaiser (Remington) shell plant. After World War II, the plant was closed and the building was torn down and sold off. In 1948, the building was reassembled here as the locomotive shops.

Across from the station is Alaska Railroad #1, an 0-4-0ST built by Davenport in October 1907. The 0-4-0ST means that the steam locomotive has no front or rear trucks (a set of wheels), just two axles that provide power to the rails to move the locomotive and the cars that it is hauling. The "ST" indicates that the locomotive is built with a saddle tank, meaning that the water tank wraps around the locomotive's boiler instead of riding in a tender behind the locomotive. This locomotive was originally built as narrow gauge #802 for work on the Panama Canal. In 1917, a large amount of equipment was transferred from the canal project to the Alaska Railroad Commission, and this locomotive arrived as #6. It was converted to standard gauge in 1930 and renumbered to #1.

Alaska Railroad #1, Anchorage. Photo by Barton Jennings.

Downtown at 9th Avenue and E Street in Delany Park is former Alaska Railroad #556. The plaque next to the steamer explains its history.

> *"Built in 1943 by the Baldwin Locomotive Works, Baldwin, Pennsylvania, thousands of the United States Railroad Association Consolidation 2-8-0 Type Locomotives were assembled in America for war service in England, Europe and Asia. Outnumbering other war-time railroad engines, they were simple to maintain with the close clearance required for the narrow bridges and tunnels on European railroads. They were stripped down for war action, and acquired the nick-*

name "Gypsy Rose Lee" locomotives after the famous burlesque dancer."

"Instead of being shipped to Europe, twelve of these locomotives were sent to Alaska by the U.S. Army to become Alaska Railroad Class 550. All twelve locomotives saw service over the 460 miles of the Alaska Railroad. For 13 years, No. 556 hauled passengers and freight from Seward through Anchorage and on to Fairbanks. In 1959, No. 556 was taken out of storage and moved to its present location, where it has been an education display and object of play for three generations of Anchorage youngsters."

"Of the thousands of U.S.R.A. Consolidation Type Locomotives originally built for war service, only three remain in North America. After service on the Alaska Railroad, several of the locomotives were shipped to Spain and are reported to still be in operation."

To the south of the station, up on the hillside, is downtown Anchorage. Fourth Avenue is a popular street to walk as it is lined with a number of interesting tourist attractions. This is the area to buy native art, souvenirs, or just about anything to send back home.

To the north of the station is the port area. Stacks of containers can be seen here. Also look for the massive fuel tanks in this area. Daily unit tank trains deliver various fuel products to this tank farm from the refineries at North Pole, Alaska. The park near C Street and the overpass to the east are both great train watching locations.

113.9 **CP1140** – This is the south end of the split between the freight main and the passenger main. The passenger main goes by the station (through freights use it, too)

Alaska Division – Anchorage to Seward

while the freight main loops through the yards. To compass north (railroad west) is South Yard Lead, off which the Northland intermodal lead and the Flint Hills loop track split.

"CP" means "Control Point," a term used in Centralized Traffic Control (CTC) signaling systems. Basically it means that the signals are controlled directly by the railroad's dispatchers, and the train crews are required to obey the instructions provided by the signals. CTC signaling exists on the Alaska Railroad from just south of Anchorage to north of Wasilla.

112.8 **CHESTER CREEK** – Chester Creek, named in 1906, is a major drainage system in downtown Anchorage. A series of parks have been built along it forming a greenbelt of more than six miles that is rated as a must-see for tourists and locals alike. Moose are a common user of the Chester Creek greenbelt and trail system.

110.7 **CP1107** – This is a new junction that serves as the north airport branch connection and the north end of Coastal Siding. **For details on the railroad branch to the Anchorage airport, please check out the Anchorage International Airport Branch route guide, found on page 183 of this book.** A limited number of passenger trains operate over this branchline, generally trains operated for various cruise ship lines taking tourists to and from their flights.

110.2 **CP1102** – This is the south airport lead connection, another part of the major track work that has taken place through Anchorage.

110.0 **SPENARD** – Nearby Lakes Spenard and Hood are one of the largest float plane bases in the world. This area was named for Joseph A. Spenard in 1916. Spenard was an early Anchorage settler and businessman. There was a post office located here 1949-1953.

Alaska Railroad: History Through the Miles

109.9 KEYSTONE – This is in the middle of an industrial area with one of the largest concentrations of rail shippers on the railroad. A 700-foot long spur was here during the early 1980s.

109.7 CONROCK – Known also as Wilder Loop, this is a spur to the west that is used for unloading rock trains. The line makes a full loop at the end of the line so trains can simply pass through, unload, and head back north for more rock.

109.5 CP1095 – Once known as Barrett, this location is now a crossover on the new double track. A crossover is a set of track and switches that allows a train to cross over from one track to another. They are often used to allow a train to pass a slower train, or to change tracks to pass a local freight train serving customers.

109.3 CAMPBELL – A one-time section house location named in 1918, Campbell is named for Campbell Creek. Campbell was also a flag stop on the railroad – if you wanted the train to stop and pick you up, you simply waved a flag at the engineer. To the east are the Chugach Mountains.

The new trackage between the south end of the former Campbell siding (milepost 109.1) and the north end of the former Turnagain siding was placed in service during June 2003. This was part of a project to double track the line through the Anchorage area. In this particular area, the new tracks will allow the railroad to keep all the gravel trains over on the old (west) track to serve the many area customers, and keep the new (east) track open for passenger trains.

108.8 GOTTSTEIN – Gottstein is a fairly common name in Alaska business communities. The leading food and drug retailer in Alaska is Carr-Gottstein Foods Company. In addition to the retail stores operated by

Alaska Division – Anchorage to Seward

Carr-Gottstein, the company also owns freight operations, which includes a 105,000 square foot warehouse and cross-docking facility in Tacoma, Washington, and a warehouse and distribution center in Anchorage, the only facility of its kind in Alaska. The company was formed in 1986 by the merger of J.B. Gottstein & Co., a retail grocery and wholesale grocery distributor founded in 1915, and Carrs Quality Centers, an Alaska grocery store company founded about 1950.

108.4 **ALAGCO** – We cross Campbell Creek here. ALAGCO was the Alaska Aggregate Corporation but is now known as QAP (Quality Asphalt Paving). The facility is served from a siding to the west.

108.0 **COASTAL** – Coastal is a 27,742-foot long siding. Long ago, there was only a small spur near here.

107.2 **CP1072** – This is another new crossover track, built after the track through here was double tracked. This crossover is designed to allow freight trains to serve customers and run around their consists.

106.2 **TURNAGAIN** – Turnagain was once a long siding between mileposts 108.2 and 105.8. It was named for nearby Turnagain Arm. This location is today marked by the Anchorage Sand & Gravel facility.

Turnagain Arm was named by William Bligh of HMS Bounty fame. At the time, Bligh served as Captain Cook's Sailing Master on his 3rd and final voyage, with the aim to discover the Northwest Passage. Hunting for the Passage, Bligh was of the opinion that Turnagain Arm was the mouth of a river and not the opening to the Northwest Passage. However, Cook ordered a full search of the area. Upon this party's return, Bligh's frustration led him to name the bay the disingenuous name "Turn Again," thus Turnagain Arm.

ARR 4011 at Turnagain. Photo by Barton Jennings.

105.1 **CP1051** – CP 1051 is the south end of Coastal Siding. The track was extended to this location during the summer of 2003 as a part of the Anchorage double track project. A sawmill was once here.

Between Anchorage, Whittier, and Seward is some of the most rugged country in Alaska, one covered by snow much of the year and glaciers all of the time. This area includes glaciers both above and below the train as it winds along ledges and crawls through mountain passes.

103.5 **RABBIT CREEK** – There are more than a dozen official Rabbit Creeks in Alaska. The railroad bridges Rabbit Creek while passing through Potter Marsh, created when railroad grade construction dammed several creeks. Today, Potter Marsh is part of the Anchorage Coastal Wildlife Refuge and is a favorite location to spot arctic tern, Canada geese, trumpeter swans, and many other species of birds. Also watch for moose which typically graze throughout the area. By the way, the average adult moose eats about 50 pounds of fresh branches and twigs daily.

To the west you can now clearly see the Turnagain Arm of Cook Inlet. The railroad operates alongside the water until about Portage.

100.6 **POTTER** – The historic Potter section house (named for nearby Potter Creek) and Potter Marsh Wildlife Viewing Area mark the junction of Cook Inlet and Turnagain Arm, so named when Captain Cook's search (1778) up the arm for the Northwest Passage ended when he had to "turn again." Watch for the bore tide, a huge wall of water rushing into or out of the arm during tide changes. Turnagain Arm is one of only about 60 bodies of water worldwide to exhibit a tidal bore. The bore may be more than six feet high and travels at 15 miles per hour on high spring tides. Turnagain Arm sees the largest tidal range in United States, with a mean of 30 feet, and the fourth highest in the world.

The 1950 Turnagain Arm Alaska Railroad relocation started here and went south to milepost 88.1 at Indian Creek. There is a 2179-foot siding to the east at Potter.

Look to the east at Potter and you will see the Potter Section House State Historic Site, consisting of a former Alaska Railroad section house (built in 1929), rotary snowplow X-900212, and a troop sleeper/kitchen car. During the summer, volunteers often maintain a railroad garden here in the tradition of railroad workers.

Rotary snowplow X-900212 at Potter. Photo by Sarah Jennings.

95.5 **BELUGA POINT** – Beluga Point is named after the Beluga whales that are often seen in Turnagain Arm near here. Beluga whales are unique in that they are the only all-white whales. Additionally, due to the food sources here, the Cook Inlet Beluga whale is a genetically distinct and geographically isolated stock.

As already mentioned, Cook's crew originally came up with the name Turnagain for the area. However, they called it Turnagain River. Captain Vancouver resurveyed the area in 1794 and changed the name to Turnagain Arm.

93.2 **RAINBOW** – Rainbow is named for Rainbow Creek, which flows into Turnagain Arm from the Suicide Peaks to the northeast. The Suicide Peaks got their name because they looked so terrifying that, according to the early railroad workers who spied them from the tent city of Anchorage, you'd have to be suicidal to try to climb them.

Close by are Hope and Sunrise gold mining districts which were founded in 1895. According to an information sign near here, gold was discovered about

Alaska Division – Anchorage to Seward

1890 by Alexander King on Resurrection Creek, across Turnagain Arm to the south. The mining area took its name from Percy Hope, a 17-year-old miner working a claim in the area. Hope was one of the largest towns in Alaska while it boomed – 1895 to 1898 – with more than 700 gold seekers. Hope shrank when Sunrise City boomed nearby as a supply base for the gold rush on Sixmile Creek, eight miles to the east of Hope opposite of Bird Point. Today there are only several dozen residents, most of which still maintain active mines.

The Alaska Engineering Commission once had a railway construction camp, dock and warehouse at Rainbow Creek, along Turnagain Arm. Later, Rainbow was a flagstop and section house location. There is a short siding to the west.

To the east, watch for Dall Sheep on cliffs above the railroad and highway. A good way to know they are up there is to look for clusters of parked cars along the highway. Wildlife photographers are very common through this area.

88.7 **INDIAN** – Home of local craftsmen and artisans, Indian offers a panoramic view of Turnagain Arm and the Kenai and Chugach mountains. Indianhouse Mountain, 4300-feet high, is to the north. Indian Valley Mine National Historic Site is located here. Indian Valley Mine represents early mining and settlement activity on the more sparsely settled north side of Turnagain Arm during the years 1920-1939, after the Alaska gold rush era of 1896-1908. Peter R. Strong developed the mine. He came to Southcentral Alaska in 1889 and mined at different camps in the area. Strong was one of the relatively small number of "98ers" who stayed in Alaska after the gold rush. He developed one of the few lode mines on the north side of Turnagain Arm that operated for any significant length of time.

Indian was first listed as a flagstop in 1922 and was named for nearby Indian Creek. The railroad had a sawmill and an icehouse here in 1920. Today, there is a 4822-foot siding to the west. The old Indian section house still exists as the back part of the Indian House Roadhouse.

The railroad is working on plans to replace three culverts on nearby Indian Creek at milepost MP 88.1.

86.6 **BIRD CREEK** – Bird Creek is a popular fishing stream for silver salmon. The railroad crosses the creek using six 14-foot timber spans and an 80-foot through plate girder. There are a large number of trails in this area, as this is the center of access to Chugach State Park, "the third largest state park in America – a half-million acres of some of the most accessible hiking, skiing, camping, wildlife viewing, snowmachining, rafting, and climbing in Alaska." Chugach State Park basically wraps around the east and south side of Anchorage and the railroad will be in the park from here to almost Girdwood.

81.7 **BROOKMAN** – Brookman is a 2511-foot siding to the west. We are entering "Avalanche Alley," a 9-mile area of winter danger. Both the highway and the railroad have recently been rebuilt to try to move them away from the avalanche danger. According to a plaque here, *"This monument is dedicated to Mr. Brookman and the men and women of the Alaska Railroad and Alaska Department of Transportation who work on the front line each winter keeping Alaska's railroad and highways safe for the traveling public. While working to clear 2 avalanches that had closed the railroad and highway east of this site, Mr. Brookman from the Alaska Railroad and 2 co-workers from the Department of Transportation were engulfed by a third avalanche. Mr. Brookman died on February 1, 2000, from injuries sustained in this tragic incident. His co-workers survived."*

81.0 **BIRD POINT** – Bird Point is named for the flood of raptors and other birds seen here during spring. Many

Alaska Division – Anchorage to Seward

of the birds follow the passes to the south and Bird Point forms a narrow part of Turnagain Arm, thus concentrating many of the birds into this area.

Bird Point is also one of several favorite viewing locations of the large tidal bores for which Turnagain Arm is famous. A tidal bore is a wave generated by a sudden influx of water rushing into an estuary following low tide. The prime ingredient for a tidal bore is a coastal tide range in excess of twelve feet. Turnagain Arm's extreme tides are over 39 feet, reportedly the second largest range in the world after the Bay of Fundy in Nova Scotia. The length of Turnagain Arm contributes to the large wave height, as the "slosh" or resonance of the water flowing into the relatively shallow arm coincides almost exactly with the nearly twelve-hour frequency of tidal movement. The largest wave occurs during the periods of lowest tides. After low tide in Anchorage, the tidal bore should reach Bird Point 2¼ hours later.

80.8 **SEWARD HIGHWAY** – The railroad passes under the Seward Highway as a part of the recent reroute of both transportation systems. The first portion of the Seward Highway was completed in 1923, and the highway was finished on October 9, 1951. The entire highway was paved in 1952. It became a U.S. Forest Service scenic byway in 1989 and was designated as an All-American Road in 2000. The highway stretches from Anchorage south to Seward, with the route from Anchorage to the Sterling Highway junction being Alaska Highway #1, then AK-9 south on to Seward.

75.9 **GIRDWOOD SNOWSHED** – This historic snowshed doesn't exist today, but for many years, it was a major feature of the Alaska Railroad. Snowsheds were built to protect the railroad from snowslides, and this was a major one. The "big" snowshed was completed during the week of November 8, 1919. Reports indicate that two streams were rerouted as part of the project. The *Alaska*

Railroad Record of December 9, 1919 stated: "Doors on snowshed Mile 75.9 are kept in closed position and will be opened by sectionmen for trains to pass. Engineers will approach this snowshed expecting to find doors closed."

On April 28, 1920, a snowslide just north of here took the lives of three section men who were cleaning up a slide from the previous day. This is just one example of the problems that the railroad faced each winter, and helps explain why years later the railroad and highway moved further to the west.

74.5 **GIRDWOOD** – Girdwood is the site of Alaska's finest ski resort, with the related condominiums, chalets, a hotel and restaurants, all located at the base of Mount Alyeska.

Girdwood was originally named Glacier City, and was founded as a gold mining town at the turn of the century with several gold claims being staked on Crow Creek, Virgin Creek, and California Creek. As the number of miners increased, a supply camp developed that also supplied a trail stop on the route between Seward and Ship Creek (Anchorage). In 1901, James Girdwood, an Irish immigrant and linen merchant, made four gold claims on Crow Creek. His business and mining success led the community to name itself after him. A post office opened here in 1907 as Girdwood, confirming the name.

Construction of the railroad spurred a boom in Girdwood as the railroad made the local businesses more profitable. Mining in the upper Crow Creek area continued into the late 1930s when mine closures by a World War II presidential order made Girdwood a near ghost town. In 1954, eleven local men formed the Alyeska Ski Corporation with the idea of creating a first-class ski resort. In 1960, a secondhand chair lift from France was acquired and installed at the resort. Then, tragedy struck. On Good Friday in 1964, an earthquake

Alaska Division – Anchorage to Seward

with a magnitude of 9.2 dropped the coastal edges along the Turnagain Arm eight to ten feet. Consequently, the townsite of Girdwood moved 2½ miles up the valley to the present location. Three years later, the resort was sold to Alaska Airlines. The Nugget Inn, the original hotel, was built and a second chair lift was constructed on the upper mountain. In October 1980, Seibu Corporation purchased Alyeska Resort and invested heavily in its development. Seibu built a new high-speed quad chair, a fixed quad and a 60-passenger aerial tramway. Today, Girdwood consists of a diverse population of outdoor enthusiasts, local businesses, services and Anchorage commuters. Girdwood has become a year-round attraction and outdoor center.

For the railroad, Girdwood is a frequent passenger stop due to the tour activity here. However, the station area is little more than a parking lot and a covered platform. Additionally, there is a frequently used passing siding (1855 feet long) to the east.

74.3   **GLACIER CREEK** – Look for the 80-foot through plate girder bridge. Glacier Creek gets its name from the many glaciers in the mountains to the north and east.

70.7   **KERN CREEK** – Kern Creek drains several small glaciers on the mountains to the east. Lately, a few crazy kayakers have been floating, or maybe more properly, sliding down the 600-foot drop to the east. Kern Creek received its name from prospectors, with the name first recorded by Lieutenant Herron in 1899.

Lieutenant Joseph S. Herron led a mapping and photography team along much of the route of the Alaska Railroad at the end of the 1800s. His team included several native guides, and he named a number of locations based upon the recognized Indian name, spelled phonetically. Herron Glacier, located in Denali National Park and Preserve, is named after him.

70.5 **KERN** – Kern is a former flag stop on the railroad, named after Kern Creek. Kern Creek Station was listed as a flagstop as early as 1912. The Alaska Northern Railway built to here by the end of 1910.

68.4 **PETERSON CREEK** – That's Blueberry Hill to the southeast as we cross the 60-foot through plate girder bridge. Lieutenant Herron confirmed the name of this stream in his 1899 report.

64.7 **TWENTY MILE RIVER** – Twenty Mile River reaches into the Chugach Mountains to reach Twenty Mile Glacier. The river is just south of Blueberry Hill and north of Beglich Peak and flows through a large marshy area which is a favorite fishing and bird watching area. The seven 70-foot deck truss spans that the railroad uses is a favorite photo spot for railfans.

For those interested in bridges, here is an explanation of some of the terms. To start with, a truss bridge uses a structure of connected bridge parts to form triangular units to carry the load of the bridge. This is one of the oldest types of modern bridges, is easy to design, and is efficient in the use of materials. When the track is on top of the truss the bridge is called a deck truss. When the truss is above and below the track and is connected in both places, it is known as a through truss since you pass through the bridge. Some truss bridges have the truss stick above the tracks but they don't connect the tops of each truss together. This design is known as a pony truss or half-through truss.

Twenty Mile River flows into Turnagain Arm and was named in 1898. There was a station stop here in 1913.

64.2 **PORTAGE** – Portage got its name by being on the portage route from the Gulf of Alaska to Cook Inlet. However, today you have to look close to find Portage. Mostly, you will see a few collapsed buildings and lots of

Alaska Division – Anchorage to Seward

dead trees. Devastated by the1964 earthquake, the old town of Portage is all but gone. Dead trees stand in silent testimony to the power of the quake (the second largest recorded in the world), which flooded the town and dropped the surrounding land 10 to 12 feet. The Alaska Railroad suffered greatly from this catastrophe. The rails in the region were torn from their ties and buckled. In one area, water covered the rails during high tide. When the water receded, the tracks were cleared and rebuilt, and the railroad resumed operations.

At one time, Portage was a motor vehicle loading area for the Alaska Railroad. Cars and trucks, along with passengers, were hauled from here to Whittier for connections to the Alaska Marine Highway. This procedure ended when the Whittier tunnel was rebuilt for both rail and highway traffic. Today, there is a small yard here along with an office building. The north leg wye switch is at milepost 64.3 while the south leg switch is at 63.8. The current passenger station at Portage is just north of the north leg wye switch.

Because passenger trains take different routes around the wye at Portage, this area has had CTC signaling installed so that trains do not have to stop to allow their crew to manually line the switches.

For those riding the *Glacier Discovery*, **the train heads east from here on the Whittier Division, and then back to here before it heads on south. Details about the Whittier Division are found on page 151 of this book.**

63.4 **PORTAGE RIVER** – This bridge consists of six I-beam spans. The Portage River drains Portage Lake, which was created by the Portage Glacier.

Portage Glacier is considered by some to be Alaska's most visited tourist attraction. The Begich-Boggs Visitor Center provides information on the Portage Glacier area. Portage Glacier was a local name first recorded in 1898 by Thomas Corwin Mendenhall of the U.S. Coast and Geodetic Survey, so called because it is on a portage route between Prince William Sound and Turnagain Arm.

The glacier has been receding for a number of years. In the last few years the glacier face has begun retreating from the lake it created. A small section in the center has exposed bedrock but much of the glacier face is still in the water and extends down more than 100 feet into Portage Lake. Portage Glacier is still considered a valley glacier. Nearby are several hanging glaciers, that is glaciers that come part way down a mountainside. Glaciers that reach the sea are called tidewater glaciers and glaciers that end in lakes are called freshwater glaciers. Portage Lake was created behind the terminal moraine of Portage Glacier as it began receding.

Portage Glacier. Photo by Barton Jennings.

63.0 **PORTAGE RIVER** – The railroad crosses two channels of the Portage River here, this being the smaller of the two. This bridge is made up of five I-beam spans. Technically we now exit Anchorage, which is the size of Delaware.

To the west is the Alaska Wildlife Conservation Center (AWCC), "a nonprofit organization dedicated to preserving Alaska's wildlife through conservation, public education, and quality animal care. AWCC takes in injured and orphaned animals year-round and provides spacious enclosures and quality animal care. Animals that cannot be released into the wild are given a permanent home at the center." Since its founding in 1993 as the for-profit Big Game Alaska, more than 3 million people have visited the wildlife center. In 1999, the center became a 501(c)3 non-profit organization with the public name of Alaska Wildlife Conservation Center (AWCC). The name was officially changed to Alaska Wildlife Conservation Center in 2007.

Visitors to the Alaska Wildlife Conservation Center can drive around the facility, or walk much of the park. The 170-acre facility provides a unique opportunity to see and photograph many Alaskan animals including brown (grizzly) and black bears, coyotes (look for them in the bear enclosures where they keep up their scavenging skills), moose, elk, musk ox, wood bison, Sitka deer, caribou, lynx, and porcupine. All of the large mammals are in enclosures covering acres of land, allowing them to wander in their natural habitat. The AWCC continues to expand and is building new enclosures to provide better viewing of the animals.

AWCC is involved in some major wildlife restoration projects. In addition to its efforts to heal and release injured animals, the facility is an active participant in restoring the wood bison back into the wilds of Alaska. Jointly sponsored by the Alaska Department of Fish & Game and other conservation groups, this effort is underway and 130 bison have already been released as the herd at AWCC has grown quickly over the past decade. Gone from the wild of Alaska for almost 100 years, the restoration of the wood bison, the largest land mammal in North America, has been underway since 2003. In November of that year, the Yukon Territory donated a herd to the AWCC, the only wood bison herd in the United States. The first wood bison calves born in the state of Alaska in over 100 years were born at AWCC in 2005. The herd has continued to expand through natural birth and via further donations from Canada. In 2012, almost 40 calves were born to the herd.

Just south of the bridge at the Portage Glacier Road grade crossing is the new Portage maintenance-of-way base.

Wild wood bison in the Yukon Territory. Photo by Sarah Jennings.

59.9 GLACIER CREEK – Glacier Creek drains several glaciers that are located to the west of Portage Glacier. The bridge includes twelve 15-foot wooden spans.

59.4 SKOOKUM CREEK – Skookum Creek is a noted salmon stream. A new bridge was built over Skookum Creek Drainage in 2011. Work to further stabilize the railroad grade in this area continues.

58.7 LUEBNER LAKE – Luebner Lake, named in 1957, is to the east and this twelve span wood trestle crosses the lake's drainage channel. There are plans to build a small station platform near here to allow summer hikers to access this part of the Chugach National Forest. The Na-

Alaska Division – Anchorage to Seward

tional Forest Service describes this area as "the centerpiece of a large, wide open, wildlife filled wetland area fed by the nearby glaciers and creeks."

55.8 **SPENCER** – Spencer is a 3054-foot siding to the west, named after a former railroad employee who seems to have everything in the area named after him. This was a flagstop by 1913. That is Tincan Peak immediately to the west. Tincan is one of the most popular areas for backcountry skiing due to its access from the Seward Highway. Spencer is one of six locations between Portage and Moose Pass getting new passenger shelters, toilets and interpretive displays. You can see the new complex to the east. This is part of a plan to provide local service during the summer for hikers and possibly winter for skiers. The plan includes purchasing self-propelled DMUs (passenger cars) that will operate out of Portage seasonally. The railroad has historically had a gravel pit at Spencer.

The Spencer facility was completed in late summer 2007, the first one built. A trail has been built from here to Spencer Glacier. Construction on the Grandview site began in 2011 and was completed in 2013 (opened in 2014). Construction of a pedestrian bridge over the nearby Placer River began in 2011 and the bridge was installed in 2012.

54.1 **PLACER RIVER** – The railroad crosses the Placer River using a 200-foot through truss bridge with three wood spans on the ends. The Placer River drains Spencer Lake, created by Spencer Glacier, as well as several small streams that flow off the smaller Bartlett glacier. Note Gun Position 8. The Alaska Railroad has its own artillery, used to blast snow to prevent major avalanches in this area. During the rebuild of the railroad in 1919-1920, there was a construction spur at this location.

Notice that the railroad begins a steep climb as it heads south. At the south end of the bridge, the railroad goes from flat track to a grade of more than 2.2%, then 3.0% south of Tunnel at milepost 51.0. Southbound the locomotives scream as they haul the trains up the hills.

53.7   **SPENCER GLACIER** – This magnificent wall of ice is less than a mile from the tracks. In 1906, Spencer, a railroad paymaster, fell into a crevasse on the glacier and died. Reportedly, he had a box of payroll with him. Neither his body nor the money were ever found.

Alaska Railroad records from late 1919 show that a snowshed existed at milepost 53.8. The snowshed protected the railroad from snowslides off the nearby mountains.

53.0   **SPENCER FLATS** – A natural wetland: watch for moose, bear and birds. This is a snowslide location, with snow coming down off the hillside to the west and down the narrow canyon. When the railroad was built, there was a snowshed at milepost 53.1 to protect the railroad from these snowslides.

The country will now immediately change as the railroad curves. Heading south, the railroad begins to follow the Placer River into a narrow gorge, climbing into the Kenai Mountains. Get your cameras ready!

52.7   **TUNNEL 52.7** – This is the first of five tunnels over the next mile, all of which help the railroad to tunnel through the eastern slope of Spencer Mountain. The tunnel is 584 feet long and is lined with shotcrete and concrete lining. In 1919, this was officially Tunnel 7.

52.6   **BRIDGE** - The railroad pops out of one tunnel and then crosses this 29-foot beam span bridge, and then back into another tunnel. Hang out on the east side and look down to the river, if you dare! By the way, the railroad has plans to replace the I-beam span.

Alaska Division – Anchorage to Seward

52.5 **TUNNEL 52.5** – This tunnel is 197 feet long. It was officially Tunnel 6 in 1919.

52.4 **TUNNEL 52.4** – This tunnel is 307 feet long and is rock lined. In 1919, this was Tunnel 5. Records show that in 1919 there was a short Tunnel 4 at milepost 52.3.

52.1 **TUNNEL 52.1** – This is the longest of the five tunnels at 955 feet long. In 1919, this was Tunnel 3. There is a short bridge over a small creek between Tunnel 52.1 and Tunnel 51.9.

51.9 **TUNNEL 51.9** – This tunnel is 310 feet long and is mostly rock lined. In 1919, this was Tunnel 2.

51.8 **PLACER RIVER** – Watch for the 133-foot deck truss plus two 14-foot wooden spans just south of the tunnel. This bridge is definitely worth fighting for a spot in a vestibule or out on the GoldStar platform. Views to the east are down into the narrow gorge of the Placer River. To the west, the river flows out of the gorge and into a wider valley.

51.1 **TUNNEL** – Tunnel was known as Tunnel Siding in 1909, taking the shorter name in 1922. It was named for the tunnels nearby and served as a camp for their construction. There was a post office here 1930-1931. A section station today, this was once headquarters for the "Loop", an engineering marvel which allowed the tracks to cross over themselves on a wooden trestle as the trains wound through the canyon. The loop bridge and route was replaced in 1951. There is a section house to the east. Also look for more of the Alaska Railroad artillery, located to the west in a tan tent facility.

This is the area of the historic **Alaska Railroad Loop**. Bernadine Prince describes the Loop in the book *The Alaska Railroad*, "A little north of Mile 48 the line passes through a tunnel of a distance of 714 feet, turning to the right on a 14 degree curve, with a total curvature of 235 degrees. Much of this turn is made on a trestle whose maximum height is 106 feet. The line continues to descend on the maximum grade, crossing various high points to Mile 54, where the foot of the heavy grade is reached. In Miles 50 and 51 a complete loop is made, the road crossing under itself." This loop was necessary due to the location of the Bartlett Glacier and the construction techniques available at the time.

A 1941 travel guide also described the loop. The report stated that "here, for over three miles, runs the famous Alaska Railroad Loop, consisting of two spirals, one of which is a complete circle, on which the track runs along the mountainside, over high bridges, trestles, and through tunnels and snow sheds, forming a complete loop over Placer River."

Over the next three decades, Bartlett Glacier receded significantly and construction techniques improved. Therefore, the Alaska Railroad decided to replace the mostly timber loop (there were five timber trestles on the loop) with a cut and fill route. The new line would allow longer and heavier trains to traverse the route and greatly reduce the track maintenance costs in this area.

Work began on the line change in late 1950 with surveyors fighting snow to locate the new line. The new line opened on November 6, 1951, and the famous Loop District between miles 47.5 and 50.8 was eliminated. A total of 1.1 miles was cut off the Seward to Anchorage run, costing the railroad $1,000,000. As Bernadine Prince states in her book, "The last rail was dropped into place at 11:06 a.m. and the final spike was driven by Colonel Johnson at approximately 11:30 a.m. Work cranes, gas cars and other equipment were shifted out of the way as freight train No. 32, an Anchorage-bound freight out of Seward, started down the new three percent grade from Grandview at 1:30 p.m. behind three puffing steam locomotives."

A result of this construction was a milepost equation due to the shorter route. Make a note that milepost 50.8 now equals milepost 49.7.

48.2 **BARTLETT GLACIER** – Named in 1907 for Frank Bartlett, Alaska Central Railroad civil engineer, the glacier is visible just 800 feet away from the tracks. Deadman's Glacier rises above.

In 1908, the Pacific Northwest Society of Engineers had a presentation entitled "Tunneling on the Alaska Central Railway and a General Description of the Alaska Central Railway with Some of the Methods Used in Locating and Constructing the Line," by G.A. Kyle, Principal Assistant Engr., Chicago, Milwaukee & St. Paul Ry. Co. The presentation included significant details about the building of the railroad and the role that Frank Bartlett played. It stated that Bartlett located much of the railroad in 1905, including the Loop and tunnel district. Bartlett is also credited with designing and supervising the construction of Tunnel #1 on the Loop, now listed on the National Register of Historic Places.

This is one of the most photographed locations on the railroad. Heading south, the railroad makes a hard right turn into a horseshoe curve, and then up a 3% grade. Approaching the curve, photos of the train passing the glacier can be made from the east side of the train. Once the train enters the horseshoe curve, photos of the train are better from the west side of the train. Passenger trains generally slow so that passengers can photograph the glacier.

Bartlett Glacier is another planned site for a summer access station.

47.6 **PLACER RIVER** – The railroad will again cross the Placer River several times as both the river and the railroad wind their way up the grade through the narrow canyons. This is a 27-foot beam span bridge, 104 feet high.

47.2 **PLACER RIVER** – We quickly cross the river again on this 60-foot deck plate girder.

46.8 **PLACER RIVER** – This is our final crossing of the Placer River, which forms on the hillside above the tracks at the north end of Grandview siding. This bridge is a 75-foot deck truss.

44.9 **GRANDVIEW** – Grandview is the southernmost stop and the turnaround point for the *Glacier Discovery Train*, a summer only passenger train that operates out of Anchorage and serves Whittier, Portage, and other area communities. Grandview is also the staging area for special winter ski-trains for cross-country skiing. There is a siding to the east at this location. The Forest Service has built a station here to provide access to the surrounding country.

Grandview is located in one of a number of narrow passes that the old Iditarod Trail used on its route between Seward and Nome. To the west is Anderson Peak, named for Paul Anderson, who was killed July 25, 1968, while working on a project to divert the waters of Ohio Creek which runs off this peak. To the east is a series of glacier-covered mountains, one of the largest collections of glaciers in the world. Just to the south of Grandview is a place called Snoring Inn. To the east is a series of waterfalls that some know as "Snow White" due to the seven smaller falls nearby.

Grandview is the top of the hill at 1063 feet. Heading south, the train starts a drop of 2.0% until Hunter, following Trail Creek down the hill. The siding at Grandview is often used to double a train up the hill, as timetables state *"all southbound trains exceeding 5,000 feet in length must double Grandview Hill, unless otherwise directed."* When a train doubles a hill, part of the train is left along the route and two trips are made to the top of the grade to get it all over the hill. The train would then be reassembled and move again as one train.

Alaska Division – Anchorage to Seward

A watchman shack was located here to provide some protection for trackmen walking the area looking for avalanches.

Grandview was listed as a station in 1908, named because it "afforded a scenic view."

44.3 **TRAIL GLACIER** – Breathtaking views of Trail Glacier, Trail Creek and Trail Canyon, all to the east. The rock and dirt in the middle of Trail Glacier is a medial moraine. According to several sources, a medial moraine is "a ridge of moraine that runs down the center of a valley floor. It forms when two glaciers meet and the debris on the edges of the adjacent valley sides join and are carried on top of the enlarged glacier. As the glacier melts or retreats, the debris is deposited and a ridge down the middle of the valley floor is created."

Trail Glacier got its name because a trail was built upon its face, since it was easier to walk the glacier than fight the brush, river, and rugged terrain down in the valley.

40.0 **HUNTER** – The railroad's 1912 station list called this Hunters, however the 1919 Alaska Railroad Guide called it Hunter. The 4527-foot long siding to the west is the bottom of the grade and was often used to double trains or to add helpers. Steam locomotives used to take water here from the large steel tank before climbing up the grade. There was a wye to the east that was used to turn helpers. For a number of years, a track maintenance gang was assigned to Hunter, and a "Mess house" also existed here.

The railroad has exited the narrow canyon country and now enters heavily wooded country.

37.0 **TRAIL CREEK** – The Alaska Railroad bridges Trail Creek (one of dozens in Alaska) on sixteen 15-foot wood spans. Trail Creek is another one of the planned station stops that will provide access to the Chugach National

Forest. The railroad has plans to rehab at least seven of the timber bridges between here and Falls Creek. The Alaska Railroad has had a program for many years to replace timber bridges with various types of steel and cement bridge types. Trail Creek heads on Trail Glacier.

33.8 **JOHNSON** – This is the location where the Johnson Pass trail, part of the original Iditarod Trail, breaks off and heads north via Johnson Creek, past Johnson Lake, and through Johnson Creek Pass. The trail then continued past Bench Lake and followed Bench Creek to the route of today's Seward Highway. This route was used when snow and avalanche conditions made the route along Trail Creek too dangerous. This location was listed as a railroad station in the 1918 Alaska Railroad Guide.

Johnson is situated at the north end of Upper Trail Lake. The railroad will run along the eastern shore of the lake to Moose Pass. Heading south, the railroad is making a turn from westbound to southbound as it circles around Lark Mountain, to the south. Lark Mountain is named for the horned lark, the only lark found in Alaska. The hillside is a favorite location for birders to see the lark.

33.0 **TRAIL CREEK** – The railroad crosses the creek again, this time using 25 15-foot wood spans.

29.3 **MOOSE PASS** – This small settlement located about where Upper Trail Lake flows into Middle Trail Lake was once a railroad section station. The community was first named in 1912 as a station on the Alaska Railroad. The name is reportedly derived from a mail carrier's team of dogs that in 1903 had considerable trouble gaining the right-of-way from a moose. A post office was established in 1928. The railroad crosses Trail Lake on a timber trestle made of 19 spans. Future plans call for the Alaska Railroad to extend their summer Glacier

Alaska Division – Anchorage to Seward

Discovery train to Moose Pass to provide access to the country north of here.

According to the official Moose Pass website, "Oscar Christensen and his partner, Mickey Natt, came by horse and dog sled to Moose Pass in 1909. They built a small log cabin, and then a log roadhouse to serve as an inn and supply house for the miners up north. The original Iditarod Trail, used to transport gold and supplies, was blazed through the area in 1910 and 1911. This small town was known for mining, logging and as a transfer point for those headed north with supplies, or south with gold. The Alaska Railroad Company built a small freight shed and receiving platform for heavy machinery in 1927."

Heading south, the railroad meets back up with the Seward Highway, now Alaska Highway 9. It will closely follow the railroad all the way to Seward. Moose Pass siding, 999 feet long, is to the west.

ARR 4324 at Moose Pass. Photo by Barton Jennings.

25.9 **LOWER TRAIL LAKE** – The last in a trio of Trail Lakes, the lower lake drains into Kenai Lake.

25.7 **TRAIL CREEK** – Look for the 24 15-foot timber spans. A 1941 travel guide states that there was a tramway and a road leading up the mountainside to the east to a gold quartz mine. The mine is probably the Crown Point Mine.

25.4 **FALLS CREEK** – The Falls Creek Mine is up near the headwaters of this stream to the east. The railroad crosses the creek on eight 15-foot timber spans. In 1906, the stream was known as False Creek. A 1910 map had it identified as Falls Creek.

24.5 **CROWN POINT** – U.S. Geological Survey agents reported a railroad station called Trail Lake Station at this site in 1912. There is a siding here to the east measuring 3707 feet long. The Crown Point Mine was on the mountainside to the northeast. At the north end of the Crown Point Siding at milepost 25.2 is a track serving a propane facility.

24.4 **PHILLIPS SPUR** – There is a short spur to the west just south of the south switch for Crown Point Siding.

23.8 **SEWARD HIGHWAY** – The railroad crosses Alaska Highway 9 at grade. The USFS Kenai Lake work center, part of Chugach National Forest, is located to the west.

23.5 **ROOSEVELT** – Roosevelt was originally located at the north end of the Ptarmigan Creek bridge. The station was named for President Theodore Roosevelt. The name came about due to the hunting and wildlife preservation history of the area.

During the several gold rushes in the area, miners relied upon local wildlife for much of their food. However, by 1905, the gold rushes were over but locals replaced the mining employment with guiding wildlife hunters. A National Park Service report states that "by 1911, one source noted that it had come to be regarded as the greatest game country in the possession of the United States. Its popularity stemmed from its accessibility, the variety of local megafauna (specifically moose, sheep, bear, and goat), and the existence of many trophy-size animals."

By 1905, construction of the Alaska Central Railroad had proceeded to the point that Seward became the primary access point to the gamelands. The Kenai Peninsula gamelands were essentially unregulated until May 1908, when Congress passed (and President Roosevelt signed) a law providing for major revisions to previous Alaska hunting laws. The new law mandated that all Alaska hunting guides be licensed and that all Kenai Peninsula sport hunters be accompanied by a licensed guide. No other Alaska hunting grounds were singled out with this requirement.

Roosevelt, a station stop on the east side of Kenai Lake, had long been a transfer point and roadhouse for hunters heading west to the game country. In 1923, Nellie Neal purchased the roadhouse. Neal, a former market hunter and cook in the railroad construction camps, soon married a Seattle electrician named William B. Lawing. The new Mrs. Lawing, hoping to cash in on the expected boom in tourist travel on the recently completed railroad, cleaned out a building that was located in the narrow strip between the lake and the railroad right-of-way. Then, according to a local news report, she "placed her entire exhibit of fine Alaskan skins and furs on exhibit." The stop, which was renamed Lawing, became increasingly well-known and thousands of Alaska tourists (and residents) stopped there during the 1920s and 1930s.

23.3   **LAWING** – Look for the building with the community name on it. The railroad begins running along the eastern shore of Kenai Lake. Lawing was listed as a station starting in 1925.

During the rebuild of the line by the Alaska Engineering Commission in 1919, there was a large gravel quarry here, used to provide ballast for the railroad from here north to near Moose Pass. Reports indicate that "Marion steam shovel No. 3" did the work.

The Marion Steam Shovel Company was established in August 1884. Its unique characteristic that differentiated it from competitors was a heavier construction, and thus the ability to move heavier loads. With the move from steam to diesel power systems, the company changed its name to the Marion Power Shovel Company in April 1946. The company was acquired by Dresser Industries in 1977.

20.2 **LAKEVIEW** – The Alaska Central Railroad construction ended here in 1904. The name Lakeview comes from the view of Kenai Lake that is available here and was used as a station name by 1927. The railroad follows Kenai Lake for the next several miles with nice views to the west.

20.0 **VICKERY CREEK** – A 1941 travel book has this listed as Vichery Creek. The railroad crosses the creek on a 123-foot long through truss span. Also known as Victor Creek, the stream starts at Mother Goose Glacier, one of a number of glaciers in the mountains to the east.

18.4 **PRIMROSE** – The Primrose campground and hiking trail are here, located on Kenai Lake. The trail leads to Lost Lake in an area of alpine tundra.

Kenai Lake forms the headwaters of the Kenai River. The lake is large (22 miles long), and stretches in a large S-shape all the way northwest to Cooper Landing. The Kenai Lake is a major attraction for fishermen as the Kenai River has all five species of Pacific salmon, and salmon overwinter in the lake. King and silver salmon are described as huge, and in 1985 a 97-pound salmon was caught on the Kenai River. Kenai Lake also is fished for rainbow trout, lake trout, and Dolly Varden, a type of char. The waters are cold with the lake being more than

540 feet deep, and it is fed by several glacial tributaries including the Snowy and Trail Rivers.

Primrose was first listed as a flag stop on the Alaska Railroad in 1919. The Seward Highway passes over the railroad at Primrose, using a man-made tunnel. The railroad will stay on the east side of the valley while the highway moves more toward the west side of the valley.

14.5   **SNOW RIVER** – This is a big river, requiring four 150-foot through truss spans plus four 30-foot beam spans to cross it. Snow River flows from the Blackstone Glacier area through the Paradise Valley, before emptying into Kenai Lake. Blackstone Glacier is one of a number of glaciers in the mountains just south of Whittier. The glacier was named by Thomas Corwin Mendenhall (one-time superintendent of the U.S. Coast and Geodetic Survey, Mendenhall was one of the surveyors responsible for determining the exact boundary line between Alaska and Canada) for a miner lost while carrying mail to Whittier in 1896. Blackstone became lost in a snowstorm and wound up cutting across the wrong mountain pass and placed him on what became Blackstone Glacier. Blackstone's body was never found, but his brother later found the mailbag on the glacier.

14.3   **SEWARD HIGHWAY** – The highway is overhead, using large culvert sections which makes it seem that the railroad passes through a tunnel. The railroad is now on the west side of the valley, and climbing grades of 2.4% as the train heads south.

12.2   **SEWARD HIGHWAY** – The railroad again is bridged by the Seward Highway, again using a modern "tunnel" instead of a more traditional bridge. This method makes the highway more stable and protects the railroad from debris thrown by the highway snow plows.

12.0 **DIVIDE** – Divide is a siding to the west, once known as Summit Station. This area has been called a small "Continental Divide" as it is at the top of railroad grades more than 2% in each direction. This is the first crossing of the Kenai Mountains at approximately 700 feet in elevation. All waters north of here to Summit (milepost 312) flow into Cook Inlet. Water to the south of here flows into Resurrection Bay near Seward.

Directly to the west is Mount Ascension at 5710 feet in elevation. To the east is Paradise Peak at 6050 feet. To the southwest are Resurrection Peaks, topping out at 4712 feet. Can you tell that someone was in a religious mood when they reached this valley?

11.4 **TUNNEL** – The *Alaska Railroad Record* (Vol. IV, No. 5, dated December 9, 1919) called this "Tunnel 0." When built, this tunnel was only 136 feet long, but it had a 426-foot snowshed on the north end and a 216-foot snowshed on the south end. The snowsheds were designed to provide additional protection from snowslides in this area.

6.9 **WOODROW** – The station of Woodrow was listed as a flagstop in 1918. A 1920 Rand McNally listing of Alaska Railroad stations showed this to be Woodrow Station. A 1912-foot long siding once existed to the west. Woodrow Wilson ordered the Alaska Engineering Commission to complete the Alaska Railroad, so it is likely that the siding was named for him.

Woodrow is located at a short level spot for the railroad. Toward Seward, the grade is between 1% and 1.7% downhill. Heading north from Woodrow, the grade is 2.2%. Early documents stated that Woodrow was to be used to release retainers on trains coming down the hill from Summit (Divide). Retainers are designed to keep brakes on even if a train runs out of air in its braking system. They are turned on and off by hand, so trains must stop to allow the train crew to adjust them.

Alaska Division – Anchorage to Seward

For northbound trains, Woodrow was used to add a helper locomotive, or to set out cars if a train was going to double the hill. When a train doubled a hill, they left part of their train along the route and made two trips to the top of the grade to get it all over the hill. The train would then be reassembled and move again as one train.

This area is considered to be a suburb of Seward. Woodrow is officially at 236 feet above sea level, although the railroad is just less than 200 feet.

6.6   **BEAR CREEK** – Look for the nine 15-foot timber spans. Bear Creek is a small stream that flows out of Bear Lake, to the east.

5.9   **SALMON CREEK** – Salmon Creek is named for, well, I guess you can come up with the answer. Salmon Creek is known for the fall Dolly Varden run. Salmon Creek starts in Bear Lake Glacier up the canyon to the east. The railroad crosses the stream using eleven 15-foot timber spans.

3.7   **WEST BRANCH SALMON RIVER** – This small bridge is the bottom of the grade that has been about one to two percent since Divide.

3.5   **SEWARD** – This is the north end of the Seward complex of tracks and its yard limits. Look for the grade crossing with Nash Road.

3.3   **MINERAL CREEK** – Another stream from the west, this one is crossed by a bridge made of an 80-foot through girder and two 33-foot I-beam spans. Mineral Creek is a very common Alaskan name.

For many years during the 1910s and 1920s, LaRochelle & Roberts operated a contract sawmill here for the railroad. Hoben & Davis were the log contractors.

3.2 **RESURRECTION RIVER** – The Resurrection River travels through a wide flood plain in this area. The railroad crosses the river using a mix of through girder and I-beam spans for a 150-foot bridge. The Harding Icefield to the west is the source for this river. Due to the heavy silt in the river, not many salmon are present. Resurrection River flows into Resurrection Bay at Seward. The name was reported by the U.S. Geological Survey (USGS) in 1904.

Mineral Creek and Resurrection River merge in this area, and the river channels under bridges 3.2 and 3.3 are shared by both streams. The names used in the route guide are based upon Alaska Railroad records.

3.0 **RESURRECTION RIVER** – Another 220-foot series of through girder and I-beam spans over the river's flood plain. Look to the west; that is Mount Benson at 4274 feet in elevation. Mount Benson was named for Bennie Benson (1913-1972) who, as a student in Seward, designed the Alaska flag in 1927. Before that, the mountain was known as Iron Mountain. To the east is 5265 feet tall Mount Alice. This mountain was named for Alice Lowell Scheffler, daughter of Captain Frank Lowell, who settled in the area during the 1880s.

2.9 **SEWARD YARD SWITCH** – This is the north end of Seward Yard and the lead to the coal and ferry docks. According to railroad documents, the yard has a capacity of 583 cars on 34,195 feet of tracks.

Passenger trains stay on the mainline and head straight to the modern Seward train station. Freight trains take the lead to the Seward Yard. East of the railyard is the Seward Airport.

2.3 **SEWARD WYE** – To the east is the Seward Yard, a small locomotive and car shop, and the line to the coal and intermodal docks.

Alaska Division – Anchorage to Seward

1.7   SEWARD STATION – The "Railhead" of the Alaska Railroad. A year-round deep-water port, Seward is the gateway to interior Alaska and is situated on Resurrection Bay's fertile, salmon and halibut-filled waters. Resurrection Bay was named in 1792 by Russian fur trader and explorer Alexander Baranof. While sailing from Kodiak to Yakutat, he found unexpected shelter in this bay from a storm. He named the bay Resurrection because it was the Russian Sunday of the Resurrection.

Seward Station. Photo by Barton Jennings.

The City of Seward was named for U.S. Secretary of State William Seward (1861-69) who orchestrated the purchase of Alaska from the Russians in 1867. Construction of a railroad at Seward was first begun in 1904 by the Alaska Central Railway. By 1960, Seward was the largest community on the Peninsula. Tsunamis generated after the 1964 earthquake destroyed the railroad terminal and killed several residents. Because of the damage, and the move of the major port facilities to their current location, the railroad was abandoned between the original depot location and the edge of town at Dock Road, milepost 1.60. Although the railroad no longer goes to the historic downtown, a number of Alaska Railroad items are still there. The original depot was built at Adams and Ballaine Streets, but was moved in 1928 after the Jefferson Street flood. Today, the building still stands and is used as part of the Alaska SeaLife Center at 4th and Railway Avenue. The former right-of-way of the Alaska Railroad is today a walking trail between the station and the new tourist part of town by the current station.

For many years former Parlor/Obs Car #5, the *Seward,* sat downtown at 3rd and Jefferson. This car was built in 1916 by Pacific Car and Foundry in Oakland, California, and acquired by the Alaska Railroad in 1935. Throughout its life it served as a Passenger Car, Club V.I.P. Car and Dining Car. It was retired from service in 1960, given to the Seward Chamber of Commerce in 1963 and used as their visitor's center. However, the car was abandoned when a new visitor center was built out near the current train station. The car was put up for sale in late 2007, and current status is unknown.

With the Alaska Railroad moving their depot and passenger trains to the north edge of town, many of the facilities which cater to the tourists the trains bring have followed the railroad. A number of hotels, restaurants, and bay tours have sprung up and the commercial docks just keep growing. Across the street from the current Alaska Railroad station is the Train Wreck, a cluster of former railroad cars used as offices, stores, and a deli. The two former military cars were once ARR 0020 (former kitchen car used as the deli) and 0037. The other two cars were built as sleepers by American Car & Foundry (ACF). Former 51 is today used as bedrooms by Whistle Stop Lodging.

To the east is the coal dock and the Alaska Railroad's intermodal dock and cruise ship port. In 2005, the Alaska Railroad Corporation Board of Directors recognized Seward resident Dale Lindsey's contributions to the Railroad and State of Alaska by naming the railroad's newly renovated **Seward Passenger Dock** the "Dale R. Lindsey Alaska Railroad Seward Dock." A former Alaska Railroad train service employee during the period of Alaska Railroad federal ownership, Lindsey also served as a member of the Alaska Railroad Board of Directors for twelve years including presiding as Vice Chair of the Board for seven of those years. Lindsey retired from the Alaska Railroad Board of Directors in 2001. His father and grandfather both worked on the Alaska Railroad and his brother Jack Lindsey was the Fairbanks Terminal Superintendent in the 1960s and 1970s.

Sign on the Seward Passenger Dock. Photo by Barton Jennings.

According to the Alaska Railroad, the railroad's Seward terminal is spread across 328 acres. Approximately 240 acres are used for railroad operations while the rest is available for lease or permit. The four major rail uses of the terminal are [1] the coal loading facility and dock (26 acres), [2] the cruise ship and passenger dock and terminal (12 acres), [3] the freight dock (35 acres), and [4] the railroad yard. Even though coal shipments are down, the freight facilities have seen a 142 percent increase in revenues since 2008. Because of this, the Alaska Railroad is in the process of expanding its freight dock in Seward to improve safety, efficiency and capacity of freight intermodal operations (ship-to-train, ship-to-truck, ship-to-barge). The current freight dock (East Dock) was built between 2000 and 2002 and is 620 feet long. Phase I of the expansion widens a portion of the dock from 200 feet to 320 feet. Later phases will widen the entire dock to 320 feet, essentially doubling the dock's 5.3 acre footprint to 10.6 acres. In 2007, the railroad placed gravel and rip rap to fill a two-thirds-acre expansion of the dock. Since 2001, the West Dock and its terminal building have been substantially improved to support intermodal passenger activity. This is the dock that many cruise ship patrons know.

The Alaska Railroad acquired the Seward Coal Loading Facility in 2003 and made subsequent improvements in order to increase facility efficiency, driving down the cost of operation, thus making Alaska's coal resources more competitive in the global market. The first phase of conveyor speed upgrades was completed in 2005. In response to community concerns over coal dust problems resulting from unusual dry, windy weather in early 2007, ARR spent $150,000 to enhance existing dust suppression and safety systems, and also hired industry experts to analyze and recommend future capital improvements as operations warrant and funding allows. The FRA provided the original $9.54 million grant, with $8.3 million spent on acquisition and associated studies and $1.24 million used for inspections, repairs and improvements. The railroad had further plans to expand the Seward Loading Facility to accommodate an increase in demand for Alaskan coal.

Seward is technically milepost 0 of the Iditarod Trail. The trail was surveyed in 1910 as a mail route between Seward and Nome. The trail, used until 1924 when it was replaced by airplanes, was 938 miles long. Today, the entire trail is a National Historic Trail.

Entrance to Anchorage Station. Photo by Sarah Jennings.

Alaska Division – Anchorage to Fairbanks
Denali Star & Hurricane Turn

114.3   **ANCHORAGE** – The name Anchorage comes from Knik Anchorage located just offshore. The town has had a number of names before Anchorage, including Alaska City, Brownville, Ship Creek, Port Woodrow, and Woodrow.

Perched on the Knik Arm of the Cook Inlet and framed by the Chugach Mountain Range, Anchorage began as a railroad construction base in 1913, saw a post office open in 1914, and saw boom times through both World War I and II as a military staging city. Anchorage has grown into Alaska's center for finance and industry. It is the state's largest city with more than 275,000 people. *Reader's Digest* recently named Anchorage one of "The Best Places to Raise a Family" in the U.S. Because it is protected by the Kenai Mountains, Anchorage is relatively dry, receiving only 15.9 inches of precipitation and 69 inches of snow yearly. Normally, snow is on the ground in Anchorage from October until April. The record high temperature in Anchorage is 86°F, set during June 1953. The coldest was set in February 1947 at -38°F.

Anchorage is an important community in world freight movements. Approximately 90 percent of the consumer goods for Alaska flow through either the port or the airport. The Ted Stevens Anchorage International Airport is the third busiest freight airport in the United States (behind FedEx in Memphis and UPS in Louisville) and among the top ten in the world. It has long been a refueling and freight consolidation center for flights from around the world. For passengers, there are more than 280 flights daily, handling more than 5 million passengers yearly.

For the rail enthusiast, there are plenty of interesting and historic sites around the Anchorage station. Just to the northeast of the Anchorage station is a small park with a number of historical markers. A visit here is a must for anyone interested in learning more about the development of the Ship Creek area, including the many railroad facilities. There is also a pedestrian bridge that you might want to walk across. The Ship Creek Pedestrian Bridge was originally built in 1916 as a 196-foot railroad bridge comprised of fourteen 14-foot spans. It was rebuilt in 1938 and 1956. Bridge 114.6 was removed from train service in 1987, when it was converted to pedestrian use only.

The current Anchorage station was built in 1942 for $261,000, and had the two-story wings added on in 1948. To the east of the station is the former freight house. Built in 1941, the 349-foot wood frame building was extended in 1948. The three-bay engine repair shop (230' x 320'), visible to the north, has a very interesting history, starting near Denver, Colorado. It was originally part of the Kaiser (Remington) shell plant. After World War II, the plant was closed and the building was torn down and sold off. In 1948, the building was reassembled here as the locomotive shops.

Across from the station is Alaska Railroad #1, an 0-4-0ST built by Davenport in October 1907. The 0-4-0ST means that the steam locomotive has no front or

Alaska Division – Anchorage to Fairbanks

rear trucks (a set of wheels), just two axles that provide power to the rails to move the locomotive and the cars that it is hauling. The "ST" indicates that the locomotive is built with a saddle tank, meaning that the water tank wraps around the locomotive's boiler instead of riding in a tender behind the locomotive. This locomotive was originally built as narrow gauge #802 for work on the Panama Canal. In 1917, a large amount of equipment was transferred from the canal project to the Alaska Railroad Commission, and this locomotive arrived as #6. It was converted to standard gauge in 1930 and re-numbered to #1.

Alaska Railroad #1, Anchorage. Photo by Barton Jennings.

Downtown at 9th Avenue and E Street in Delany Park is former Alaska Railroad #556. The plaque next to the steamer explains its history.

> "Built in 1943 by the Baldwin Locomotive Works, Baldwin, Pennsylvania, thousands of the United States Railroad Association Consolidation 2-8-0 Type Locomotives were assembled in America for war service in

England, Europe and Asia. Outnumbering other war-time railroad engines, they were simple to maintain with the close clearance required for the narrow bridges and tunnels on European railroads. They were stripped down for war action, and acquired the nickname "Gypsy Rose Lee" locomotives after the famous burlesque dancer."

"Instead of being shipped to Europe, twelve of these locomotives were sent to Alaska by the U.S. Army to become Alaska Railroad Class 550. All twelve locomotives saw service over the 460 miles of the Alaska Railroad. For 13 years, No. 556 hauled passengers and freight from Seward through Anchorage and on to Fairbanks. In 1959, No. 556 was taken out of storage and moved to its present location, where it has been an education display and object of play for three generations of Anchorage youngsters."

"Of the thousands of U.S.R.A. Consolidation Type Locomotives originally built for war service, only three remain in North America. After service on the Alaska Railroad, several of the locomotives were shipped to Spain and are reported to still be in operation."

To the south of the station, up on the hillside, is downtown Anchorage. Fourth Avenue is a popular street to walk as it is lined with a number of interesting tourist attractions. This is the area to buy native art, souvenirs, or just about anything to send back home.

To the north of the station is the port area. Stacks of containers can be seen here. Also look for the massive fuel tanks in this area. Daily unit tank trains deliver various fuel products to this tank farm from the refineries at North Pole, Alaska. The park near C Street and the

Alaska Division – Anchorage to Fairbanks

overpass to the east are both great train watching locations.

114.8 **CP1147** – This switch, located just north of the Cordova Street grade crossing, is the north end of the Anchorage station complex. The freight main heads through the yard on the north side of Ship Creek while the passenger tracks are off to the railroad-east (compass-south) by the station. At the Anchorage passenger station, several tracks exist. Passenger 1, located just east of the mainline and running between CP1147 and CP 1140, is 4096 feet long. Passenger 2 comes off of Passenger 1 and is 2760 feet long. Passenger 3, located next to the Anchorage depot, comes off of Passenger 2 and is 2334 feet long.

"CP" means "Control Point," a term used in Centralized Traffic Control (CTC) signaling systems. Basically it means that the signals are controlled directly by the railroad's dispatchers, and the train crews are required to obey the instructions provided by the signals. CTC signaling exists on the Alaska Railroad from just south of Anchorage to north of Wasilla.

115.2 **SHIP CREEK BRIDGE** – The railroad passes over Ship Creek, and the Ship Creek Trail bridges over the railroad just to the north. Ship Creek is a favorite local spot for fishing and shorebird viewing near downtown in the industrial environment of the Port of Anchorage. Two miles upstream from the mouth of the creek is the Elmendorf State Hatchery. The lake and adjacent pond provide salmon viewing in the spring and summer. King salmon are present from late May through July, and coho salmon from August through mid-September.

The Ship Creek Trail is a popular walking route as it follows the stream through a green space from downtown to the northeast. It is not unusual to see moose or even bear along the trail, especially during salmon season.

115.4 CP1154 – This control point is the south end of two tracks through the Elmendorf area, and is located just north of Whitney Road.

117.0 CP1170 – This is a new set of crossovers, part of the new CTC Elmendorf Siding heading northward to CP 1213. This is essentially a split of the mainline. The west track enters the yard here as North Main. North Main loops around the railroad west (compass north) side of the yard and becomes South Main before rejoining with the passenger tracks just south of the station. Freights typically take the west track into the yards while passenger trains typically proceed on the east track to the Anchorage station. Look for the Air Force guard gate on the east side of the train.

119.0 ELMENDORF – This is the official milepost of the 23,533-foot siding. Historically, the Elmendorf station was near milepost 117. However, there recently has been an Elmendorf sign at milepost 118. Initially Elmendorf Air Force Base was an Army Air Corps field. After World War II, the Army moved its operations to the new Fort Richardson and the Air Force assumed control of the original Fort Richardson and renamed it for Captain Hugh M. Elmendorf who was killed in an air accident on January 15, 1934. It is the largest Air Force installation in Alaska and home of the Headquarters, Alaskan Command (ALCOM), Alaskan NORAD Region (ANR), Eleventh Air Force (11th AF) and the 3rd Wing.

119.1 WHITNEY – The railroad station at Whitney was here by 1918. The rail line passes through Fort Richardson in this area. In 1996 an AWACS airplane crashed a mile north of here, just barely making it across the tracks. Much of the track through Fort Richardson was realigned and straightened during the 2003 work season. Originally, this area included some of the Alaska Rail-

Alaska Division – Anchorage to Fairbanks

road's most curvy track. Ernie Piper, railroad assistant vice president of operating safety, told the Alaska Journal of Commerce that "historically, the greatest degree of derailments has been on these curves."

Fort Richardson was named for the military pioneer explorer, Brigadier General Wilds P. Richardson, who served three tours of duty in the rugged Alaska territory between 1897 and 1917. Richardson, a native Texan and an 1884 West Point graduate, commanded troops along the Yukon River and supervised construction of Fort Egbert near Eagle, and Fort William H. Seward (Chilkoot Barracks) near Haines. As head of the War Department's Alaska Road Commission from 1905 to 1917, he was responsible for much of the surveying and building of early railroads, roads and bridges that helped the state's settlement and growth. The Valdez-Fairbanks Trail, surveyed under his direction in 1904, was later named the Richardson Highway in his honor.

Fort Richardson was built during 1940–1941 on the site of what is now Elmendorf Air Force Base. Established as the headquarters of the United States Army, Alaska (USARAK) in 1947, the post moved to its present location in 1950, Fort Richardson. The majority of USARAK combat forces are at Fort Wainwright, 300 miles to the north, with Fort Richardson as the primary support base. The post's largest military tenant is the Alaska National Guard, with facilities at Camp Carroll and Camp Denali. Fort Richardson also hosts several non-military activities, including a United States National Cemetery and a state-owned fish hatchery. The post has 3300 soldiers, as well as over 3200 family members, and employs about 1200 Army and Department of Defense civilian employees.

The fort encompasses 62,000 acres, which includes space for offices, family housing, a heliport, a drop zone suitable for airborne and air/land operations, firing ranges and other training areas. Nearby mountain ranges offer soldiers the opportunity to learn mountain/ glacier warfare and rescue techniques.

119.8 CP1198 – These are some crossovers between the siding and main line tracks, built as part of the track improvements in this area. The original railroad route through this area curved about trying to avoid the need for major excavation work. However, track improvements over the last decade have straightened the route and created a series of cuts and fills.

Just north of CP1198 is a grade crossing with Davis Highway. Further north is the Fort Richardson track, curving off to the east.

121.3 CP1213 – This is the north end of Elmendorf Siding. Through this area, it is easy to see some of the old grades for the railroad. The new route is much straighter, has more gentle curves, and passes through a number of deep cuts to avoid short but steep climbs over these low ridges.

122.9 LOOP ROAD – Note that the new bridge abutments here are built for two tracks. The new bridge was completed in October 2006. A second track to the west has been installed, but is not completed. North of here, there are a number of places where the old grade crosses the new grade.

126.0 EAGLE RIVER – This was the station for the town of Eagle River (post office opened 1961), a suburban community about 10 miles from Anchorage and about a mile to the east. Eagle River has become a popular suburb of Anchorage and has seen the recent development of the typical strip malls, gas stations, and box stores. That big mountain off to the east is Mount Magnificent.

127.6 EAGLE RIVER BRIDGE – This is a big bridge, composed of two 74-foot deck plate girder spans, two 40-

foot deck plate girders spans, and one 80-foot deck plate girder span. The Eagle River drains the Eagle Glacier basin and flows west into Cook Inlet, for about 40 miles in length. It is a popular stream for whitewater fans and the Iditarod National Historic Trail follows the river for some distance.

In 1898, the Indian name for the river was reported to be "Yuklahina", which some sources says means "Eagle River." There are three rivers officially known as Eagle River in Alaska.

128.0 REEVES – This is the south switch to the siding. According to the *John's Alaska Railroad* website, the 5748-foot siding of Reeves (located to the west) is dedicated to "the conductor who was killed in the September 20, 1994 accident where the caboose he was riding was hit by a tractor trailer. The siding was formerly known as Eagle River siding." The Alaska Railroad has been working hard to improve their track north of Anchorage. During the fall of 2004, a number of realignment projects were completed between Reeves and Anchorage and the speed limit was increased to 45 mph.

131.0 POWDER SPUR – Once known as Fire Creek Valley, there is a short spur to the east that has historically been used for explosives storage. Just north of here was once a railroad gravel pit. This area had a line change in 1957. Much of the track north of here was moved to a new route between the late 1950s and early 1980s.

136.3 BIRCHWOOD – This is the north switch to a 6163-foot siding to the east, plus a five-track yard, an LPG dock, and a lumber yard. The yard is often full of maintenance-of-way cars, retired equipment, and track material and supplies. The railroad has an office here. The Alaska Railroad routinely auctions off old equipment, and items like used ties and materials. The auctions are normally conducted at Birchwood. To the west is the Birchwood Airport.

According to several sources, a wood frame railroad station was built here in 1916. It was later moved to Willow and sold in 1963, and is today used as a private business.

North of here between miles 137.5 and 139, the railroad parallels the south shore of Knik Arm, an estuary of Cook Inlet. During the late 1960s, the railroad was moved away from Knik Arm as it was eroding the railroad grade. Cook Inlet branches into the Knik Arm and Turnagain Arm at its northern end, almost surrounding Anchorage. Directly west of here is Mount Susitna (4379 feet), sticking out above the Susitna River lowland. About milepost 139 is the location of the old town of Knik. Before the Alaska Railroad was built, Knik was the upper limits of navigation for shallow-draft vessels on Knik Arm, thus the supply center for the Willow Creek mining district.

140.8 EKLUTNA RIVER – The Eklutna River, earlier known as Eklunta Creek, starts at Eklutna Glacier, about 20 miles to the east. It flows through Eklutna Lake before passing under the railroad and flowing into the Knik Arm of Cook Inlet just west of here. The U.S. Geological Survey (USGS) showed the spelling to be Eklootna (Eklut River) in 1906.

The railroad bridge is an 80-foot through plate girder. This is getting to be prime moose country. Just south of here at milepost 140 was once a railroad ballast pit to the west.

141.8 EKLUNTA – Eklunta is named for the Eklunta Indians and is the site of their village and cemetery, as well as a Russian Orthodox Church. The Eklutna area was the site of many Athabascan Indian villages as long as 800 years ago. Russian Orthodox missionaries arrived in the 1840s. Today's residents are descendants of the Tanaina tribe and the community is known for its brightly-colored "spirit houses" in the Russian Slavic style.

Eklutna is located at the head of the Knik Arm of Cook Inlet, near the mouth of the Eklutna River, 25 miles northeast of Anchorage. Eklunta is the location of one of the state's few hydroelectric projects and the source of fresh water for Anchorage.

A railroad station was originally built here in 1918. A post office existed here 1926-1945. Today, there is a 5531-foot siding to the west. A quarry for rip-rap was once here, and old documents show a powder house here also. The railroad has plans to reduce the curvature of the mainline track and siding at this location. The project will relocate a maintenance spur track from the north end of the curve to the south, and lengthen the spur from 130 to 1000 feet.

142.3   REED – This was once a flag stop that served the nearby hydroelectric plant that supplied Anchorage and the Alaska Railroad repair shops with power. Today, this is close to the north switch of the Eklunta siding.

142.4   GLENN HIGHWAY – The railroad passes under this main highway, built to interstate highway standards. The Glenn Highway splits just north of here and heads east while the Parks Highway continues on north. Glenn Highway is the main route between Anchorage and Glennallen and on to the Alaska Highway at Tok.

This part of the Glenn Highway originated as the Palmer Road in the 1930s, built to reach the agricultural colony at Palmer. During World War II it was completed to Glennallen as part of a massive program of military road and base building that also resulted in the Alaska Highway, and connected Anchorage to the continental highway system. It is named for Captain Edwin Glenn, leader of an 1898 U.S. Army expedition to find an Alaska route to the Klondike gold fields (the eventual Richardson Highway). The highway was paved in the 1950s.

The railroad's track surface and line are difficult to maintain in this area because the area is basically silt materials. The track surface and line were badly damaged by the 1964 earthquake. The 112-foot wooden trestle (now a culvert) at milepost 142.9 was compressed and arched 8.5 inches by lateral spreading of the silt materials.

145.5 OLD GLENN HIGHWAY – The railroad passes under the Old Glenn Highway, which became a scenic roadway after the new highway was completed.

146.4 KNIK RIVER – This bridge used to consist of ten 80-foot through plate girders and four 14-foot timber spans. However, the railroad has been slowly rebuilding the bridge with a great deal of work taking place in 2004. The railroad constructed ten new concrete piers to replace the existing timber piers. Borings indicate that there is a thick layer of outwash gravel (50 to 80 feet thick) covered by another thick layer of silt in this area.

Knik is reportedly an Inupiaq term for fire (igniq). The river starts at Knik Glacier, about 25 miles to the east, and flows into the Knik Arm of Cook Inlet just to the west. As the Knik River flows under the railroad, it is basically merging with the Matanuska River. The Matanuska River has numerous channels across this delta area, and one connects with the Knik River here.

147.4 MATANUSKA RIVER FLOOD CHANNEL – The Alaska Railroad crosses this flood channel on a bridge that consists of a 123-foot pony truss and two 27-foot beam spans.

For those interested in bridges, here is an explanation of some of the terms. To start with, a truss bridge uses a structure of connected bridge parts to form triangular units to carry the load of the bridge. This is one of the oldest types of modern bridges, is easy to design, and is efficient in the use of materials. When the track is on

Alaska Division – Anchorage to Fairbanks

top of the truss the bridge is called a deck truss. When the truss is above and below the track and is connected in both places, it is known as a through truss since you pass through the bridge. Some truss bridges have the truss stick above the tracks but they don't connect the tops of each truss together. This design is known as a pony truss or half-through truss.

147.5 **MATANUSKA RIVER FLOOD CHANNEL** – The bridge is made up of five 123-foot pony trusses and two 27-foot beam spans. The bridges through here were originally all wooden trestles. However, seasonal flooding quickly damaged them and the newer steel bridges eventually replaced them, providing more clearance and strength.

Just north of here is a short spur known as Bridge Spur which allows bridge and track forces to work in the area and park their equipment close to these bridges.

148.3 **MATANUSKA RIVER** – Look for the two 125-foot through truss, two 70-foot through plate girder, and 63 14-foot timber spans. The railroad has modernized this bridge over the past decade by replacing most wood components with steel or concrete. The Matanuska River starts about 70 miles east of here with the Matanuska Glacier. This is one glacier that you can drive right to and then walk out on the ice without the need for climbing equipment. You can get to it from near Sheep Mountain, an area known for its small resorts and hills covered with Dall Sheep.

150.5 **SOUTH MATANUSKA** – This is the south switch to the Matanuska track complex, located on the east side of the mainline. The mainline is basically a new track built to bypass the Palmer Junction wye. The Palmer Branch technically begins here. **Each year in late August and early September, the Alaska Railroad operates the *Fair Train* to take people from Anchorage to the Alas-**

ka State Fair near Palmer. Details about the Palmer Branch are found on page 139 of this guide.

151.0 MATANUSKA – The current spelling of Matanuska dates from 1897. Matanuska means "people," thus the local Ahtena Indians were called "Matanuska." The term also was used to imply a route or territory between Cook Inlet and the Copper River. A railroad station was established here in 1914 and the townsite was surveyed in 1916 as a railroad junction community.

Some say that Matanuska is a corruption of Russian for "copper river." Matanuska is located at the lower end of Matanuska Valley. The Matanuska River flows down through the valley, starting at the Matanuska Glacier. The big mountain peak east of Palmer is Matanuska Peak. There is also a *Matanuska* ferry boat operating as a part of the Alaska Marine Highway. The word does seem to be somewhat popular.

The Matanuska-Susitna (or Mat-Su) valley was settled by many homesteaders as part of an experiment in the 1930s. While most soon failed and moved away, enough stayed to develop the region. Agricultural crops and natural resources sustained growth and development in the valley.

Matanuska is home to world-record vegetables and the center of agriculture for Southcentral Alaska. The valley includes Palmer and surrounding communities. The Matanuska coal mines once provided fuel for the Alaska Railroad.

151.0 PALMER JUNCTION – This is the old connection to the Palmer Branch and is now located on the old tracks closer in to Matanuska. South of here is the Matanuska Siding, 4566 feet long, off to the east.

151.5 NORTH MATANUSKA – This is the north junction with the line to Palmer. A line breaks off and heads east to Matanuska. When looked at on a map, this junction

Alaska Division – Anchorage to Fairbanks

looks like a huge wye, with each leg almost a mile long. Much of this area was rebuilt in 2003 as a part of plans to upgrade major sections of the railroad.

151.6 **GLENN HIGHWAY** – The railroad passes under the Glenn Highway (Alaska Highway 1) / Parks Highway (Alaska Highway 3) interchange. Heading north from here, the railroad starts a long climb of a 1% grade to Cottonwood Creek (milepost 158.7).

154.9 **WASILLA CREEK** – The railroad crosses the creek in the middle of a curve. Wasilla Creek forms north of Palmer, off to the northeast. There was once a gravel pit spur to the west at milepost 155.6. This area has been developing quickly with housing and small retail stores as Wasilla grows.

158.7 **COTTONWOOD CREEK** – The top of the grade is just north of this small stream, about where the railroad passes under the Palmer-Wasilla Highway. Cottonwood Creek is known for rainbow trout fishing. On the north side of the highway and on the west side of the tracks is the restoration shop for the Engine 557 Restoration Company. This group is restoring Alaska Railroad 557, the last steam locomotive to operate on the railroad. Details about the group can be found on page 265.

159.8 **WASILLA** – Wasilla is a regular passenger train stop and the station is to the west, now also serving as the local Chamber of Commerce. The station was built in 1916 and is listed on the National Register of Historic Places. Wasilla was named after the respected local Dena'ina Indian, Chief Wasilla. In the Dena'ina Athabascan Indian dialect, "Wasilla" is said to mean "breath of air." Other sources claim the Chief derived his name from the Russian language and that "Vasili" is a variation of the Russian name "William." Wasilla is world famous as being the headquarters of the famed Iditarod

Sled Dog Race and the home of Sarah Palin and about 7000 other folks.

The townsite was established in 1917 at the intersection of the Knik-Willow mining trail and the newly-constructed Alaska Railroad at an elevation of 330 feet. It was a supply base for gold and coal mining in the region through World War II.

As stated elsewhere, the Alaska Railroad has been realigning 44 miles of mainline track south of here, straightening about 70 curves between Wasilla and Anchorage. The project increased the speed that trains can safely travel. When all of the work is done, travel time between Anchorage and Wasilla is expected to drop from 90 minutes to less than an hour, making rail commuter service feasible. The project was substantially complete in 2006, except for the Knik River Bridge and straightening of curves at MP 133. The Anchorage-to-Eagle River budget was funded primarily by the U.S. Department of Defense while work north of there was primarily funded by the Federal Transit Administration.

When this work is completed, the Alaska Railroad has plans to straighten curves along the mainline track in South Wasilla, between mileposts 154 and 158. The track relocation would eliminate five at-grade crossings, reduce operational and maintenance costs, and allow for faster train speeds.

163.7 MUSEUM OF ALASKA TRANSPORTATION AND INDUSTRY – The Museum of Alaska Transportation and Industry is to the west. The collections include trains, boats, planes and trucks that were part of Alaska's transportation history. As the train passes by, you should be able to see part of the rail collection which includes ARR 1500 (F-unit), ARR 1000 (RS-1), several former U.S. Air Force Baldwin locomotives, and a large number of military and railroad passenger cars. More details about this Museum are found on page 261.

Alaska Division – Anchorage to Fairbanks

View from a Gold Star car on a northbound *Denali Star*. Photo by Barton Jennings.

164.3 PARKS HIGHWAY – The George Parks Highway, Alaska Highway 3, reportedly the widest and best maintained road in the state, passes overhead. Many people think the road is named for the Alaska parks along the route, but it is instead named for George Parks. The road opened in 1971 as the Anchorage-Fairbanks Highway but was renamed for Parks in July 1975.

George Parks (1883-1984) first came to Alaska in 1907 as a mapmaker but became a mineral examiner for the U.S. Land Office from 1908 to 1917. During World War I, Parks worked in a chemical warfare division and eventually attained the rank of captain. Upon the end of the war, he was made chief of the Land Office from 1920 to 1923, and then assistant supervisor of surveys, Public Lands for Alaska in Anchorage (1924 to 1926), where his duties included helping to lay out the emerging city of Anchorage. George Parks does have a railroad related connection to the area. On May 15, 1916, Parks was riding the Tanana Valley Railroad when the train wrecked. He was one of the twelve passengers who survived a derailment at Morino, even though the passenger car was totally destroyed.

In 1925, President Calvin Coolidge appointed Parks as Alaska's Territorial Governor and he served in that position until 1933. He then returned to service with the federal government and worked again as a mapmaker for the Bureau of Land Management until his retirement in 1949. Parks then split his time between private business and his love of the outdoors. For the next thirty years, he worked on many engineering and construction projects across the state.

164.4 **CP 1644** – This switch serves the large aggregate loading facility to the east.

165.6 **PITTMAN** – This is a former railroad passenger station built in 1918 and named after Senator Key Pittman of Nevada. In 1918, Pittman pushed through The Pittman Act, a bill ordering the U.S. Treasury to melt down silver coins and then sell the bullion for $1 an ounce to Great Britian. To replace the silver dollars, the bill also ordered the mint to buy domestic silver at $1 an ounce, above the current market value, and then mint new coins. The Act basically acted as a federal subsidy to the silver mining industry. Later (1933-1940), Pittman, who represented Nevada in the Senate as a Democrat, was the President pro tempore of the Senate, chairman of the powerful Committee on Foreign Relations, and a member of the Committee on Territories. In 1940, Pittman suffered a severe heart attack just before the election. His aides were told that death was imminent, but they announced that he was being hospitalized for exhaustion so he could still win the election. He won, but died a few days later.

There was a water station here in 1920. Today, there is a rock quarry to the east and a 6183-foot siding.

169.0 **LINE CHANGE** – This is one of many line changes that have happened along the Alaska Railroad. However, this one is a bit interesting. In 1969, this curve was reduced

Alaska Division – Anchorage to Fairbanks

from six degrees to three degrees, meaning that it is less sharp than it once was. When the original roadbed was excavated, it demonstrated some of the construction methods originally used in building the railroad. When the track was moved, an old beaver dam was found beneath the ties. Apparently, it was more solid than some of the soils in the area, or it was too difficult to remove, as the original Alaska Railroad track was just built right over the beaver dam.

173.0   **PARKS HIGHWAY** – The railroad crosses the highway on an overpass. In June 1996, Alaska's most destructive wildfire started near here. What was called the Big Lake Wildfire burned 37,500 acres and almost 450 homes and buildings valued at $8.9 million.

173.4   **CASTLE MOUNTAIN FAULT** – The railroad crosses an active fault line at this location, trending east-northeast along the Little Susitna River valley and the southern front of the Talkeetna Mountains. It is about 125 miles long and is one of many large, linear faults in Alaska.

173.5   **PORT MACKENZIE LINE WYE** – A 2007 study favored Houston (milepost 175.3) as the approximate site for the connection to the proposed Port MacKenzie line. The actual location chosen was just south of the Little Susitna River bridge. A 2011 permit allowed the railroad to extend the Houston siding and build a second bridge over the Little Susitna River as a part of the work. In late March 2013, a contract was let to start construction of the line to Port MacKenzie. This construction includes a new wye and siding on the west side of the mainline. By late 2015, the earthwork here was completed and the siding and some wye tracks installed.

Some years ago, the leaders of the Mat-Su Borough realized that the Port of Anchorage was surrounded by the city, and that there was little land to develop. Additionally, it was recognized that if the port was moved, some very expensive land would become available for commercial development. Therefore, the Borough began looking for alternative port locations that could be easily accessible by both rail and highway. A site was chosen, and the facility, known as Port MacKenzie, is now in limited service and is located almost directly across Knik Arm from the Port of Anchorage. The new port has access to deepwater, both borough and state lands are available for development, and the site is close to the Anchorage port and airport systems, if the Knik Arm Crossing bridge is built.

An important factor in this plan is the proposed Knik Arm Crossing project. The Knik Arm Crossing Project is being developed to meet the current and projected transportation needs of the Municipality of Anchorage and the Mat-Su Borough. The goal of the project is to construct a railroad and vehicle bridge of about 2 miles across Knik Arm to join the Port of Anchorage area and Port MacKenzie area. The Alaska Railroad is on record stating that this alignment would likely be their new mainline between Anchorage and Fairbanks. The Port MacKenzie to Houston alignment is a much more direct route north from Anchorage than the existing alignment (approximately 25 miles shorter) and could be expected to reduce travel times between Anchorage and Fairbanks by perhaps an hour or more.

174.3 LITTLE SUSITNA RIVER – The railroad crosses the river on an 80-foot through plate girder bridge. The current bridge was installed in 1927. Before that, the old bridge had 1652 feet of timber trestle on the south end of the bridge and 1358 feet on the north end.

The Little Susitna River often floods with disastrous results. For example, in 1971, the river cut into the grade here resulting in the roadbed collapsing under a northbound freight train and causing a serious derailment.

Alaska Division – Anchorage to Fairbanks

The Little Susitna River starts in the Talkeetna Mountains to the northeast and flows 110 miles into Upper Cook Inlet. The river is famous for its king salmon and silver salmon runs, some of the largest in Southcentral Alaska. Salmon need sandy streams to reproduce. Susitna is an Indian word for sandy river. It was shown on an 1898 U.S. Coast and Geodetic Survey (USC&GS) map.

175.3 **HOUSTON** – This was once a railroad station and section house location, named after Congressman William Cannon Houston of Tennessee, constructed in 1917. Congressman Houston was chairman of the United States House Committee on Territories 1913-1919, so the name certainly had some political importance.

A spur was constructed from here to the Athans & Jandos coal mines in 1918. The coal was used in Anchorage and also by U.S. Navy ships. There was a 2493-foot siding to the east in 2010. "Houston Siding" was first listed on a blueprint map of the Alaska Railroad in 1917. The area was homesteaded during the 1950s. In 1966, Houston became an incorporated city. Each August, Houston celebrates Founder's Day with fireworks, a barbeque, and various other events.

176.3 **COAL SPUR** – This area is at the western edge of the Matanuska coalfields in the Little Susitna mining district. In 1917, several attempts were made to develop the thin coal beds located in the benches to the east. During the early 1950s, strip mining was attempted in this area and the coal was loaded into railroad cars on a spur track at this location. However, the coal seams were too thin and the coal quality was poor, and mining ceased in 1954 and the spur track was removed.

Construction records for May 20 to August 24, 1917, noted that frozen borrow material was used to build the main line in this area. This is permafrost country.

Alaska Railroad: History Through the Miles

180.7 NANCY – Nancy Lakes State Recreational Area, a chain of lakes and streams, lies to the west. The nearby lake was shown on a 1917 Alaska Railroad survey blueprint and Nancy was listed as a station in 1919. The track here is built through a glacial moraine, causing there to be excessive water and problems with frost heaves in the track. Great lakes views exist to the west.

182.6 PARKS HIGHWAY – The highway is overhead at highway milepost 66.5. The railroad knows this location as "Whites Underpass." For the next few miles, the railroad curves between a chain of lakes.

185.7 WILLOW – Look for the grade crossing with Willow Station Road. There is a 6273-foot siding to the east. To the west is a now abandoned wye track, with its switches removed but some ties and rail still in place. A railroad section house is also located here. Willow should be bigger as it was the planned state capital of Alaska. In 1976, Alaskans selected Willow for their new state capital site. However, funding to enable the capital to move was defeated in the November 1982 election.

Historically, the Dena'ina Indians have occupied this area, living in semi-permanent villages. However, the permanent community got its start when gold was discovered on Willow Creek in 1897. Supplies and equipment were brought in by boat to Knik on the Knik Arm of Cook Inlet. From there, a 26-mile summer trail went northwest, up Cottonwood Creek, and across Bald Mountain to Willow Creek. The winter sled trail went north, crossing the present line of the Alaska Railroad at Houston, and up the west end of Bald Mountain for 30 miles. This trail, dubbed the "Double Ender Sled Trail," is still being used by skiers, hunters, backpackers and snow machine (snowmobile) enthusiasts. The sleds then followed a trail along Willow Creek in an easterly direction, now Hatcher Pass Road. The Talkeetna Trail also passed through Willow and was used by dog teams

Alaska Division – Anchorage to Fairbanks

and pack horses. Cabins to accommodate freighters and mail carriers were located at Nancy Lake, Willow and other points north. This route was the forerunner of the Parks Highway.

During construction of the Alaska Railroad, surveyors, construction crews, homesteaders and other settlers came to Willow. A railroad station house was constructed in 1920, soon followed by an enclosed water tower. During World War II, a radar warning station and airfield were built in this area. To the west is the old Willow Auxiliary Airfield, constructed during World War II on a gravel terrace of the Susitna River.

A post office opened at Willow in 1948. By 1954, Willow Creek was Alaska's largest gold mining district, with a total production approaching $18 million. The construction of the Parks Highway spurred growth in the area with today's population being about 2000. Willow serves as the official restart location for the Iditarod Trail Sled Dog Race after a ceremonial start in Anchorage (making the route 1049 miles long).

186.9   **FISHHOOK-WILLOW ROAD** – Also known as Hatcher Pass Road, the railroad crosses this road at grade. The road heads east into the Talkeetna Mountains, passes the Independence Mine State Historical Park at Hatcher Pass, and then turns south to Palmer. Operated by the Alaska Pacific Consolidation Mine Company 1938-1941, the mine site includes a number of buildings that remain from this company mine and town. The gold mine is definitely worth a visit, and the road is a great country drive through a gold mining area.

187.1   **WILLOW CREEK** – Willow Creek is a very common Alaska name. Look for the 80-foot deck plate girder bridge. Willow Creek is listed as one of the best king salmon streams in Alaska.

Just north of here at milepost 187.6 is the short bridge over Iron Creek. Iron Creek is at the bottom of grades from both directions.

190.4 **JOHNSON'S HOMESTEAD** – According to *John's Alaska Railroad*, "These historic Alaska Railroad buildings are the oldest continuously used buildings along the entire route. The log shed was built in 1914 to house horses and mules used during the railroad's construction."

190.5 **LITTLE WILLOW CREEK** – The railroad crosses an 80-foot deck plate girder. Little Willow Creek is fished for both salmon and trout and was named by 1906.

193.9 **KASHWITNA** - Kashwitna is a Tanaina Indian name reported in 1906 and adopted by area miners. However, Captain Glenn's 1898 expedition reported two Indian names: Kiswitno and Kochuitno. Kashwitna is a common name in the area with Kashwitna Lake to the south and west (where the railroad and Parks Highway briefly come together) and the Kashwitna River to the north. There was once a short 1615 foot long siding to the west at this location. The name was first used by the Alaska Railroad in 1920 in *The Alaska Railroad Guide*.

In 2010, the arrangement of tracks at Kashwitna changed. The siding to the west was abandoned and a new siding was installed to the east. This new siding measures 10,590 feet, reportedly the longest siding on the railroad.

199.0 **KASHWITNA RIVER** – The Kashwitna River starts in the Talkeetna Mountains to the east and flows to the west until joining the Susitna River. A 200-foot through truss bridge is used by the railroad to cross it. To the east is the Willow Mountain Critical Habitat Area. Located in the Talkeetna Mountain Range east of the Parks Highway between the Kashwitna River and Wil-

Alaska Division – Anchorage to Fairbanks

low Creek, the Willow Mountain Critical Habitat Area supports some of the largest concentrations of moose found anywhere in the state. Located along the western slopes of Willow Mountain, the area includes both the upper extent of mixed forest and the lower alpine zone. This characteristic broadens the range of wildlife that can survive in this area.

202.3   **WOLF** – Formerly known as Caswell, this is the site of a former section headquarters. There is a 1322-foot long siding to the east. This area now has several subdivisions, all accessed off of Hidden Hills Road.

203.3   **SHEEP CREEK** – Look for the 80-foot deck plate girder bridge. There are dozens of Alaska streams by this name.

206.2   **PARKS HIGHWAY** – The railroad crosses the highway at grade. This is milepost 91.7 on the highway.

Less than a mile north of the highway crossing is what is known as the "Dr. Seuss House." Look to the west to see it. There are several legends about this house. The structure starts with a normal house, and then almost 100 feet of odd towers built on top. The reported owner calls the building the "Goose Creek Tower," named for the nearby stream. An Anchorage attorney reportedly started building the house and tower in the late 1990s. In a television show, he stated that the exterior is basically complete, but the interior still has much to be done. He also stated that the house is an observatory, and he plans to place a telescope in the top of it. Sources report that the "tower is 185 feet high with unfinished metal decks that wrap around almost every story. It's natural wood and more than 60,000 pounds of steel." Other sources say the structure was started after a forest fire. When the trees grew, the idea of the tower started and just grew out of control. This story version says that the owners died and a new owner is trying to restore the property. Either way, it is a weird house.

207.8 GOOSE CREEK – The railroad originally crossed this stream using thirteen 14-foot long timber spans. However, in 1981, the wood trestle was replaced by a clear-span bridge with steel girders that were salvaged from another bridge. There are almost twenty Goose Creeks in Alaska. About a mile north of here look for the five former military railroad cars to the west.

209.3 MONTANA – Montana Siding (4144 feet long) is to the west. First known as Montana Creek, Montana became a small Dena'ina village about 1915 during construction of the Alaska Railroad. Montana was one of the first construction camps and later the location of a section house and water tower (built May 1920). In 1918, a spur was constructed to a coal mine in the area. It was homesteaded during the 1950s, bringing its population up to about 500.

To the west across a field at Montana is a former troop sleeper, one of many that the Alaska Railroad acquired and used as bunk cars for employees, and housing for tourists. A bit further north and to the east is a former enclosed railroad water tower. The water tower is on the 2015 Alaska Association for Historic Preservation list of the state's Ten Most Endangered Historic Properties. The "Alaska Railroad Montana Station Water Tower" has been listed several times over the years. An enclosed water tower had an external shell built around it so a stove could heat the building, keeping the water from freezing.

211.0 MONTANA CREEK – There are 16 recognized Montana Creeks in Alaska. The bridge has a warning system to alert people in the area of the approach of a train. Why all of the people? This is the location of the Montana Creek State Recreational Site.

This Montana Creek is formed by the merger of North Fork (forming on Bald Mountain to the northeast), and Middle and South Forks (both form in the

Alaska Division – Anchorage to Fairbanks

glaciers on the southeast side of Bald Mountain). None of these forks are more than a dozen miles long. Combined, the waters flow west, eventually entering into the Susitina River just west of here. In 2014, it was selected as one of "The 10 Waters to Watch" by a team of the nation's leading authorities on aquatic conservation. Sources state that this "alluvial system has high quality spawning gravels and provides critical spawning, rearing, and overwintering habitats for Chinook, coho, pink, and chum salmon." Another says that Montana Creek is "one of the more productive clear-water tributaries to the Susitna River."

214.3 **PARKS HIGHWAY** – The railroad rejoins the Parks Highway with this at-grade crossing, located at Parks Highway milepost 100.4.

215.3 **SUNSHINE** - Sunshine Depot was established in 1918, with a gravel pit being worked here in 1919 to provide material for track ballast and for bank widening. The station was moved to higher ground in 1936. A section house was once located here. Today, there is a 5823-foot siding to the west. To the east of the tracks is a small lake, known as Section House Lake.

North of the siding, the first curve was once known as "Boomer's Curve" by the Alaska Railroad. A "boomer" is a railroad employee that frequently changes the railroad that they work for. There was once a powder house for explosives on the west side of the tracks, at the north end of the curve, on the bank of Sunshine Creek.

217.5 **ANSWER CREEK** – You will find this small stream by the five 14-foot timber spans. Answer Creek starts on Bald Mountain and flows into Question Creek just west of here. Answer Creek is first shown on a 1917 Alaska Railroad map.

217.7 QUESTION CREEK – Look for several concrete box culverts. It is not clear what the question is but the answer must be Answer Creek to the south. However, Question Lake is to the east. Question Creek was first shown on a 1915 Alaska Railroad map.

221.3 FISH LAKE – This is the location of a former flag stop. The stop was for Fish Lake (named by Alaska Railroad surveyors in 1917), a small lake off to the east. To the west is the Sustina River. West of that is a series of bogs and swamps, trapped between the river and the Alaska Range.

Just south of Fish Lake, the railroad crosses Birch Creek. Birch Creek starts in the low ridges to the east and flows through Fish Lake, passes under the railroad, and flows into the Sustina River just west of here.

223.3 MCKINLEY SIDING/GRAVEL PIT – There is a new 2322-foot siding to the west, named McKinley, at the location of an old gravel pit and log loading facility. Currently, cruise ship trains unload passengers here for bus trips to nearby hotels. Many railroaders know this location as the Woodpecker Facility, or East Woodpecker. The name Woodpecker comes from Woodpecker Avenue, which connects the site with Talkeetna Spur Road to the east.

McKinley Siding is located at the top of a short but steep grade from both directions. The grade is 1% in both directions. Heading north from here for the next mile, there are some great views to the west of the Sustina River. Looking to the northwest, there can also be some great views of Denali/Mount McKinley.

225.7 TALKEETNA SPUR ROAD – This is the only road into Talkeetna. The railroad crosses it at grade just north of the Talkeetna Alaskan Lodge. Just south of here you can look to the northwest and see a number of the major peaks in Alaska. From north to south, they are Denali/

Alaska Division – Anchorage to Fairbanks

Mount McKinley (20,320 feet); Mount Hunter (14,960 feet); Mount Foraker (17,000 feet); Mount Russell (11,600 feet); and Mount Dall (9,000 feet).

226.1 TALKEETNA STATION – This is the new station built at Talkeetna to provide more room for longer passenger trains and the many tour buses that meet the train here. It can be a bit noisy at times as it is located at the end of the Talkeetna airport, where a number of charter companies fly climbers, hikers and tourists to Denali/Mount McKinley.

Talkeetna Station. Photo by Sarah Jennings.

226.7 TALKEETNA – Welcome to what legend says was the inspiration for the television show *Northern Exposure*. It is also a popular base station for assaults on Mount McKinley. The Talkeetna and Chulitna Rivers join the Susitna River at Talkeetna, an Indian word meaning "where the rivers join." Originally the site of a Tanaina Indian village, Talkeetna was established as a mining town and trading post in 1896, before either Wasilla or Anchorage existed. A gold rush to the Susitna River brought prospectors to the area, and by 1910, Talkeetna became a riverboat steamer station. According to a history of Talkeetna, "a USGS report stated that most steamboats could ascend the Susitna as far as Talkeetna. From there to Indian River shallow-draft steamers could navigate, but only during periods of high water." Problems with service on the Susitna River included low water in summer, ice in winter, and constantly moving gravel bars.

At about the same time, the Alaska Commercial Company was operating pack teams out of the Talkeetna area, having established a relay station here for their Susitna-Valdez Creek route. Costs were so high that packers from Valdez took most of the market and the Alaska Commercial Company abandoned the relay station in the early 1910s. In 1915, Talkeetna was chosen as a construction camp for the Alaska Engineering Commission and the building of the Alaska Railroad, and the community peaked near 1000 residents.

Downtown Talkeetna. Photo by Barton Jennings.

A post office opened here in 1916 and a railroad station officially opened at Talkeetna in 1920. However, World War I and the completion of the railroad in 1919 dramatically decreased the population. Several of its old log buildings are historical landmarks, and Talkeetna was placed on the National Register of Historic Places in April 1993. The railroad has a 1518-foot siding to the east. It is all uphill from here to the summit of Broad Pass. Talkeetna is at an elevation of 346 feet.

Alaska Division – Anchorage to Fairbanks

In July, the Moose Dropping Festival gives contestants a chance to see how far they can throw a moose "chip."

Heading north, the railroad is far away from highways until near Hurricane, 50 miles away. To serve this area, the Alaska Railroad runs a regular summer train – the *Hurricane Turn* – that stops anywhere that is needed.

227.1 **TALKEETNA RIVER** – The railroad crosses this river using two 200-foot through truss spans. The Talkeetna River heads at Talkeetna Glacier to the east, and flows west into the Susitna River just west of the bridge. The Talkeetna Mountains are to the north. This was the end of track by March 4, 1919.

227.9 **BILLION SLOUGH** – Old Alaska Railroad records show this as Nickolai Creek, and even as Larson's Slough. However, neither name is listed in any USGS records for this location. Billion Slough was a name recognized by the USGS by 1958. The slough actually serves as a shortcut and overflow route between the Talkeetna River and the Susitna River.

In the early 2000s, the bridge over Billion Slough was made up of eleven 14-foot spans. The railroad replaced the timber structure with a new 120-foot through plate girder bridge in 2007-2008. It was built with a pedestrian bridge on the west side as a part of the Chase Trail.

232.0 **GRAVEL PIT** – This gravel pit is shown on most topographical (topo) maps. There is an unused siding to the east. This gravel pit area is identified by the Alaska Department of Fish and Game as the Upper Susitna River freshwater fishing location. A 4-wheel drive road heads east to Wiggle Creek.

The gravel pit was in operation by 1920 as "Steamshovel No. 2, Marion 60" started working here on May 7, 1920, as reported by the *Alaska Railroad Record*.

The Marion Steam Shovel Company was established in August 1884. Its unique characteristic that differentiated it from competitors was a heavier construction, and thus the ability to move heavier loads. With the move from steam to diesel power systems, the company changed its name to the Marion Power Shovel Company in April 1946. The company was acquired by Dresser Industries in 1977.

The Marion Model 60 steam shovel was designed in 1902 and was a popular shovel for mid-to-heavy construction. This shovel had a capacity of 2½ yards and formerly worked on the Panama Canal project. It was declared surplus by the railroad by October 1928.

236.2 **CHASE** – Chase, named by the railroad by 1922, is a 6235-foot siding to the west and also a small bush community along the Susitna River. The railroad is the only access to this location, although a few snow machine (snowmobile) and ATV roads reach into the area. A section house was once located here to house workers maintaining the track through this canyon.

According to the Alaska Community Database, Chase was originally named Nanchase, taking the name from Nancy Chase. Nancy was the daughter of R.D. Chase, who was a special disbursing agent for the Alaska Engineering Commission at Anchorage.

Heading north from Chase, the railroad closely follows the Susitna River on its east bank.

241.7 **LANE CREEK** – Lane Creek starts up about fifteen miles to the northeast against the ridge in that direction. The railroad crosses it on a 60-foot through plate girder bridge. The stream was first identified on a 1915 railroad survey map.

Rail was being laid northward through this area in late June 1920. A spur was built in this area at the same time to store freight cars loaded with track materials.

Alaska Division – Anchorage to Fairbanks

242.6 LANE – Lane is another bush location with only the railroad as access. It was naturally named for nearby Lane Creek and was listed as a flagstop in 1922. In 1920, a siding was installed at Lane to allow construction and ballast trains to pass.

244.2 McKENSIE CREEK – McKensie Creek is another small stream in this marshy area. The railroad crosses it on six 14-foot wood spans. Also often spelled McKenzie, the name comes from early prospectors. The railroad still follows the Susitna River closely.

245.8 PORTER CREEK – Porter Creek isn't much and it takes only four 14-foot spans to cross it.

248.1 CURRY LOOP – Today, the Alaska Railroad is developing a 10-acre quarry site located within its Curry Reserve. The quarry will provide ballast, riprap, armor stone and other rock materials for construction and maintenance of the railroad's track. The project includes a 1½ mile truck access road. The access road was constructed in 2005 and 2006. In 2007, new facility tracks were constructed and the site prepared for mining. The facility includes an entire loop so trains can be turned as they load.

South of here at milepost 246.7 is the former Curry rock quarry. Located to the east, the old quarry involved the large granitic intrusion that rises 1200 feet above the valley floor. Reports indicate that all of the granite material in the area is of excellent quality, but the height of the granite wall creates some safety problems.

248.5 CURRY – Welcome to Dead Horse Hill, named because a team of horses ran off a cliff near here when they became frightened at seeing a bear. Today a ghost town, Curry recalls a bygone era when a rail trip from Anchorage to Fairbanks involved two days of travel and an overnight stay in a hotel. Curry served as a planned hotel stop for the train. However, Curry effectively died on Tuesday, April 9, 1957, when a fire burned the 75-room hotel to the ground, killing three people. Reportedly, "all that remained of the historic structure were smoldering ashes, two tall chimneys and a tangle of pipes." The rest of the buildings were torn down almost immediately by the railroad. Today, all that remains is a large meadow and a few interpretive sign boards.

Curry, Alaska. Photo by Barton Jennings.

Curry was founded as a maintenance-of-way section station. In 1922, A.E.C. Chairman Fredrick Mears named the station after Congressman Charles F. Curry of California. Curry was then the Chairman of the Committee on Territories and was a major supporter of the railroad in Congress. Because Curry was halfway between Seward and Fairbanks, it presented an ideal spot for travelers and rail workers to spend the night during the two-day steam train trip. Furthermore, a new stylish resort would hold the potential to draw additional passenger revenue. Billed as "a palace in the wilderness where accommodations are modern, inviting and comfortable and the cuisine of highest order," the Curry Hotel opened in 1923, standing two stories tall and con-

Alaska Division – Anchorage to Fairbanks

nected directly to the railroad by a large train platform. As the popularity of the resort grew, so did its offerings. A 537-foot long suspension footbridge across the Susitna River was built in the summer of 1924. Across the bridge, atop a 2600 foot mountain, a shelter house was erected for the benefit of tourists and others. By 1925, Curry was already becoming a very popular resort.

On July 18, 1926, the engine house and power plant at Curry were destroyed by fire caused when coal dust came in contact with the overheated stack. A rotary snowplow and one locomotive were damaged. A new engine house and power plant were built in two separate buildings. In 1926 a two-story annex 36 feet by 72 feet, connected by a 65-foot covered balcony to the hotel, was constructed, and tents erected to take care of the increased tourist business. The hotel grounds were improved by clearing and removing stumps from a small additional area in view of the hotel and a three hole golf course, a tennis court and a small swimming pool were constructed. In 1927 a chicken house, hog house and barn were built. With the Curry Hotel being turned into a resort it was proving to be one of the best attractions along the entire railroad.

A creamery was also constructed at Curry in 1927. This created a market for milk produced in the Matanuska Valley. Most of the butter was sold through hotels operated by the Alaska Railroad. In 1933, the creamery equipment was transferred to the Matanuska Experiment Station in Palmer.

The Curry engine house was again destroyed by fire in 1933. Construction of a 24 foot by 242 foot engine house took place soon thereafter. In 1935-1936, an addition was built on the hotel which connected it to the annex. The expansion added twelve rooms with private bathrooms, four private bathrooms to serve four rooms in the main hotel and six multi-bedrooms without private bathrooms.

With the construction of the McKinley Park Hotel in 1939 and faster train service later on, the popularity of Curry began to decline. However, in 1944 the railroad built employee's dormitories and in 1945 the lobby and several rooms were remodeled to permit the installation of a cocktail lounge and bar. On June 6, 1945, a hand fired locomotive-type steam boiler in the power plant exploded due to low water in the boiler. The plant building was demolished and a new similar building, 62 feet by 44 feet, was constructed as a replacement.

After World War II, the railroad also began marketing weekend excursions to Curry. These proved to be very popular so a ski slope and jumping area were cleared and a cabin built. In 1948, Army-type barracks were assembled at Curry as well as Anchorage, Healy and Fairbanks. Also that same year, the railroad began promoting a "Fisherman's Special." Fishermen could catch a train from Anchorage to Curry and back. They would leave on a Saturday, return on Sunday. Fishermen could get off any place along the line and were picked up on the return trip. However, these efforts failed to make the facility economically viable and the 1957 fire ended any hope for Curry's future. The final closing of Curry happened on December 26, 1960, when the agency at Curry was closed and moved to Talkeetna.

Each year, the Nordic Ski Association of Anchorage operates the Nordic Ski Train to Curry. The train provides access for "Alaska backcountry skiers, telemark skiers and snowshoers" to "hundreds of acres of untracked snow and the sort of virgin Alaska wilderness we all search for." The train stays at Curry during the day selling meals and providing a warm place to sit. The bar car is generally considered to be one of the most popular sports of the event.

The Alaska Railroad has looked several times at Curry as a possible tourist attraction. Years ago, a series of trails with signs explaining the history of Curry was created. Some of these still exist. A "station" of sorts is

Alaska Division – Anchorage to Fairbanks

here, a small screened shelter with a station sign on the roof stating the elevation as 546 feet. Additionally, several pieces of railroad equipment have been placed on display at Curry. In the mid-2010s, this included Alaska Railroad Rotary snowplow #3, bunkcar 1039E, caboose 1086, and a tank car.

248.7 **DEAD HORSE CREEK** – Deadhorse Creek, as it is shown on the topo maps, is a short stream that flows into the Susitna River near here. The railroad crosses the stream on eight 14-foot timber spans.

251.0 **DEADHORSE** – There is a 6758-foot siding to the west at this location, named for Deadhorse Creek.

257.7 **SHERMAN** – There is a 1447-foot siding to the west. Look for the blue house to the east marked "Sherman City Hall." A section house once stood next to the tracks. Sherman was listed as a station in the 1916 timetable.

258.3 **SHERMAN CREEK** – This bridge was replaced a number of years ago using three beam spans. The cuts in this area are a regular winter problem for the railroad. The ground has a great deal of moisture, and the walls of the cuts can easily get lined with ice. The railroad has tried many techniques, including trying to drain off the water, regular ice scrapings, rock salt, and even setting up charcoal grills to keep the water flowing.

263.2 **GOLD CREEK** – Gold Creek is a 5223-foot siding to the east and was named for the stream nearby. Between Gold Creek and Curry was the Gold Creek Mining District, an old placer mining region dating back to 1903. A section house was once located here.

In 1921, this station was called Susitna River Station by the Chamber of Commerce of Seattle, Washington. The railroad called it Gold Creek in their 1922 list of stations.

Alaska Railroad: History Through the Miles

264.1 SUSITNA RIVER – The railroad uses almost 800 feet of bridge to cross the Susitna River – a 504-foot through truss, two 70-foot through plate girders, a 60-foot through plate girder, six 14-foot timber spans, and one 10-foot timber span. The *Alaska Railroad Record* of February 10, 1920, stated: "The Alaskan Engineering Commission has awarded contract to the United States Steel Products Company for furnishing and erecting the 504 foot steel truss span over the Susitna River at Mile 264." The bridge is on the National Historic Register since the main span was once the longest single span west of the Mississippi River, and it was the first steel bridge built north of Anchorage.

The Susitna River heads in the Susitna Glacier in the Alaska Range between Mount Hess and Mount Hayes. It flows 260 miles to the southwest into Cook Inlet. Susitna first appeared on Russian maps in 1847. The name is reportedly a Tanaina Indian word meaning sandy river.

266.7 INDIAN RIVER – The Alaska Railroad crosses the Indian River four times in the next three miles. Here, the river is crossed using a 200-foot through truss span. For trains heading north, this is the beginning of a long uphill climb to Hurricane, with grades up to 1.75%.

268.4 CANYON – Founded and named about 1916, today it is a 1819-foot siding to the west, reached only by the railroad.

269.2 INDIAN RIVER – The river is again crossed, this time using a combination bridge made up of a 40-foot deck truss, a 125-foot through truss, and a 55-foot deck truss.

269.9 INDIAN RIVER – The river is crossed again using a 125-foot through truss bridge. The railroad and river are closely sharing a narrow canyon, both winding their way alongside Kesugi Ridge, which is immediately to the west. Kesugi Ridge is a 35-mile long north/south alpine

Alaska Division – Anchorage to Fairbanks

ridge bordering the Parks Highway. "Kesugi," a Tanaina Indian dialect word meaning "The Ancient One," is an appropriate description for this granite alpine ridge that dominates the eastern half of Denali State Park.

270.0 INDIAN RIVER – The Indian River is crossed using an 80-foot through plate girder. The name of this river was first reported in 1951 by the USGS.

Heading northwest, the railroad starts up a 1.75% grade that runs to near Hurricane at milepost 280. While the steep grade is not desirable, it was necessary to avoid several additional major river crossings and other construction projects. For example, early plans for the railroad showed several different alignments, including one which involved building six tunnels.

273.8 CHULITNA – Located just south of Chulitna Pass, Chulitna is a 2105-foot siding to the east where a gravel pit once operated. A grade for an old wye can be seen to the west. South of here, several line changes were made in 1968.

The railroad joins the Indian River, which comes in from the northeast, near here. The Indian name of Chulitna was first reported in 1898, and the station took the name in 1916. The gravel pit at Chulitna was used by the railroad until the 1950s. When the railroad abandoned the gravel pit, the community basically disappeared. A series of summer and winter trails still intersect at Chulitna.

Chulitna is located on a short flat stretch of track. The 1.75% grade starts again at the north switch and goes until milepost 280, except for another flat area between milepost 275 and Pass Creek.

276.3 PASS CREEK – The railroad crosses this stream on seven 14-foot timber spans. Pass Creek is a common name in Alaska. There are eighteen Pass Creek listings in the *Dictionary of Alaska Place Names*.

Alaska Railroad: History Through the Miles

279.7　PARKS HIGHWAY – This is an at-grade crossing, located near milepost 169 on the Parks Highway. This is the first public grade crossing since Talkeetna, 50 miles south of here. Notice the solar collectors used to power the crossing signals. Denali/Mount McKinley is visible to the northwest, only 46 miles from this point, the closest the railroad gets to the mountain.

281.4　HURRICANE – There is a 5976-foot siding to the east. Hurricane is a short stretch of CTC signaling, the only such section of track except for between the Anchorage and Wasilla area, and at Portage.

This station was named in 1916 after the nearby Hurricane Gulch. The railroad has a number of facilities here for their maintenance-of-way forces, including a modern section house and several storage buildings and tracks.

CTC signaling near Hurricane. Photo by Barton Jennings.

284.2　HURRICANE GULCH BRIDGE – One of the line's best photo vantage points, the bridge spans 918 feet, some 296 feet above the creek. The rail line curves to the west at the south end of the bridge, so a photo for-

Alaska Division – Anchorage to Fairbanks

ward or back can get the train with the bridge. Ready for the details? Built in 1921, it is made up of one 150-foot deck plate girder, two 120-foot deck plate girders, one 384-foot arch span, three 60-foot deck plate girders, and two 30-foot deck plate girders. It contains more than 100,000 rivets. During the mid-2010s, the bridge was heavily inspected and upgraded.

There is some disagreement about where the name Hurricane comes from. One source says that an Alaska Railroad construction crew named it in 1916. However, the USGS states that prospectors named it before the railroad arrived. Reportedly, the name comes from the strong winds that can blow through the gorge.

The stream at the bottom of the gulch flows into the Chulitna River less than a mile to the west. Heading north, the railroad drops to Honolulu and then begins to climb again all the way to Broad Pass.

View from Hurricane Gulch Bridge. Photo by Barton Jennings.

287.3 LITTLE HONOLULU CREEK – Look for the three 14-foot wooden spans. We are now in the center of the Chulitna Mining District which produced gold, copper, tin, silver, coal, and a number of other minerals. This mining lasted well into the 1930s since the district was never taken over by the larger mining companies. Even today, a number of the operations are active and worked by individuals or families. Prospectors reportedly named the stream in 1913, and the name was first published in 1919 in a USGS report.

287.7 **HONOLULU CREEK** – Honolulu Creek flows out of Honolulu Pass in the hills to the east, and runs about twenty miles until it enters the Chulitna River. The railroad uses a 150-foot through truss bridge to cross the creek. The name was reported in 1913 as coming from prospectors.

288.7 **HONOLULU** – Halfway point between Anchorage and Fairbanks, the area has a very active beaver population and dams can be seen along the tracks. There is a 5338-foot siding to the west. Reportedly, this access point to several area gold districts was named for a location where many of the miners would have rather been. It was listed in the 1922 Alaska Railroad timetable and station guide. There was once a section house and water tower located at Honolulu.

292.3 **EAST FORK CHULITNA RIVER** – This is a good-sized bridge. It is made up of one 80-foot long deck plate girder, two 50-foot deck plate girders, and two 30-foot deck plate girders. The East Fork merges with the Middle Fork to create the Chulitna River. Chulitna was first reported as its name in 1913 by the USGS. There is a small gravel pit just north of this bridge on the east side of the railroad.

297.1 **COLORADO** – Colorado was a flag stop listed in the 1922 timetable, serving an access route to once dormant gold mines that are becoming active again. To the north up Costello Creek is the Dunkle Mine. The Dunkle

Alaska Division – Anchorage to Fairbanks

Mine was a coal mine built to supply nearby gold and copper operations with coal for their boilers. Reports indicate that some of the coal was loaded on the railroad at Colorado Station. Today, it is within the Denali Park property and is listed as a hazardous location. There is a 10,074-foot siding here to the west of the mainline.

Colorado is just west of the George Parks Highway, and has become the location of a number of summer cabins. Colorado Lake is to the east. The area to the northwest is the Alaska Range, and Denali National Park. The views explain some of the interest in the Colorado Lake area.

Also to the northwest is the Golden Zone, an area of gold mines opened up by Wesley Earl Dunkle starting in 1936. Dunkle had earlier worked for Kennecott, exploring copper ore seams for them. He went independent and opened several mines before settling on the Broad Pass area to explore. He built a hydroelectric plant to power his plans, and opened or helped to open the Golden Zone Mine, Dunkle Mine, and Silver King Mine. Dunkle's timing was poor as his finances could not hang on during World War II, especially after the War Production Board ordered such mines closed. To survive, Dunkle immediately opened up a coal mine north of Golden Zone and shipped bituminous coal to the military bases in Anchorage. He even worked as a laborer in the mine to pay his bills. Dunkle died in 1957 while attempting to open additional coal mines in the area.

North of here, the railroad follows the route of the Middle Fork Chulitna River, staying just east of the stream to near Broad Pass. Be on the lookout to the east for a huge white igloo. This is Igloo City, a planned theme hotel that never opened due to engineering and building code issues.

301.6 FOURTH OF JULY CREEK – There are more than a dozen streams by this name in Alaska. This one was first shown on an Alaska Railroad map dated 1918. The stream is crossed on 56 feet of timber spans. Just south of here there is an old gravel pit to the west. This pit has been described as one of the few locations in the Broad Pass area where the gravel is clean enough to produce crushed-gravel ballast. A powder house once stood near the spur track that served it.

304.3 **BROAD PASS** – This is the southern end of the broad, treeless pass that is the lowest traveled pass in the Rocky Mountain chain from Mexico to Alaska. The railroad once had a section house at Broad Pass. There is a 7530-foot siding to the west and a wye to the east. The Alaska Railroad has plans to connect the siding at Broad Pass with the siding at Colorado, about six miles to the south.

Southbound train at Broad Pass. Photo by Barton Jennings.

Broad Pass was formed when the south branch of the Nenana Glacier moved southwest to join other glaciers in the area. Broad Pass also serves as a spillway for weather. Large low-pressure systems moving into the Gulf of Alaska bring heavy precipitation and develop strong winds north of the pass. During long periods of intense cold in the Tanana Valley, a pressure gradient develops, and cold winds spill through the pass from

Alaska Division – Anchorage to Fairbanks

the north. These winds can last for weeks and exceed 40 mph.

The northbound and southbound *Denali Star* trains often meet at Broad Pass. When this happens, the on-board crew is swapped so they can return home each evening. A unique part of the staffing of the trains on the Alaska Railroad is the number of young people, many learning about the tourism industry. Each year, about 16 students are part of a program where they get college credit at the University of Alaska Fairbanks, credit that transfers to the University of Alaska Anchorage.

Crew swap on the *Denali Star*. Photo by Sarah Jennings.

305.5 PARKS HIGHWAY – This is milepost 194.3 on the Parks Highway. This area is mostly treeless, and there are great mountain views in all directions. Much of the ground around here is covered in blueberries. Moose and caribou are commonly seen in this area.

305.7 MIDDLE FORK CHULITNA RIVER – At almost 400 feet long, the eleven I-beam spans cross this stream on a 1951 line change. You can see parts of the old grade to the east.

The Chulitna River originates between the Alaska and Talkeetna Mountain ranges. The Middle Fork forms off to the east near Caribou Pass. The Center Fork starts about 10 miles south of Caribou Pass. The Middle and East Forks of the Chulitna River are both clear and fast and are popular whitewater streams. Downstream of their confluence, the main channel becomes glacial, faster and everchanging. After 77 miles of whitewater, the Chulitna River joins the Susitna River at Talkeetna, Alaska.

310.1 **SUMMIT OF GRADE** – Look for the sign – this is the actual top of the grade at an elevation of 2363 feet above sea level.

312.5 **SUMMIT** – This location was first known as Summit Lake when it was a construction camp in 1919. It was known as Summit Broad Pass Station when the railroad opened. The summit of the Continental Divide (located two miles south of here) is at 2363 feet and is the lowest rail pass in the Rocky Mountain chain. However, Summit is the beginning of a short flat area which was truly the summit for trains fighting from the north. There is a 2867-foot siding to the west at this location, where in the 1970s was just a 40-car spur track. A section house once stood here.

Heading north, the railroad first passes Summit Lake and then Edes Lake (on the east side of Mirror Lake), all on the east side of the tracks. Summit Lake is truly at the summit of the hill as it eventually drains both into the Pacific Ocean to the south and the Bering Sea to the north. Summit Lake, the largest of several lakes in this area, used to be called Edes Lake but was renamed Summit Lake in 1927 when Edes Lake took its name. Edes Lake, located on the east side of Mirror Lake across from the Summit Airport, is almost 1.5 miles long and was named for William C. Edes, chief engineer

Alaska Division – Anchorage to Fairbanks

and chairman of the Alaskan Engineering Commission from 1914-1920.

This area has great views of the Alaska Range to the west and lakes to the east. In summer and fall, there should be a great deal of wildlife and birds here, stocking up for winter.

314.0 PARKS HIGHWAY – Recently the highway received a new bridge to pass over the railroad at this location. Known as Summit Underpass by the railroad, this is milepost 202.1 on the Parks Highway.

316.4 CANTWELL RIVER – Look for the single span deck plate girder bridge, 80 feet long. The Cantwell River drains a large swampy area in the mountains to the west and eventually flows into the Nenana River. During the early years of Alaska, the Nenana River was also known as the Cantwell River until the two were separated by name.

The Cantwell River was named in 1885 for Lieutenant John C. Cantwell, an early military explorer working for the United States Revenue Cutter Service (USRCS). The USRCS had been formed in 1790 as a part of the Treasury Department to collect customs along the coasts of the newly formed United States of America. The USRCS was THE U.S. government for many in Alaska during the late 1800s, with their ships covering the coast and inland rivers. In 1915, the USRCS was merged with other marine-related government services to become the U.S. Coast Guard.

Cantwell served for many years on the *Corwin*, commanded by Captain Michael A. Healy. One of his responsibilities was the exploration of the Kowak River. He later explored the Yukon River while commanding the *Nunivak* in 1899-1901. According to his bio, his 1902 report was declared "one of the finest books ever written about Alaska" by the explorer General Adolphus

Greely. Later is his life, Cantwell was also a key player in getting reindeer established in Alaska.

319.5 CANTWELL – Cantwell was named for the nearby Cantwell River. The earliest inhabitants of the area were nomadic Indians who trapped, hunted and fished throughout Interior Alaska. Cantwell was a small settlement and starting point of the Valdez Creek gold mining district. Today's Cantwell began as a flag stop on the Alaska Railroad in 1922. There is a 6200-foot siding to the east and the railroad has an office and locomotive barn located here at an elevation of 2190 feet. Also, here is the first of six new Section Maintenance Facilities (SMF) that the railroad is building along the line. The SMF here was completed in 2006. Other SMFs are planned for Hurricane, Talkeetna, Wasilla and Nenana. The sixth SMF was built at Portage in 2012.

Cantwell is a full-service community that provides lodging, camping, food and fuel right along the Parks Highway to the east, with much of the housing to the west of the tracks. Also to the west of the railroad is the Cantwell Airport. Almost 90 years apart, Cantwell was the setting for the filming of a movie. During the 1920s, Cantwell was used for the filming of *Lure of the Yukon*. In 2007, Cantwell was used for scenes in the movie *Into the Wild*.

Heading east out of Cantwell is the Denali Highway (Alaska Highway 8), the original road into the Denali Park region. This road, still a mix of dirt and gravel, opened in 1957 and was the only road to Denali National Park until the Parks Highway was completed in 1972. The Denali Highway goes from Cantwell east to Paxson on the Richardson Highway. Most of the highway is unpaved, 110 miles of the 135 mile road, but the drive across the mountains and the views that come with them is worth it. The road crosses Maclaren Summit, at 4,086 feet, the second highest road in Alaska. While the road is closed in winter, and little traveled during much

Alaska Division – Anchorage to Fairbanks

of the rest of the year, it can see traffic jams during the annual fall hunting season.

As the railroad continues to the north from Cantwell, it follows the Jack River. The Jack River starts in Caribou Pass, just a few miles from where the Middle Fork Chulitna River forms, and eventually flows northward into the Nenana River. It was named for W.G. Jack, a local prospector, by USGS employees Eldridge and Muldrow in 1898.

323.0 SOUTH BOUNDARY OF DENALI NATIONAL PARK – The Alaska Railroad enters Denali National Park from the south by crossing Windy Creek. Windy Creek starts to the west with many forks draining the area. One of the main forks flows out of Foggy Pass. It flows into the Jack River a few miles to the east of here. Look for the two 60-foot through girder spans.

In 1977, Alaska Railroad documents show that there was a powder house on the east side of the tracks at milepost 323.6. Further north, the Jack River will be in the canyon to the east.

325.0 McKINLEY STRAND OF DENALI FAULT – The railroad crosses this fault line at a slight angle. This large and active fault line starts in Canada, follows the crest of the Alaska Range to near here, then turns southwest and continues through Foggy Pass and down the Alaska Range toward Bristol Bay.

326.7 WINDY – There is a 5470-foot siding to the east. At one time, there was also a spur and wye track to the east at Windy. The grades can barely be made out in the woods. There was a railroad station here as early as 1922. Windy has also been known as Windy Creek and Bain Creek. It is located at the junction of Bain Creek and the Nenana River. The Jack River flows into the Nenana River just to the northeast of here.

Just to the north of Windy the rail line squeezes between Panorama Mountain to the east and an unnamed hill to the west. This is one of several main passes through the Alaska Range. For those who are interested, those are the Reindeer Hills to the southeast. At Windy, the Nenana River comes in from the east between Panorama and Reindeer Mountains, and will be to the east of the tracks.

329.6 **CLEAR CREEK** – It takes a 60-foot through girder span to cross this stream. Clear Creek was named by the Alaska Railroad in 1923. To the east is Panorama Mountain (5778 feet above sea level). The Parks Highway is squeezed between Panorama Mountain and the Nenana River.

About a mile north of here is an old gravel borrow pit on the west side of the track. A quarry for rip-rap was once located a bit farther north at milepost 331.

334.4 **CARLO** – There is a 2191-foot siding to the west. Carlo Creek is nearby and flows westward into the Nenana River from the hills to the east. The siding is named for Carlo Creek, which was named by the Alaska Railroad. To the east across the Nenana River are several cabin and resort facilities for visitors to the National Park.

340.9 **COAL TIPPLE** – There was once a spur track and coal tipple to the west at this location. The facility was built during an early attempt to develop a local coal seam.

341.7 **YANERT** – This station was named for nearby Yanert Glacier, located to the east on Mount Deborah. Recently, the glacier changed its characteristics and became a surging glacier, which differs from most glaciers in Alaska. After grinding along for decades, surging glaciers suddenly move with unexpected speed. For example, Yanert may have crept the length of a football field each year since its last surge in 1942, but during the

Alaska Division – Anchorage to Fairbanks

2001 surge the glacier was covering the same distance every day.

Yanert was first shown to be a flagstop in 1922. The name Yanert comes from Sergeant William Yanert, a member of Captain Glenn's 1898 expedition.

342.7   **OLIVER** – The site was named for former Railroad Roadmaster Thomas Oliver. There is a 6202-foot siding to the west at the top of the grade out of the Denali area.

343.7   **LAGOON** – Lagoon was once a flagstop (1920s) that allowed access to the Denali area. However, its future may be even busier than the past. The Alaska Railroad has looked at building a wye or balloon track to allow trains to turn around at Denali National Park, which is currently not possible. This need has been created by the large number of passenger trains being operated for cruise ship companies that originate in Anchorage, Whittier, and Seward. To make room for a 3000-foot balloon track, it has been proposed that the railroad exchange a small parcel of land located near Moody Tunnel for an equal sized parcel of National Park Service land near Lagoon. Such land swaps require U.S. Congressional and Alaska State Legislature approval.

347.4   **HINES CREEK STRAND DENALI FAULT** – The railroad crosses another part of the Denali Fault system.

345.1   **PARKS HIGHWAY** – The Alaska Railroad and Parks Highway (highway milepost 235.1) again meet, this time at grade. To power the crossing signals, the railroad uses both solar panels and wind generators (glow-and-blow). There are a lot of these through the Denali Park area.

346.6   **PARKS HIGHWAY** – The railroad crosses over the Parks Highway on a bridge about 210 feet long.

347.4   RILEY CREEK – This is an impressive way for northbound trains to enter the main part of Denali National Park. The railroad crosses Riley Creek using a curving bridge consisting of five 30-foot spans and seven 60-foot spans, all deck plate girders. The Riley Creek Bridge is the railroad's second highest, it was also the next to last bridge completed on the railroad.

Riley Creek Bridge. Photo by Barton Jennings.

The National Park Service states that the steel bridge looming high above Riley Creek "looks much the same as it did upon its completion in early 1922, with one exception. Gone is a wooden trestle – 400 feet long and 60 feet high – that originally connected the steel structure to the north bluff. In the 1950s, hundreds of tons of rock and earth were hauled and dumped here to extend the bluff to the edge of the first concrete and steel support. Except for increased vegetation, the view of the bridge to the south is unchanged."

"The Riley Creek Bridge, manufactured in Pennsylvania and shipped north on 24 rail cars loaded with 600 tons of steel via the Panama Canal, consisted of seven steel towers decked with 30-foot and 60-foot steel plate

Alaska Division – Anchorage to Fairbanks

girders. When finished, the creek crossing would measure 900 feet in length."

"In the first week of January 1922, despite blizzards, sub-zero cold, and limited daylight hours, workers installed the first steel "bent." Less than a month later, a steam crane crossed the bridge from south to north." Reports indicate that the track on the bridge was completed by February 5, 1922. The NPS describes the event on their website. "A few days later, with a minus 30°F wind chill, a celebratory train left Seward for Nenana, arriving on February 5. With the completion of the bridge, Camp Riley quickly emptied and soon resembled an abandoned gold camp."

Riley Creek is a 22-mile long stream that flows into the Nenana River just east of here. The stream and name were first shown on the 1921 Mount McKinley National Park Survey and it flows in from the southwest. A second stream, Hines Creek, flows in from the west. The creeks flow together almost directly below the railroad trestle. According to the National Park Service, "both streams were important to pioneer residents. Riley Creek provided access to the mountains for hunters and wood gatherers. A trail on Hines Creek led west toward the park."

The NPS also tries to explain the names of the streams. "Hines Creek was originally called Maurice, or Morris, Creek, after Maurice Morino. Because the first government use of an alternative name appears in park service communication, we can assume that the park's first Superintendent Harry Karstens changed it. He may have named it for an old friend, Frank J. Hines, who had died recently. Both Karstens and Hines had been dog team mail carriers in the early 1900s, and had connecting routes. The two likely had met earlier in Dawson City during the Klondike gold rush of 1897-98. In late May 1922, Frank Hines and his partner drowned when their canoe capsized on Birch Creek in Interior Alaska. Almost three weeks passed before searchers found Hines' body. His partner's remains were never found."

"The source of the name Riley Creek, a significant park landmark, also remains speculative. Maurice Morino was a long-time business associate of miner and entrepreneur J.E. Riley, of Fairbanks, whose nickname was "George." Riley was tough, smart, and capable, exploiting almost every gold strike in Interior Alaska, and one of the few to profit from such ventures. It appears that Riley refinanced Morino after a catastrophic bankruptcy. The next year, during the 1914 Broad Pass stampede, Morino built his first cabin on the stream that was soon named Riley Creek."

Riley Creek Bridge from stream level. Photo by Barton Jennings.

347.7 DENALI PARK STATION – After the railroad was built, a small town grew up here known as McKinley Station. It disappeared in 1932 as the park expanded, but the name remained. Until 2001, the Denali National Park Hotel stood to the west of the tracks where today's park visitor center and related facilities stand. The hotel was originally built in 1939. The National Park Service started construction but the railroad finished it. Shortly after it was completed, the U.S. Army took

Alaska Division – Anchorage to Fairbanks

possession of the facility and used it as a rest facility for troops assigned to Alaska. After a disastrous fire burned the hotel in September 1972, retired AAR sleeping cars, the new west wing which did not burn, and temporary structures were used to replace the burned hotel until it closed in the September 2001. Today, the area houses an excellent visitor center, a restaurant, and offices for park management.

ARR 4324 southbound at Denali Park Station. Photo by Barton Jennings.

The railroad has a siding to the west of the mainline, measuring 2618 feet long. It is used to serve the modern station complex at what is now called Denali Park Station. In 2014, 102,786 (about one in five) of the park's 531,315 visitors arrived by train. To handle the crowds, the Alaska Railroad built a complex of station buildings so that the cruise ship companies could each have a covered waiting area for boarding. Gone are the wye track and several other tracks used to park passenger cars.

The National Park Service has a good description of the history of Maurice Morino and his development of the original Mount McKinley Park Hotel. It states that "the hotel was the first thing visitors saw stepping down from the train. The 120-acre homestead of hotel proprietor Maurice Morino straddled the railroad tracks. One visitor described the unusual, flat-roofed, two-story log building as "Italian-Alaskan." It featured exposed balconies, glass windows, and electric lights. Inside were two-dozen sleeping rooms, a mercantile, lunch counter, kitchen, and storeroom."

"The Mount McKinley Park Hotel was not Morino's first foray in the local hospitality sector. Five years earlier, just two years after he first settled here in 1914, Morino learned that his home on the banks of Riley Creek was right on the newly selected route of the Alaska Railroad. Quick to spot an opportunity, Morino added on to his cabin and turned it into a roadhouse and trading post. With the news of the establishment of Mount McKinley National Park in 1917, he renamed it the Park Gate Roadhouse."

"In late 1920, business booming, Morino realized that the roadhouse was unsuited to handle the volume. By late summer 1921, he was hard at work on a new hotel at a new location on the bluff near the tracks. After completion of the railroad, Morino planned to cash in on park tourism, envisioning a lively business."

"When park boundaries came east and absorbed McKinley Station in 1932, Morino kept his homestead listed as a park in-holding. The title passed to the Park Service in 1947. Three years later in 1950, the dilapidated remains of his hotel were destroyed in a fire started by a transient."

The first mention of the Denali/Mount McKinley massif was by Captain George Vancouver, who, after seeing it from Cook Inlet in 1794, referred to the "stupendous snow mountains." The Russians descriptively called the mountain "Bolshaya (Bulshaia) Gora" or "big mountain." The mountain was a common topic of discussion by trappers and prospectors. In fact, prospector Frank Densmore spoke so enthusiastically of the mountain that it was known for years among prospectors as "Densmores Peak." The Tanana Indian name was reported as "Denali" or "Doleika" or "'Traleika." All of these names mean "the big one" or "the high one."

Mt. McKinley was named in 1896 by prospector William Dickey "after William McKinley of Ohio, who had been nominated for the presidency, and that fact was the first news we received on our way out of that wonderful wilderness!" Soon after, McKinley became the 25th President of the United States. Today the park is actually three different parks: a wilderness, a preserve, and a national park. The vast majority of the park is only accessible on foot.

The fabled Denali (Mt. McKinley) massif. Photo by Barton Jennings.

Just to the east of the tracks is the McKinley National Park Airport, so you can expect to see airplanes as well as the trains and buses here.

348.2 DENALI PARK ROAD – This is the entrance to Denali National Park and Preserve. This is the only road into the National Park and most of the route is restricted to approved vehicles only.

Across the valley to the east is McKinley Park, Alaska. Also known as Glitter Gulch, the community is on the George Parks Highway at the entrance to Denali National Park. Officially, the community has a population of about 150, and has developed around National Park Service employment and tourism-related facilities. During the few months of summer, McKinley Park is a very busy place with a number of hotels, restaurants, and shops serving the needs of thousands of tourists.

During winter, the hotels and most visitor services at McKinley Park are closed.

With the park being established in 1917 as McKinley National Park, there was soon a need for basic housing for the park's employees. A settlement was reported near here in 1920 known as Riley Creek. At the same time, the Alaska Engineering Commission (AEC) established Camp Riley on the south bank of Riley Creek to build the Riley Creek bridge. In 1922, a post office was established here and the name was soon changed to McKinley Park.

Heading north, the railroad passes Horseshoe Lake (to the east) then almost immediately enters the Nenana River Canyon, also called the Healy Canyon, that stretches to near Healy, ten miles north of here. Get ready for scenery! The river is to the east and a number of magnificent mountains views are to the west. If you plan to hang out of the train on the west side, watch your head as there is often little clearance between the train and the bluffs alongside the track.

349.0 NENANA RIVER CANYON – The railroad hangs onto a small ledge above the Nenana River, dropping on a grade that approaches 1%. Watch for Dall Sheep on the far side of the canyon and rafters in the river below. Across the river you can see "Glitter Gulch," the name often given to McKinley Park, the tourist town where almost all park visitors stay. Just as with most such places, there is an interesting mix of fancy hotels, tourist souvenir stores, sandwich shops, and enough support facilities for the large summer work force. During winter, it is hard to find anyone living here except for a few caretakers.

350.5 CASCADE – There is a short spur to the east known as the Cascade Outfit Track, often full of track maintenance equipment as the railroad works to hold this grade together.

Alaska Division – Anchorage to Fairbanks

351.4 BRIDGE – This three-span steel bridge (each span is 124 feet long) was built in 1948 to cross an erosion area, once crossed using a timber trestle. Even with its modern construction, it has been a constant problem for the railroad. In fact, the piers have been slowly moving toward the river, creating a need to adjust the bridge every decade or so.

352.7 SHEEP CREEK – This bridge is almost 200 feet long and crosses another stream flowing off the east face of Mount Healy. The *Dictionary of Alaska Place Names* lists 28 streams with the name Sheep Creek. The USGS noted this stream in 1950, saying that it flowed 1.5 miles northeast and into the Nenana River. Just north of here is a large area where spoil materials are placed, explaining the large flat spot inside this narrow canyon.

Southbound *Denali Star* near Sheep Creek. Photo by Barton Jennings.

353.1 MOODY – There was once a 1920s flag stop near here, named for nearby Moody Creek. Moody Creek flows into the Healy River near here. To the west are the eastern slopes of Mount Healy. A number of wet streams flow off this hillside, creating an active slide area, and the railroad crosses them with a number of substantial bridges. To the east, across the river, is Sugar Loaf Mountain.

353.2 NORTH BOUNDARY OF DENALI NATIONAL PARK – In 1908, Charles Sheldon, a hunter and naturalist, described in his journal the idea of a park that would allow visitors to enjoy the beauty he saw while visiting Alaska. Between 1906 and 1908, Sheldon had roamed the present day park gathering vital information about Dall Sheep. It was during these travels that Sheldon developed the concept of protection and preservation of these wild lands.

At the time, all of Alaska seemed wild. Wildlife was plentiful in many areas. Majestic mountains were not hard to come by. But here, just north of the Alaska Range, one could find a region with a magic combination of wildlife and scenery that typified the territory. The territory, however, was changing just as the landscape had changed in the Lower 48. Miners combed drainages throughout the region looking for gold and other valuable minerals. A railroad would soon connect Fairbanks to the coast. Early park proponents realized that the vast quantities of wildlife found north of the Alaska Range would come under increasing hunting pressure to feed railway workers, miners and populations of growing communities.

Created by Congress in 1917, the original Mount McKinley National Park preserved roughly two million acres. Wildlife protection was the backbone of the park's legislation, which set the stage for Denali's modern role as a wildlife refuge of international importance. At first, park visitation was actually discouraged but it soon became evident that visitors were going to come no matter what. Therefore, plans began to focus on limiting the impact that visitors would have on the park. This meant that there would be few lodges and campgrounds in the park, something very different from many other parks at the time.

Alaska Division – Anchorage to Fairbanks

Passage of the Alaska National Interest Lands Conservation Act in 1980 expanded the park boundaries, added preserve lands and changed the name to Denali National Park and Preserve. Boundaries were expanded in part to accommodate migration patterns of caribou and other wildlife, and to take in the entire Denali/Mount McKinley massif.

353.5 MOODY HIGHWAY BRIDGE – Just south of the old Moody Tunnel, you should look up. This is the Parks Highway, Alaska Highway 3, as it crosses the Nenana River, 174 feet above the valley floor. There is a wind sock mid-span to warn drivers of the high winds that often blow through here. Look for Dall Sheep which often cover the hillsides. A great photo spot is on the bluff across the river to the south, if you can hang on to the tree while working a camera!

Moody Highway Bridge. Photo by Sarah Jennings.

353.6 MOODY TUNNEL – This 262-foot former tunnel, originally known as Tunnel 8, was removed between 2006 and 2009. It was built during the 1920s through somewhat unstable soils. Lined with 12 inch x 12 inch

Alaska Railroad: History Through the Miles

timbers, it was located in the middle of a ten degree curve. The south portal collapsed in 1992 and the north portal during June 2005.

Northbound *Denali Star* near Moody Tunnel. Photo by Sarah Jennings.

355.7 GARNER – Garner, shown as a flag stop in the 1922 timetable, served several local mines. Today, it is simply a siding to the west. Heading south, trains face grades of up to one percent. Garner is a short flat location in the middle of this climb, making it an important location for heavy southbound trains.

356.2 GARNER TUNNEL – Look to the west to see the tunnel, or at least its remains. The railroad was rerouted and the tunnel removed in 2005 at an expense of $1.9 million. The south wooden portal is still visible while the north portal is buried.

Note the new track construction at milepost 357. In 2011, the railroad moved the track away from the Nenana River as a part of a grade stabilization project.

358.7 HEALY – Healy lies at the mouth of Healy Creek, named before 1906 for John J. Healy of the North American Trading and Transportation Company, on the Nenana River, and is the start of a 4-mile branch line that once

Alaska Division – Anchorage to Fairbanks

served nearby coal mines (there is a description on page 147 for that branch). Watch for dark coal seams in the exposed rocks to the east. The coal fuels electric power plants in the interior and is also exported to Korea. One-fifth of the railroad's freight revenue comes from hauling this coal. The elevation here is approximately 1300 feet.

Healy was a mining camp by 1905. At one time, Healy was also an important railroad station with shops and maintenance-of-way facilities due to the nearby coal mines. Healy was developed by the Healy River Coal Corporation in 1918 and a post office opened here in 1921. The coal traffic required lots of railroad support. The 250 by 50-foot roundhouse at Healy was destroyed by fire on May 10, 1952, destroying two diesel locomotives (1015 and 1016) and a railroad crane. A more modern engine house replaced the structure and is still used by the railroad. Healy also had a lunch counter to serve the passenger trains, with the cost of a lunch meal in 1941 being $1.00.

Healy Shops. Photo by Barton Jennings.

Since the two locomotives were mentioned, here are more details. Both were built by Alco as model RSD1. Number 1015 was built in 1943 (cn #70656) as U.S.

Army 8035 and transferred to the Alaska Railroad in 1948. Number 1016 was built in 1942 (cn #70647) as U.S. Army 8026 and sent to Alaska in 1949. After the fire, both were rebuilt into B-units known as an RF1B. 1016 was rebuilt into RF1B #1067 and was scrapped during the mid-1960s. 1015 had a more entertaining career. In 1952, it was rebuilt into RF1B #1065. During the mid-1960s, the unit had its traction motors disabled and it was connected to Rotary #3 as a power generator for the two traction motors that were installed in the Rotary to drive the wheel, replacing the steam boiler and engine works. 1065 was eventually scrapped in 1973.

To the west is Otto Siding, measuring 5881 feet. To the east is the longer Love Siding – 8769 feet. This is complex, so here are the details. The SSS (south siding switch) for Love Siding is at MP 358.27 while Otto SSS is at MP 358.82. The NSS (north siding switch) for Love Siding is at MP 359.96 while the NSS for Otto Siding is at MP 359.93. The Suntrana Branch breaks off from Love Siding at MP 359.24. There are additional tracks here known as East Tracks and West Tracks. The Healy River Airport is also to the east between the railroad and the Nenana River.

If the *Denali Star* has cruise ship cars on the rear, the train often makes a stop at Healy to load or unload their staff. Southbound trains will stop to board the crew so they can prepare to board their passengers at Denali. Northbound, the staff have cleaned their cars and are dropped off at Healy to be bused to their sleeping quarters nearby.

360.4 POKER – There is a short wye to the west at this location. Princess cruise ship trains reportedly turn here when they do not go on to Fairbanks. These trains are often known as HAP trains, for Holland America and Princess.

Alaska Division – Anchorage to Fairbanks

360.9 **DRY CREEK** – Look for the three 60-foot through plate girder spans. The *Alaska Railroad Record* stated that the track reached here November 1919.

362.3 **USIBELLI TIPPLE** – The Usibelli tipple is a special loading facility with a railroad track running through the center for coal loading. The coal is mined across the river and transported to the tipple by conveyor. The coal is sub-bituminous with a relatively low BTU per pound, but it is relatively clean burning due to its low sulfur and nitrogen content and high calcium content. The siding to the east is 8479 feet long.

In 1935, Emil Usibelli came to Alaska and worked as an underground miner in the Evans Jones Mine near Palmer. Eight years later, Emil and his friend, Thad Sanford, went into the coal mining business for themselves. In 1948, Emil bought out his partner and incorporated the Usibelli Coal Mining Company (UCM). Over the next few years, UCM increased its share of the military's coal demand and began its first commercial sales to Fairbanks area utilities. In 1961, UCM purchased Suntrana Mining Company and became the predominant supplier to the military. In 1964, at age 70, Emil was killed in a mining accident. Joe Usibelli, his only son, took over operations at the age of 25.

In 1967, the construction of Golden Valley's electrical plant was complete, thus supplying UCM with another large customer. In 1971, UCM purchased the neighboring Vitro Mine and became the sole producing coal mine in Alaska. In 1977, UCM purchased an enormous dragline capable of removing up to 37 cubic yards of dirt with each bucket. In 1981, construction was completed on the new train loading coal tipple along the Nenana River. A fifteen-year contract was signed with Korea Electric Power Corporation in 1984. This resulted in the construction of the Seward coal loading facility. In May of 1995, construction began on the Healy Clean Coal Project, a 50-megawatt power plant adjacent to Golden Valley's existing 25-megawatt plant. This plant began operations in 1998 and completed a successful demonstration in 1999.

As of June 2004, the production rate is about 1 million tons of coal per year. Once the coal is removed from the ground it is shipped via the Alaska Railroad to various military bases and power plants as well as the Seward Loading Facility for shipment overseas. UCM currently has 90 full-time employees and another 291 jobs are linked directly to its products. UCM's financial expenditures pumps $21.5 million into the Alaskan economy.

362.6 LIGNITE – Originally called Dry Creek, this station was named Lignite by 1922. Lignite is named for the low quality coal, often referred to as lignite, found in this area. The railroad crosses Lignite Road here.

364.7 PAN CREEK – Actually Panquinque Creek, the stream is crossed on a four-span timber trestle. The creek was named for a Philippine card game. In 1952, the USGS called the stream Pangengi Creek.

370.7 NENANA RIVER – The tracks cross the river using two 200-foot long through truss spans as well as an 82-foot long through girder span. This is actually the third bridge at this location.

This river was originally known as the Cantwell River, named by Lieutenant Allen in 1888 for Lieutenant John C. Cantwell. In 1898, the USGS reported that the native name was Tutlut, while the same year another report called it the Nenana River, a version of the Tanana Indian tribal name. A few years later, Father Julius Jette wrote that the river's name "remains unexplained and seems as much a puzzle (to the Indians) as it is to me." The river starts at Nenana Glacier and flows 140 miles to the Tanana River.

Alaska Division – Anchorage to Fairbanks

There is a sizeable community at the south end of the bridge. Older documents show that the Alaska Railroad once had a flag stop station here. There was another station at the north end of the Nenana River bridge. North of here, the railroad runs close to the eastern shore of Nenana River. There are some terrific photos to the west throughout this area.

371.2　**FERRY** – There is a siding here to the east. The name was originally published as a railroad station in 1922 and experienced a small population boom when it was a railroad work camp. The name Ferry comes from the ferry that used to exist here that was used to cross the Nenana River to access the gold fields to the east. In 2012, Ferry was the staging site for Alaska's largest wind farm. The Eva Creek facility produces 25 megawatts of power and is located 10 miles to the west of here.

374.6　**GRIZZLY** – Grizzly is a 6197-foot siding to the west named for the local bear, which is very common in this area. There used to be a station named Moss toward the south switch of the siding. There is still a Vertical Angle Bench Mark (VABM) at this location known as Moss. There used to be a number of placer gold mines to the east up Moose Creek.

381.2　**BROWNE** – There was a siding to the east, named by 1922 for F. D. Browne, a locating engineer of the Alaska Railroad. The Nenana River is immediately to the west. As the railroad follows the river, watch for locations where the railroad has tossed in a few old freight cars to try to maintain the embankment. Recently, the railroad has been removing a number of these cars for environmental reasons and to make it safer for rafters.

386.2　**PARKS HIGHWAY** – The highway passes overhead on a new overpass (known as the Rex Overpass by the railroad), a part of a construction project on the highway's

Nenana River crossing. This is Parks Highway milepost 276. The railroad has just left the Alaska Range and is entering the Tanana lowlands as it works its way north.

387.2 REX – Rex is named for Rex Dome (4155 feet high) which is to the southeast. Other domes in the area are Walker and Jumbo to the east. On a 1925 map, this location was identified as Kobi. Rex Dome was named for nearby Rex Creek, which reportedly received its name from prospectors by 1906.

388.2 CLEAR GRAVEL PIT – A wye to the east serves a large gravel pit.

388.8 SOUTH END OF CLEAR SITE LINE CHANGE – In 1959, the railroad was realigned beginning here to make room for the Clear Site radar facility. The old grade is clearly visible to the north. Look for the Ramsey Homestead to the west with their large wooden train and their "We Love Trains" sign.

392.9 CLEAR SITE – The first railroad station located here was named Clear when it was established as a construction site in 1918. Eventually it became known as Clear Site.

Today, this is the location of a BMEWS (Ballistic Missile Early Warning Site) radar site, which is one of three in the world. Built in 1959, Clear Site was used to detect enemy missile attack. It is now used to track satellites and space debris. Air Force personnel stationed there receive overseas pay and their families are not permitted on the base for security reasons.

To the east is a 6212-foot siding. A wye track is to the west, connecting with several spurs into the facility. Reportedly, the Alaska Railroad shoves coal loads to the property gate and then pulls empties from the same location. The military handles all switching inside Clear Site.

Alaska Division – Anchorage to Fairbanks

394.4   NORTH END OF CLEAR SITE LINE CHANGE – Because of the realignment, moving the mainline to the east, the length of the mainline changed. **The result of this is it is 15,945 feet between milepost 394 and 395. Yes, that means mile 394 is about three miles long. To handle this, mileposts 394A and 394B were added.**

   Just north of here is the community of Anderson, settled in the late 1950s and named for homesteader Arthur Anderson. Anderson divided his 80-acre homestead into ¼-acre lots and sold the majority of these lots to civilian workers from nearby Clear Air Force Station. The community quickly grew and was incorporated in 1962.

394.8   CLEAR – This was the original location of Clear, and there are still some signs of the former community off to the east.

401.1   JULIUS – Named for nearby Julius Creek, Julius is a short spur to the west. Julius Creek drains a large area to the south. Julius was a named station in the 1922 timetable.

408.5   PRUDHOE BAY EXTENSION – As the oil boom exploded at Prudhoe Bay, the railroad took a look at building its own line to the oil fields in 1970. This 580-mile line would leave the mainline here and head west across the Nenana River to the Yukon River near the village of Tanana. From there, the route would head north to the Koyukuk River, then along the Middle Fork Koyukuk River to Atigun Pass through the Brooks Range. At Atigun Pass, the railroad would almost parallel the route used by the Trans-Alaska Pipeline to Prudhoe Bay. In addition to the line to Prudhoe Bay, there were plans to build a 140-mile line from near the village of Alatna across a low divide to the rich copper deposits at Bornite on the upper Kobuk River. Obviously, nothing was built.

North of here, the railroad follows the wandering Nenana River, including a number of channels such as the Seventeenmile Slough, Lost Slough, and Julius Creek. Approaching the town of Nenana, the railroad passes several barge docks near where the Nenana River flows into the Tanana River.

411.4 **PARKS HIGHWAY** – That is the Parks Highway high above the railroad on the Tanana River bridge built in 1968. It is known as the "Nenana Underpass" by the Alaska Railroad, and is milepost 304.5 on the Parks Highway.

411.7 **NENANA** – Originally an Indian village, Nenana is located on the south bank of the Tanana River at the confluence of the Nenana River at 400 feet of elevation. Nenana is in the western-most portion of Tanana Athabaskan (or Athabascan) Indian territory. It was first known as Tortella, an interpretation of the Indian word "Toghotthele," which means "mountain that parallels the river." Some sources say that the Athabaskan word Nenana means "a good place to camp between the rivers." However, the "na" sound at the end of the word means stream or river. Information from the University of Alaska Fairbanks native language center indicates that the town's name likely came from the river that joined the Tanana here. Early explorers first entered the Tanana Valley in 1875 and 1885.

The discovery of gold in Fairbanks in 1902 brought intense activity to the region. A trading post/roadhouse was constructed by Jim Duke in 1903 to supply river travelers and trade with Indians. St. Mark's Episcopal mission and school was built upriver in 1905, bringing native children from other communities to Nenana. A post office opened in 1908. Nenana was a railroad construction camp in the early 1900s, and by 1915, construction of the Alaska Railroad doubled Nenana's population. Records indicate that during the early 1920s, the railroad had shops and a roundhouse, stores, docks, a hospital, a power plant, corrals, and a mess house here. The community incorporated as a city in 1921. Completion of the railroad was followed by an economic slump. The population dropped from 5000 residents in 1923 to 291 in 1930.

Nenana Depot. Photo by Sarah Jennings.

For years, the White Pass & Yukon provided service to Nenana. Yes, the WP&Y! In 1910, the WP&YR set up a river division, the British Yukon Navigation Company (BYN). Within three years BYN owned all but three boats on the upper river. The BYN operated regular service between Nenana and Dawson. Steamers owned and operated by the Alaska Railroad served the river below Nenana. Today, Nenana still serves as a hub for barge operations, serving communities up and down the Yukon River and connecting waterways for hundreds of miles.

The Nenana Ice Classic takes place each winter. Bets are made on the exact day and time the river ice will break up. The winnings exceed $200,000 and are usually split between multiple contestants. The contest began in 1917 among surveyors for the Alaska Railroad.

Ice Classic props - the Tanana River and towers. Photo by Sarah Jennings.

In 1961, Clear Air Force Station was constructed 21 miles southwest, and many civilian contractors commuted from Nenana. A road was constructed south to Clear, but north, vehicles were ferried across the Tanana River. In 1967, the community was devastated by one of the largest floods ever recorded in the Tanana Valley. In 1968, a $6 million bridge was completed across the Tanana River, which gave the city a road link to Fairbanks and replaced the river ferry.

Today, the railroad has a 3195-foot siding to the west as well as a small yard. The railroad depot, listed on the National Register of Historic Places, was completed in 1923, when President Warren Harding drove the golden spike at Nenana. The depot, still in use, now houses the Alaska State Railroad Museum with displays about the early years of the Alaska Railroad. Watch for several former Alaska Railroad passenger cars across from the depot. There was once a wye to the west at the south end of the yard.

The Alaska Railroad has plans to realign the railroad mainline track around the downtown area of Nenana, following a route outside of the existing right-of-way, north of the airport and southeast of town, over the Parks Highway. The track structure through Nenana would be maintained to support port activities.

Alaska Division – Anchorage to Fairbanks

413.7 MEARS MEMORIAL BRIDGE – The railroad crosses the Tanana River using the Mears Memorial Bridge, the last part of the railroad built between Seward and Fairbanks. The bridge marked the completion of the Alaska Railroad, completed on February 22, 1923, and the Golden Spike was driven by President Warren Harding on July 15, 1923. The bridge includes a 704-foot steel through truss span (the longest through truss in the world when built, presently the world's third longest), six 60-foot deck plate girder spans, four 30-foot deck plate girders, and a 118-foot deck truss span. The bridge was designed by the firm Modjeski & Angier and fabricated and built by the American Bridge Company. When built, the south end also featured a long timber trestle which created the curved, climbing approach that is now a large fill. The bridge is named for Frederick Mears, Head of the Alaska Engineering Commission that built the railroad.

Mears Memorial Bridge over the Tanana River at Nenana. Photo by Barton Jennings.

415.4 HARDING – Formerly known as North Nenana, there is a 4172-foot siding to the west that has been renamed to honor President Harding. The tracks are located on a hillside above much of the surrounding countryside. The railroad was built southward from Fairbanks to this point by 1919. The Tanana River, immediately to the south, halted further railroad construction for several years. If you look west across the Tanana River, you see two smaller streams flowing into the Tanana. The close stream is the East Middle River and the one farther away is the West Middle River. The highway bridge you see is the Alaska Native Veterans' Honor Bridge, a part of the Parks Highway.

The Alaska Railroad reached this point in late 1919, being built from the north about fifty miles away at Happy. The track was built to standard gauge standards, but the rails were laid to 3-foot gauge. For a few years, passengers and freight, including coal, were barged across the river in summer and used a temporary track built on the ice during winter. Starting in early April of 1923, the railroad was shut down north of here as the track was regauged to standard gauge.

417.7 PARKS HIGHWAY – This is the George Parks Highway, Alaska Highway 3, above, on a new and improved route. This location was a 1920s flagstop known as Mahon. This marks a transition point for the railroad between the boggy lowlands below and the ridge which the Tanana River curves around.

420.4 MANLEY – A one-time railroad stop, Manley is today a 6088-foot siding to the west. The stop served a trail that headed west toward Manley Hot Springs, a service and supply point for miners in the Tofty and Eureka mining districts.

The name Manley obviously comes from Manley Hot Springs. In 1907, Frank Manley built a hotel named the Hot Springs Resort Hotel. The community was then known as Hot Springs, but the post office changed to Manley Hot Springs in 1957.

423.1 BERG – The Parks Highway comes in from the east at Berg. To the west is the Minto Flats State Game Refuge, which encompasses approximately 500,000 acres.

Alaska Division – Anchorage to Fairbanks

The refuge was established by the Alaska Legislature in 1988. Minto Flats is a large wetland complex lying along a northerly loop of the middle Tanana River in interior Alaska. The area is fed by waters from the Tatalina, Chatanika, and Tolovana rivers and Goldstream and Washington creeks. It drains into the Tanana River in a generally southwest-west direction. The flats are bounded on the north by an escarpment which rises abruptly from the lowlands. The Tanana River forms the southern boundary.

Minto Flats is one of the highest quality waterfowl habitats in Alaska. It supports high density duck nesting, one of the largest trumpeter swan breeding populations in North America, geese, swans, sandhill cranes, loons, bald eagles, peregrine falcons, grouse and ptarmigan. Minto Flats has also historically supported large numbers of moose and provides excellent habitat for black bear, beaver, muskrat, river otter, lynx, wolverine, red fox and mink.

There were once two stations in this area. What is today Berg was once Little Goldstream. Berg was once a separate station to the north. Sometime in the 1920s the two were combined into today's Berg.

431.6 **DUNBAR** – This place took the name Dunbar by 1922. The Dunbar Trail, a winter road, left the railroad here leading to the Livengood gold camp. Today, there is a 6230-foot siding at this location, to the west of the tracks. The railroad crosses Goldstream Creek at milepost 432.1. A railroad section house once stood nearby at milepost 432.6.

433.2 **CALIFORNIA** – There isn't much information on this location except that it was a named flagstop during the 1920s. However, there are a number of stations along the Alaska Railroad named for other states. This was probably the case, named for the home of a local miner.

Several maps show this location as being named Section House.

439.5 STANDARD – A siding to the west, Standard was named for nearby Standard Creek, which forms in the hills to the northwest and eventually flows into the Tanana River to the south. Standard was listed in 1922 as a station.

442.1 MUSKEG – Located in the Goldstream Creek Valley, Muskeg was a 1920s flagstop. Muskeg is probably an appropriate name for this area as the word means grassy swamp in Chippewa. Like a soggy blanket draped over the landscape, muskeg, or peat bog, covers more than 10 percent of southeast Alaska. Muskeg itself consists of dead plants in various stages of decomposition. The water level in muskeg is usually at or near the surface. Stepping on muskeg is like stepping on a sponge. Muskegs need two conditions to develop: abundant rain and cool summers. A dead plant that falls on dry soil is attacked by bacteria and fungi and quickly rots. If that plant lands in water or on saturated soil, it faces a different fate. Air can't get to it, so the bacteria and fungi can't function well. The cool temperatures slow them down even more. All this slows decomposition, and the plant debris accumulates to form peat and eventually, a muskeg.

447.7 CACHE – An Alaskan cache is a small log building on tall legs, designed to protect food from bears. It looks like an overbuilt deer stand. The term is based upon a French word which means a storage building. Cache was once a flag stop on the railroad, named for nearby Cache Creek.

450.8 SAULICH – There is a 6374-foot siding to the east. The railroad once had a station here. Goldstream Creek has been following the railroad to the east of the tracks since

Alaska Division – Anchorage to Fairbanks

about Dunbar, and will continue to near Happy. Goldstream Creek starts in the former gold mining region near Fox, north of Fairbanks. In this area, Goldstream Creek can best be described as a wandering bog. It is a popular winter trail.

452.8 **MARTIN** – There is not much at Martin today, just a few houses off the road from the north. However, Martin was once a flagstop providing access to several area trails into the gold fields. Before the railroad arrived, this area was known as Spinach Creek, named for a nearby stream.

455.5 **BARTLETT** – Bartlett was a flagstop 1922-1923. It was apparently replaced by Dome. Ed Bartlett operated a large Oats Farm near here during the early 1900s.

456.2 **DOME** – There is a spur track here. Dome was once a railroad stop for miners heading to gold camps near Pedro Dome. Dome was also once the railroad stop used to service the Cold War Air Force Aircraft Control and Warning radar site located on top of nearby Murphy Dome. There was a passenger shack here. The railroad built a new grade in 1950 and installed some bridge pilings to the east as part of a proposed line change.

459.0 **ESTER** – This Ester is a new 6727-foot siding (opened in 2004) on the west side of the tracks, often used to hold trains out of the Fairbanks terminal. In 1908, the Tanana Valley Railroad had a siding at milepost 465.4 named "Ester Siding." By 1922, the TVRR siding was renamed Ester. The name Ester comes from the nearby Ester mining camp, which dates from 1903.

463.0 **HAPPY** – Nearby Happy Creek was named by local prospectors, and this station first appeared in the railroad's list of stations in 1922. The first Happy was at milepost 461.4, and was a short siding used to store cars containing explosives. To the compass northwest is the old grade of the Tanana Valley Railroad and its narrow-gauge line serving remote mining districts around Chatanika. The line was abandoned in 1930 as roads were built. Until the branch was abandoned, the track between here and Fairbanks had three rails to handle both the standard gauge and narrow gauge trains. The old spur to the east (compass-south) is now gone.

Happy is located at the top of a 1% grade up from Fairbanks and as much as 0.4% from Ester. Don't get confused by directions here. Heading railroad north toward Fairbanks a train is actually heading compass south for some distance.

Heading north to Fairbanks, the line passes through miles of black spruce bottoms, land that is not what many people think of as being Alaska. However, these black spruce bottoms are a key part of Alaska. These woods, known as taiga, a Russian word for northern evergreen forest, are a sure sign of permafrost. Permafrost soil stays frozen all year. Because of this, when the thin top layer does thaw each year, moisture is unable to sink further into the ground. This leads to the ground becoming swamp-like, drowning most ordinary trees.

465.6 OLD ESTER – What most people identify as Ester is off to the south on the main highway. Ester, sometimes known as "The Republic of Ester," is a collection of dirt streets, rambling log homes and tailing piles from a time when dredges were busy removing gold. Today, it is a bedroom community for Fairbanks. However, in 1906, Ester was a raucous mining camp with a population of more than 5000. The Fairbanks Exploration Company built Ester Camp in 1936 to support a large-scale gold dredge operation. The dredge closed as an active operation during the late 1950s but soon reopened as a tourist operation which still operates today.

Here are the details. The first gold claim was staked on Ester Creek in February 1903. However, it wasn't un-

Alaska Division – Anchorage to Fairbanks

til November that gold was actually found. A social hall was completed in 1907 and was well known throughout the mining district for its dance floor. Besides dancing, the hall was used for religious services, movies, card games, parties, and other entertainment. The town had five saloons and a couple of hotels. By 1909 Ester City had a baseball field, a doctor, a mine workers' union local, and a teacher, but gold production was beginning to decline. The Berry Post Office moved in 1910 from two miles away into J.C. Kinney's general store in Ester. The post office retained the name of Berry until 1965, when it was finally changed to that of the town it had been in for 55 years.

In the mid-1920s, the Fairbanks Exploration Company began buying claims on Ester Creek, started operations in 1929, and in 1933 built a mess hall for their camp in Ester (now a historic landmark used until 2008 as a tourist attraction and hotel). The F.E. Company revitalized the town, but they also literally reshaped it, doing large-scale open-pit mining using enormous floating dredges and draglines, removing in the process much of the original sites of Berry and Ester. In 1958, the F.E. Company sold their Ester camp and it reopened under new management as an historic resort, the Cripple Creek Resort, which later became the Ester Gold Camp. In 1987, the gold camp was designated the Ester Camp Historic District by the National Register of Historic Places.

466.0 UNIVERSITY FARM – A working farm and experimental station on the University of Alaska Fairbanks campus, the facility produces dairy, meat and vegetable products. Look to the north and you can glimpse the flower and vegetable gardens as well as the pens often filled with reindeer and musk oxen.

466.8 FAIRBANKS – A Fairbanks sign and the south end of yard limits.

467.1 COLLEGE – College is the location of the world's northernmost institution of higher education – the University of Alaska Fairbanks. College was so named because it is the location of the university, established in 1915. The Tanana Valley Railroad once had a line heading to the southwest to the river port of Chena. To the west side of the tracks are the University of Alaska Fairbanks power plant and Alaska Center for Energy and Power.

467.9 NOYES SLOUGH – South of here the railroad is a single track mainline. North of here the railroad starts adding tracks as it enters the rail yards.

The railroad crosses this stream using eighteen 14-foot timber spans and a 125-foot through truss bridge. The slough was known simply as being a part of Chena Slough until about 1910, when the name Noyes Slough was accepted and adopted. Noyes Slough was named after Fred Noyes, who arrived in Dawson, Canada, via the Chilkoot Trail in 1897. Fred Noyes remained in Dawson from 1897 to 1902 and then went west to Fairbanks, Alaska. Noyes operated two sawmills off the Chena River in Fairbanks. However, Fred Noyes was best known for his riverboat, the *Idler*, which he built in 1911 and used to move logs from along the slough to his mills on the river. Noyes returned to Seattle in the mid-1920s and died an accidental death in 1928. The house of Fred Noyes still stands today on Illinois Street in Fairbanks.

468.5 FAIRBANKS YARD – Located between Noyes Slough and the Johansen Expressway overpass (milepost 469.1), this is the main rail yard in town.

469.1 JOHANSEN EXPRESSWAY – The line to the Fairbanks passenger train station breaks off from the mainline just north of the Johansen Expressway overpass. The Eielson Branch (see page 165), heading off to North Pole, Alaska, breaks off just a bit farther north at milepost 469.5, thus bypassing the new station and allowing passenger

Alaska Division – Anchorage to Fairbanks

trains to park overnight at the station. Tracks head off in the other direction to connect to the new balloon track to turn trains at the station, and to enter the yard and service tracks near the railroad shops.

Just north of here is the Fairbanks Intermodal Yard. The Alaska Railroad has been making numerous improvements to this facility to make it more secure and user friendly.

469.8 **FAIRBANKS PASSENGER STATION** – Timetables generally show Fairbanks to be at milepost 470.3. However, that milepost is the old station near downtown. The new $22.5 million station is located on a 32-acre site adjacent to the railroad's operations yard, near the intersection of the Johansen Expressway and Danby Street. It opened in May of 2005, replacing the terminal near the intersection of Driveway Street and Phillips Field Road. The new facility was funded through a combination of Federal Transit Administration and Federal Railroad Administration funds. The new station eliminated the need to block traffic on Phillips Field Road while loading and unloading and made turning trains easier. It also provided much better facilities for the growing cruise ship business that was regularly adding cars to the passenger consists at the time.

Current Fairbanks Passenger Station. Photo by Barton Jennings.

Located inside the Fairbanks station is the Tanana Valley Railroad Club. The club was founded in 1984 and fills a 26' by 32' room with their HO layout, modeling the Alaska Railroad from North Pole to Denali Park's Riley Creek bridge. The layout is often open for viewing.

The "Capital of the Interior" and Alaska's second largest city (population of approximately 32,500 – 100,000 in the region), Fairbanks began as a trading post and mining town in 1901, known as Barnette's Cache. It is the northern terminus of the Alaska Railroad and southern terminus of the infamous Haul Road to the North Slope oil fields. Located in somewhat of a bowl at 439 feet of elevation, Fairbanks can be hot during the summer and cold in winter. During the summer, it has as much as 21 hours of daylight. Snow averages about 5 feet a winter with a record of 12 feet.

Koyukon Athabascans have lived in the area for thousands of years. In 1901, Captain E.T. Barnette was forced to establish a trading post on the Chena River. His actual plan was to travel farther up the river as far as present day Tok, but the stern-wheeler he chartered could not navigate the fast-moving, shallow Tanana River beyond the mouth of the Chena River located on Chena Slough. Since his contract stated that the end of water was the destination, he was set off at what is today 1st Avenue and Cushman Street in downtown Fairbanks.

A year later, gold was discovered 16 miles north of the post by Felix Pedro. With the gold discovery, Barnette decided that this location was a better store location. The town grew up around the Chena River steamboat landing as many prospectors and supply companies arrived during the Pedro Dome gold rush. Fairbanks was renamed in 1902 after Indiana Senator Charles Fairbanks, who later became vice president. By 1910, the official population had grown to 3541 with more than 6000 miners living and working their claims on creeks north of town. Barnette moved to California

Alaska Division – Anchorage to Fairbanks

in late 1910 and shortly thereafter his bank (Washington-Alaska Bank) failed, creating a number of rumors, making Barnette the "most hated man in Fairbanks."

Fairbanks lies on the floor of the Tanana River Valley straddling the Chena River. This situation has resulted in several floods.

Fairbanks is the base of operations for the north end of the Alaska Railroad and serves as a transportation hub to serve North Slope oil fields and Arctic villages. The railroad has a large yard here, reportedly designed to handle extra freight that would arrive should the proposed connection to Canada ever be built. There are both car and engine shops here.

Alaska Railroad passenger trains generally pull directly into the passenger station on what is known as the Golden Heart Lead when arriving from Anchorage. They often park at the station overnight and then head south by pulling around the new balloon track, often called the F.E. Loop. This loop track was built as part of the new station construction, extending a spur around the ramp area to another industrial spur which connected to the former mainline just north of the previous station. For those wanting the distance, here are the details.

0.2 miles - **Fairbanks Station** to **F.E. Loop Track Switch**
0.3 miles - **F.E. Loop Track Switch** to **Charles Street Grade Crossing**
0.2 miles - **Charles Street Grade Crossing** to **Original Main Line Switch**
0.3 miles - **Original Main Line Switch** to **North Roundhouse Switch**
0.2 miles - **North Roundhouse Switch** to **Shops Driveway**
0.5 miles - **Shops Driveway** to **Johansen Expressway Overpass**

This means that a train taking the Balloon Track travels 1.7 miles between the Fairbanks station and Johansen

Expressway compared to 0.7 miles when taking the station track.

The term F.E. comes from the Fairbanks Exploration Company. The Fairbanks Exploration Company operated gold mining operations throughout the area, including a number of dredges. For more than 30 years, the Fairbanks Exploration Company maintained a company community just east of the loop on Illinois Street. The west side of the street, on land where the loop track exists today, was where the company's office and industrial facilities were located. Company housing lined the east side of Illinois Street. At least 11 company houses used to stand there, but now only eight survive. All of the existing houses, as well as the office building and machine shop near the tracks, are included in the Illinois Street Historic District, established in 2001. Of the surviving company houses, the oldest is the Noyes house at the corner of Illinois and Minnie Streets. Built about 1911 by Fred Noyes (who owned the Tanana Mill lumber yard), the house was purchased by the F.E. Company in 1925 and used to house company employees.

Photo by Barton Jennings.

Photo by Sarah Jennings.

Palmer Branch
(A Branch)

The Palmer branch of the Alaska Railroad was completed in 1917, at the time known as the Matanuska Branch of the Alaska Railroad. At one time, the line went much further than Palmer, passing through Sutton (twelve miles to the north) and on to the Chickaloon Mine (another dozen miles). This line initially served several coal mines supplying coal to the U.S. Navy as well as various communities around Alaska. The line beyond Sutton was abandoned during the 1920s after the U.S. Navy changed to oil to power their ships, as the mines at Chickaloon were operated exclusively for the Navy. However, coal from the privately-owned Evan Jones, Jonesville, and Eska mines fueled the Sutton and Palmer economies until 1968, when the military bases in Anchorage converted their power systems to oil, and coal mining ceased.

A visit to the Alpine Historical Park at Sutton will provide the opportunity to learn about these mines and the railroad that served them. At the park are the remains of the Sutton Coal Washery, built by the Alaskan Engineering Commission and Navy Alaskan Coal Commission, and operated 1920-1922. In addition to the washery, the park includes mining cars and equipment, a former railroad bunk house, and many other buildings from the railroad and mines.

Traffic on this line has changed from coal to gravel. Just as the coal shipments ended about 1970, gravel moves began. Gravel is hauled to the Anchorage area for construction. One of the techniques to build on ground where permafrost exists is to cover it with layers of gravel to allow air flow, thus gravel is actually used state wide. Because of this regular activity on the Palmer Branch, and the growth of residential areas along the line, the Alaska Railroad, Alaska Department of Transportation & Public Facilities (DOT&PF), City of Palmer and Matanuska-Susitna Borough have discussed various solutions to blocked crossings. Plans are being developed to improve the adjacent Glen Highway (Alaska Highway 1) and possibly rebuild parts of the railroad branch to reduce or eliminate the problems of blocked grade crossings and traffic congestion.

Railroad directions for this line are north to Palmer and south to the mainline at Matanuska. The Alaska Railroad uses the letter "A" to note that the mileposts are for the Palmer Branch. The only passenger trains that operate over this line are the yearly *Fair Trains* to the Alaska State Fair.

Alpine Historical Park at Sutton. Photo by Barton Jennings.

A0.00 MATANUSKA – This location is also known as CP SSS (South Siding Switch) or South Matanuska, mainline milepost 150.55. This is also the south switch of the Matanuska Siding. The north switch of the siding is at milepost 151.45. The Palmer Branch climbs northward toward Palmer on grades of about one-half of a percent.

Palmer Branch

A0.47 NORTH LEG OF WYE – SD70MAC locomotives are prohibited on the north leg of the wye, and also beyond milepost A4.0. Passenger and gravel trains are also prohibited on the north leg of the wye.

A1.44 QAP SWITCH TO GRAVEL LOOP – This is the location of the former Alaska Aggregate Company (ALAGCO) quarry. This is a spring switch. The normal position for this switch is lined for the gravel loop, with trains passing through QAP (Quality Asphalt Paving) to load, and then re-entering the Palmer Branch at the Wilder Switch, heading south toward Anchorage. Trains can pass through the spring switch without stopping.

To the north is Echo Lake. The Palmer branch follows South Glen Highway (Alaska Highway 1) from here to Palmer.

A2.46 WILDER SWITCH TO GRAVEL LOOP – This switch was once known as Conrock, the site of another quarry. Today, it is the other end of the 9387-foot long Gravel Loop Track.

A3.30 OUTER SPRINGER LOOP – Just south of here is the AS&G tipple, loading gravel trains directly on the branch's main line. Anchorage Sand & Gravel (AS&G) has their large Palmer Pit in this area. AS&G operates a number of facilities around the state, providing stone and cement products for all types of construction. The material is essential as it is used to insulate the permafrost under buildings, thus stabilizing the ground. The Alaska Railroad operates unit trains from this facility, primarily to the Anchorage facility of AS&G, but also to their facility in Fairbanks.

According to the railroad, the "Inner and Outer Springer Loop roads experienced a reprieve from daily summer gravel train activity since 2009, when Alaska Sand & Gravel (AS&G) temporarily relocated to develop a small Birchwood gravel mine. The Birchwood pit will eventually be depleted, and AS&G plans to return to its Palmer pit on the east side of the Glenn Highway just south of the highway intersection with Outer Springer Loop."

McLeod Lake is to the northeast.

A3.70 **INNER SPRINGER LOOP** – This road heads east to access a few housing subdivisions, turns to the north, and then back west, again crossing the railroad in just over a mile at milepost A4.90.

A4.20 **FAIRGROUNDS** – Known as South Palmer, the Alaska Railroad has a shelter here for the yearly trains that serve the State Fair (held in late August and early September) at the fairgrounds. The Alaska State Fair Intermodal Commuter Center opened at the Alaska State Fairgrounds in Palmer in August 2004. The new facility, initiated by the State Fair, included a "new rail station, restrooms, handicap parking and convenient and safe drop-off traffic flow through a new fair gate."

ARR 31 at Fairgrounds. Photo by Barton Jennings.

A5.02 **INDUSTRIAL PARK LEAD** – The switch here is spiked and lined for the Industrial Park Lead, also known as the Airport Spur.

A5.10 **OUT OF SERVICE** – The line north of here is out of service. As of early 2017, there are some discussions to

Palmer Branch

allow the Engine 557 Restoration Company to use this line as a base of operations.

A5.30 **EAST COMMERCIAL DRIVE** – Tracks now follow South Colony Way on into downtown Palmer.

A6.20 **PALMER** – Palmer was established around 1916 as a railway station on the Matanuska Branch of the Alaska Railroad. Named for George Palmer, an area trader in the late 1800s, there was a post office named Palmer from 1917 until 1925. A post office was reestablished here in 1931 with the name Wharton, but it was renamed Palmer in 1935. That same year, Palmer became the site of one of the most unusual experiments in American history: the Matanuska Valley Colony. The Federal Emergency Relief Administration, one of the many New Deal relief agencies created by President Roosevelt, planned an agricultural colony in Alaska. More than 200 families, mostly from Michigan, Wisconsin and Minnesota, were invited to join the colony. They arrived in Palmer in the early summer of 1935. Although the failure rate was high, many of their descendants still live in the Matanuska-Susitna (Mat-Su) Valley today.

The wooden depot from the 1930s still stands here and is used as the Palmer Community Center. On display next to it is former Premier Coal Co. #5, a 36-inch gauge 0-4-0T. This locomotive operated at the Premier Mine just north of Moose Creek, five miles above Palmer. Reportedly, the locomotive was once owned by the Alaska Engineering Commission. There is a 1240-foot long siding at this location.

To the east is Lazy Mountain. The highest peak is Matanuska Peak, at over 6000 feet in elevation.

Steam engine at Palmer. Photo by Barton Jennings.

A7.0   END OF TRACK – The Palmer Branch once extended twelve more miles to a wye at Sutton, and then about the same distance on to Chickaloon. Chickaloon was named for the Chickaloon River, which was named after Chief Chiklu. It was established around 1916 in this coal-rich region as the terminus of the Matanuska Branch of the Alaska Railroad. However, the line east of here to Sutton was removed in 1969-1970. There were a number of coal mines in the Sutton and Moose Creek area, but when they closed, so did the rail line.

Premier Coal Company operated a coal mine north of Moose Creek (milepost 12.1). There were two mines above Sutton. Sutton was located at milepost 18.7 and founded around 1918 as a station on the Matanuska Branch of the Alaska Railroad. The post office was established in 1948. The Evan Jones Coal Mine was at the top of a 6 percent grade rising from Sutton on the Matanuska River. A junction about one mile from the Evan Jones tipple branched off to the Eska Coal Mine (operated by the Alaska Engineering Commission during the late 1910s and early 1920s). The Eska mine was closed by the late 1940s and all of these operations closed by 1967 when the power plants at Anchorage, Elmendorf and Fort Richardson were converted to natural gas.

Palmer Branch

At Sutton, the Jonesville-Eska Branch headed north three miles to the Jonesville and Eska coal mines. This branch had grades of more than four percent uphill to the mines, so at least the loads were downhill. This branch, the "B" Branch, was also abandoned and had its track removed in 1969.

Alaska Railroad: History Through the Miles

Southbound *Denali Star* near Healy. Photo by Barton Jennings.

Nenana River Valley. Photo by Sarah Jennings.

Suntrana Branch
(D Branch)

The Suntrana Branch was built in 1922, soon after the Alaska Railroad was completed between Seward and Nenana after the construction of the Riley Creek Bridge at McKinley Park. The 4.4 mile railroad spur was built up Healy Creek to reach the Suntrana Mine. In 1944, the line acquired a second loader when Emile Usibelli and T.E. Sanford opened a strip mine on Healy Creek, east of the Suntrana Mine, under a U.S. Army license. The branch's future began to look bleak when the Suntrana Mine closed because of serious fires in 1962. Later, the Usibelli mine stepped up its strip mining efforts and built a conveyor system to a new coal tipple off the Alaska Railroad's mainline, thus avoiding the steep grade off the branch. Today, little moves on the line besides a bit of explosives to a storage facility for the coal mine.

Railroad directions for this line are north to the end of track and south to the mainline. Employee Timetable No. 136 states that the entire line is excepted track, thus no passenger service is allowed. Mileposts on this line are designated by a "D".

D0.0 MAIN LINE – Located at milepost 359.35, the current Suntrana Branch heads east from Healy for about 1.7 miles, although it once went further. The railroad drops down to the Nenana River on a grade of approximately one percent. The Healy River Airport is to the east.

147

D0.9 NENANA RIVER – The railroad crosses the river using two 80-foot through plate girder spans and a 240-foot through truss bridge. Heading east the railroad climbs out of the valley on grades up to two percent. The Nenana River is one of the most popular destinations for whitewater rafting in Alaska. It starts in the Nenana Glacier in the northern Alaska Range, southwest of Mount Deborah, approximately 100 miles south of Fairbanks. The river briefly flows west, then north, forming the eastern boundary of Denali National Park. It emerges from the mountains into the broad marshy Tanana Valley and joins the Tanana at Nenana, Alaska, approximately 35 miles southwest of Fairbanks. In 1898, W.J. Peters and A.H. Brooks of the USGS, reported that the river was called "Tutlut" by the natives. The Tanana Indian name was spelled "Nenana" on a later map.

In December 1968, the highway department decked the railroad bridge to allow motor vehicle traffic to cross the river. Gates were installed on the road to close the bridge to highway traffic when trains were due.

D1.2 RUNAROUND TRACK – Located here is a double tipple used to transfer Ammonium Nitrate (a fertilizer also used as an explosive, or is it the other way around?) from railcars to trucks for the Usibelli mine.

Across Healy Road is Golden Valley Electric Association's (GVEA) Healy #1 power plant, a small 25-megawatt facility that burns coal from the nearby Usabelli mining operation. Also here is the Healy Clean Coal Project (HCCP), a 50-megawatt power plant adjacent to GVEA's Healy No. 1 plant. HCCP grew out of a nationwide competition sponsored by the Department of Energy (DOE) to test new technologies that would help solve the international problem of acid rain. The HCCP consists of a power plant utilizing a combustion system that burns coal in stages to minimize the formation of nitrogen and sulfur oxides. Pulverized limestone is added to the combustor and converted by heat in the flue gas to lime, which reacts with the sulfur dioxide in the gas and removes it as a sulfate. A second technology catches the unreacted lime and sulfates, which are recycled to scrub the flue gas, and further reduce the sulfur dioxide content. The process uses a conventional boiler that produces steam for a conventional turbine to produce approximately a nominal 50 megawatts of electricity.

In 1991, GVEA entered into a 30-year power purchase agreement with AIDEA (Alaska Industrial Development and Export Authority). GVEA's obligation to purchase power from the facility was subject to a demonstration that the plant could be operated on a sustained basis on commercial standards as defined in the power purchase agreement. However, since about 2000, AIDEA and GVEA have been in a running battle over the success of the facility and whether GVEA must buy the power.

D1.7   **END OF OPERATIONAL TRACK** – ARR reports that the end of serviceable track is milepost 1.7.

D3.7   **SQUAW POINT** – Squaw Point was once a staging yard for the Usibelli Mining Company's Suntrana operation. Much of this area is now being reclaimed.

D4.4   **SUNTRANA** – This is the location of the old Usibelli Mining Company. Since its founding, at least five different tipples have been in operation here. The Suntrana mine was established in 1922 and the community listed as a mining camp in the 1930 census. By 1928, it produced nearly half of the total coal mined in Alaska and by 1940 it had become the largest coal mine in the Alaskan Territory. The mine was purchased by Emile Usibelli (Usibelli Coal Mining) in 1961. The mine at this location later closed due to a fire. In 2007, the State of Alaska requested bids to remove the remaining grizzly and tipple at this location.

D4.7 END OF TRACK – This is the historical end of track.

Cruise ship and train at Whittier. Photo by Barton Jennings.

Whittier Division (F Branch)

Once known as the Whittier Cutoff or Whittier Branch, this line is becoming more important to the Alaska Railroad as it is the major connection to the Lower 48. Barges from Seattle and Prince Rupert dock here, as well as a growing number of cruise ships.

Plans for this line began in 1914, but the rough terrain made the route seem impossible. Railroad manager Otto Ohlson championed this route because of its ability to provide a shortcut to a deep-water port (a trip to Seward added 52 more miles), but the Whittier Cutoff didn't become a reality until World War II. In 1941, the U.S. Army began construction of the line from Whittier to Portage. On April 23, 1943, the line was completed. The route provided many challenges, including a one-mile tunnel through Begich Peak and a 2.5-mile tunnel through Maynard Mountain. Anton Anderson, an Army engineer, headed up the line's construction and the main tunnel bears his name.

For the military, Whittier provided a shorter voyage, reduced exposure of ships to Japanese submarines, reduced the risk of Japanese bombings, and avoided the steep railroad grades required on the Seward line. When completed, the Whittier Cutoff became Alaska's main supply link for the military. However, commercial vessels continued to use Seward. In 1960, the U.S. Army relinquished all control of Whittier and turned the port and the Cutoff over to the Alaska Railroad.

Parts of the 1985 movie *Runaway Train* were filmed on this line. Railroad directions for this line are south to Whittier and north to the mainline at Whittier Junction. The Alaska Railroad began an effort to CTC signalize the entire line in 2011. Mileposts on this line are designated by "F".

F0.0   **END OF TRACK** – The Whittier Branch ends/begins along Depot Road near an independent barge service on Passage Canal, which leads to Prince William Sound. Whittier is on the northeast shore of the Kenai Peninsula, at the head of Passage Canal, a location that is ice free throughout the year. While a wonderful port area, the issue has always been access to the interior of Alaska since this area is surrounded by glacier-covered mountains.

F0.3   **BARGE TERMINAL** – The Alaska Railroad conducts most of its railcar interchange through the slips at Whittier. The Alaska Railroad operates weekly service to Seattle using special barges built by Gunderson of Portland, Oregon. Their names are Anchorage Provider, Fairbanks Provider and Whittier Provider. Each barge has 8 tracks of about 400 feet in length. The barges are designed to handle the railcars on the deck with containers stacked on frames above. Each roundtrip requires three weeks. Besides the ARR service, barge service is also provided by Canadian National's AquaTrain. This service operates between CN's northwestern terminus of Prince Rupert, B.C., and Whittier.

       The barge slip is like a bridge, one end is on the land side and the other end rests on the edge of the barge. There are three sets of tracks on it. The two towers by the barge slip are the slip towers that have the cables and counter weights on them. Due to the incredibly fast and high/low tides, the window of time to unload and reload the barge is rather short, leading to an intricate ballet of trains, barge, tug and their crews.

On the south side of the yard there was the Alaska Railroad Whittier Cutoff Monument. The monument has been damaged by weather and removed until it can be restored. To save you time in hunting down its message, it reads:

ALASKA RAILROAD WHITTIER CUTOFF 1941-1943

The Alaska Railroad built by the United States Government for the development of Alaska.

Whittier Cutoff sponsored by the Alaska Railroad and approved by the War Department because of it's strategic advantages and reduction of railroad distance by 52 miles to Fairbanks. Construction supervised by Corps of Engineers, US Army contractor West Construction Company, Boston, Massachusetts.

1908 – Wilford B. Hoggatt, Governor of Alaska, requested Congress to investigate the feasibility of constructing a railroad from tidewater to the interior of Alaska.

1912 – Congress granted territorial government to Alaska and authorized President William Howard Taft to appoint the Alaska Railroad Commission to investigate railroad routes in Alaska.

1913 – The Alaska Railroad Commission submitted its report to the President.

1914 – Congress authorizes President Woodrow Wilson to build the railroad.. He appointed the Alaskan Engineering Commission for its construction.

> *1919 – President Wilson selected the route from Seward to Nenana with a branch line to the Matanuska coal fields. An extension to Fairbanks was later authorized.*
>
> *1923 – President Warren G. Harding drove the golden spike at North Nenana, signifying the completion of the railroad from Seward to Fairbanks.*
>
> *1941 – President Franklin D. Roosevelt signed the act appropriating funds for the construction of Whittier Cutoff.*
>
> *1943 – Whittier terminal and railroad completed and placed in operation.*

On the hillside to the south is a large white building about six stories tall overlooking the harbor. This is the Buckner Building, built in 1953, damaged in the 1964 earthquake, and now vacant. (Whittier was severely damaged by tsunamis triggered by the 1964 Good Friday Earthquake; thirteen people died due to waves that reached 43 feet.) It once held 1000 apartments, a hospital, a bowling alley, theater, gym, swimming pool, bank, post office, rifle range, and shops for Army personnel. For many years it was the largest building in Alaska, and was sometimes called the "city under one roof." It still stands due to the difficulty of demolition as the building contains great amounts of asbestos.

Whittier Division

Buckner Building, Whittier. Photo by Barton Jennings.

F0.8 **WHITTIER YARD** – Whittier Yard contains about a half dozen tracks as well as a small intermodal facility. The yard was designed to provide space for cars moving on and off the barges.

This is the heart of the town of Whittier. If the sun is out, consider yourself lucky. Whittier averages 197.8 inches of rain a year and 249.1 inches of snow. December is the wettest month with September signaling the start of the rainy season.

The Alaska Railroad worked for a decade on their Whittier Master Plan, an attempt to improve the railroad infrastructure in Whittier. Among the projects completed was [1] a new pedestrian underpass under the rail yard (2002); [2] the construction of a new equipment maintenance facility (2002); [3] improvements to the Delong Dock (2002); [4] the construction of barge slip side-loading structures (2002); [5] demolition of the old transit shed (2003); [6] construction of a new cruise ship passenger spur and platform (2004); [7] increased security measures including cameras and fencing (2006/07); [8] demolition of the marginal wharf (2008); and [9] the extension of the barge slip ramp and the replacement of the stern (rear) unloading area to include hydraulic lifts and pass/pass features (2009-2011). In 2012, there were plans to install a full security fence around the Whittier Yard with a $311,224 Homeland Security grant and $82,000 from railroad.

The name Whittier was officially assigned to the community on September 4, 1941, when a U.S. Army press release stated that the "name of 'Whittier' was approved by Secretary Ickes today for the townsite to be constructed at the new southern terminus of the Alaska Railroad, originally known as Portage Bay. The name Whittier was suggested by the town's proximity to Whittier Glacier, named after the poet by the Coast and Geodetic Survey." Before that, the area was known as Portage Bay because it was the access point to the trail over Portage Pass. There was not really a town here, it was just a handy place for boats to land and people to walk across the mountains to reach the gold fields around Hope. The trail over Portage Pass has been historically used by Alaska Natives, Russian fur traders, and early settlers, and still exists as a recreational trail. Portage Bay became known as Passage Bay with the presence of the military during World War II, but then was again renamed Passage Canal, used by the USGS and nautical charts.

The Great Pacific Seafoods facility is on the south side of the yard. Here you can see Alaska Railroad mechanical reefer 11507. In 1966, the Alaska Railroad purchased 11 mechanical reefers from Pacific Car and Foundry. These 57-foot reefers were used to ship juice into Alaska and fish to the lower 48 states. When they ended their useful life, most of the reefers had their roofs cut off, were filled with scrap and sent south. Today, mechanical reefers have disappeared on the Alaska Railroad except for 11507 which is used as a storage shed.

To the south is another large building dating from the military era of Whittier. Originally called the Hodge Building, and now known as the Begich Tower, this

14-story structure was at one time the tallest building in Alaska. Built for family housing, it was completed in 1956, only four years before Whittier was inactivated and mothballed by the U.S. Military. The building initially held 177 apartments and now consists of condos in which most of Whittier's residents live. The first floor contains the city offices, grocery, library, post office, and so forth. The interior was 1950s institutional until a recent upgrade. The building was renamed in 1973 for Congressman Nick Begich, who was killed in a plane crash the previous year.

To the north of the yard is the ferry terminal for the Alaska Marine Highway. Ferry service is available from Whittier to Valdez, Cordova, Juneau, and even Dutch Harbor. With an increase in cruise ship activity in Whittier, there has also been some recent development of tourist facilities around the ferry terminal. Several restaurants and souvenir stores can now be found here.

Also to the north is the Whittier U.S. Coast Guard Auxiliary – District 17, with their ex-ARR caboose 1076, which was built by Pacific Car and Foundry of Renton, WA, in 1949.

Whittier. Photo by Barton Jennings.

Alaska Railroad: History Through the Miles

F1.2 **WHITTIER CREEK** – The railroad crosses Whittier Creek on a 9-span wood trestle. Whittier Creek drains the northeast corner of Whittier Glacier. Whittier Glacier, to the south, was named for the American poet John Greenleaf Whittier in 1915, and the creek and community also took the name. Take a look around, especially to the south. Whittier is surrounded by the Chugach National Forest, the second largest in the United States and a vast wilderness.

The main road into town crosses the tracks just east of the Whittier Creek bridge.

F1.3 **WHITTIER STATION** – The original Whittier station was located next to the docks where passengers could easily transfer to trains from arriving ships. However, today's rail station, actually a collection of frames covered in canvas during the summers, is about a mile further west, across from the new cruise ship terminal. Just across the highway is the new cruise ship facility, opened on May 15, 2004, when the Coral Princess docked. The Alaska Railroad operates dedicated passenger trains from here to Anchorage and Denali for the cruise ship lines.

ARR 3009 approaching Whittier station. Photo by Barton Jennings.

Whittier Division

The station and cruise ship dock are not the first structures at this location. Colombia Lumber Company operated a steam sawmill here from the mid-1940s until it was destroyed in the 1964 Alaska earthquake. The mill operated seasonally because of the heavy snows in Whittier. They cut timber and dimensional lumber as well as ties for the Alaska Railroad under contract. Whittier Creek used to pass between the slash burner and the mill. A dock was used for loading flats with finished lumber and servicing tow boats and small tugs used to bring log floats of spruce in from logging operations at remote sites in Prince William Sound. The new cruise ship dock occupies the space where the old wood dock served the tow boats.

To the south during the late 1950s was a Koopers Creosote Plant, built inside the railroad wye at Whittier Creek. They had a contract with the ARR to treat ties cut by the Colombia Lumber mill.

F2.1 SHAKESPEARE GLACIER CREEK – This area is known as "West Camp" or "Head of the Bay." This delta area is created by creeks flowing from Portage Pass, Shakespeare Glacier and Learnard Glacier. The railroad bridge is just over 200 feet long. Shakespeare Glacier was named in 1915 for William Shakespeare by the USC&GS.

F2.2 PETROLEUM TERMINAL – To the north is a former U.S. Army jet fuel tank farm, today listed as a Defense Fuel Supply Point. The facility has been slowly removed.

F2.6 WHITTIER TUNNEL WHITTIER PORTAL (DOOR 1) – Traffic through the tunnel is closely monitored and scheduled to prevent accidents since the route is single lane throughout. According to the tunnel's website, "two complex computer systems are dedicated to help the tunnel operations staff operate the tunnel in a safe and efficient manner. One of the most complicated aspects of tunnel construction and operation is the Tunnel Control System (TCS) and Train Signal System (TSS). These two computer-based systems make it possible for cars and trains to safely take turns traveling through the tunnel."

"The TCS is responsible for all vehicle movement within the tunnel. An intelligent traffic system, the TCS tracks each vehicle and meters traffic through the tunnel. One of its main functions is to monitor the direction of vehicle movement and, through its control of the traffic signals and gates, allow vehicles to travel only in one direction at a time. The TCS also monitors tunnel operations via live video covering the length of the tunnel. If a car stops for any reason, the vehicle detection equipment will alert the tunnel control operator in the Tunnel Control Center, direct the video cameras automatically to display that area of the tunnel, and shut appropriate gates. The TCS also continually monitors and adjusts the lighting and ventilation systems."

"In a similar fashion, the TSS is responsible for train movement through the tunnel. This system controls train switches and signals and ensures that trains only move through the tunnel in one direction at a time and only when there are no vehicles in the tunnel."

"Because these systems are linked, the TCS and TSS together ensure that cars and trains never meet in the tunnel. When the tunnel is in the railroad mode, the TSS controls the trains and locks out the operation of the TCS system. All highway gates are closed and the highway signals are set to red. When the tunnel is in the highway mode, the TCS locks out the TSS until highway vehicles are cleared from the tunnel."

F5.1 **WHITTIER TUNNEL BEAR VALLEY PORTAL (DOOR 2)** - Today known as the Anton Anderson Memorial Tunnel, the tunnel passes under Maynard Mountain and is the second longest highway tunnel and longest combined rail and highway tunnel in North

Whittier Division

America. The rail line was originally opened on April 23, 1943, linking Whittier to the Alaska Railroad's main line at Portage. In the mid-1960s, the Alaska Railroad began offering a shuttle service for automobiles thru the tunnel between Whittier and the former town of Portage. As traffic to Whittier increased, the shuttle became insufficient, leading in the 1990s to a project to convert the existing railroad tunnel into a one-lane, combination highway and railway tunnel. Construction on this project began in September 1998, and the combined tunnel was opened to traffic on June 7, 2000. To coordinate movements through the tunnel, traffic is scheduled in 20 minute blocks – twenty minutes each for eastbound highway traffic, westbound highway traffic, and the Alaska Railroad. By the way, the tunnel is now a toll route with a fare collected on the eastbound move for a roundtrip.

Eastbound ARR 4324 exiting Portage Tunnel into Bear Valley. Photo by Barton Jennings.

Notice the alpine look of the portal. The engineering report on the tunnel states that "the portals are built of structural steel and concrete to safely absorb the shock of any potential avalanche and are shaped like A-frames to split any snow slide. Each portal building will house two portal fans (for tunnel ventilation), emergency vehicles and equipment, power distribution equipment, furnaces to heat ice-control panels within the tunnel and remote operations consoles (the main operations center is in a separate facility). Each portal building has a train-sized 'garage' door that rolls up and down to let automobiles and trains in and out of the tunnel. Due to the potential for avalanches, the portal roof on the Whittier side has been constructed to withstand forces of 1000 pounds per square foot. The roof is made with 14-inch-thick concrete panels. On the Bear Valley side, the roof is designed to withstand forces of 220 pounds per square foot which is equivalent to about 11 feet of new snow. For comparison, the building code for Anchorage requires that building roofs can be constructed to withstand a load of 40 pounds per square foot."

The tunnel was also rebuilt with other concerns such as ventilation, escape rooms (called "safe houses" – rooms at 1600 foot intervals for use in case of an emergency), and pull-outs for broken down vehicles.

The tunnel is named after Anton Anderson, an army engineer who in 1941 headed up the construction of the railroad line from Whittier to Portage. The tunnel is listed as being 14,361 feet long in some materials while the official Anton Anderson Memorial Tunnel website states that it is 13,300 feet long.

F5.3 **BEAR VALLEY** – There is a siding to the north, a relatively new feature. Bear Valley has been described as a desolate bowl full of willows, rocks and tundra south of Boggs Peak, aptly named for the wildlife that roam the area. To the south you can view Portage Glacier and Portage Lake, favorite day trip destinations for people out of Anchorage.

Whittier Division

ARR 3013 in Bear Valley, with Learnard Glacier visible above. Photo by Barton Jennings.

F5.7   **PLACER CREEK** – The railroad crosses Placer Creek on a new girder bridge, replacing a 17-span timber trestle in October 2006. Placer Creek drains Bear Valley and flows into Portage Lake.

F5.8   **PORTAGE TUNNEL BEAR VALLEY PORTAL (DOOR 3)** – At approximately 4905 feet long, this tunnel passes under Begich Peak.

F6.7   **PORTAGE TUNNEL WEST PORTAL (DOOR 4)** – Between Portage and Portage Tunnel, the railroad follows Portage Creek through a narrow but marshy valley, heavily impacted by the 1964 earthquake.

F7.1   **MORAINE** – A former siding location, originally a railroad engineering camp, named for the glacial moraines in the area. MORA Block, named for Moraine, begins here for eastbound trains.

F11.3 **COHO** – This is a siding and yard (often known as New Yard) just off of the mainline to the south. It generally is used by maintenance-of-way trains, but can also be used by mainline freights to drop off or pick up cars. The New

Yard term comes from the fact that it replaced the old Portage Yard which sank with the earthquake. Coho is a species of salmon.

F12.4 **WHITTIER JUNCTION** – This is the junction with the main line.

North Pole, Alaska, Post Office. Photo by Sarah Jennings.

Eielson Branch (G Branch)

The 29-mile line between Fairbanks and Eielson Air Force Base, beyond North Pole, was built during World War II. Railroad directions for this line are north to Eielson and south to the mainline at Fairbanks, although Eielson is south of Fairbanks. Note that these mileposts are "G" mileposts. Passenger trains normally do not operate on this line. However, at least one charter train has operated here, and the line is visible south of Fairbanks from the Richardson Highway.

G0.0   **MAIN LINE CONNECTION** – The old Eielson Branch broke off from the original mainline at milepost 469.5.

G0.2   **FAIRBANKS STATION** – This is the new Fairbanks station, built to provide adequate train space for the new longer trains with private cruise ship cars. The station opened on May 15, 2005.

        The new $22.5 million station is located on a 32-acre site adjacent to the railroad's operations yard, near the intersection of the Johansen Expressway and Danby Street. When it opened in 2005, it replaced the terminal near the intersection of Driveway Street and Phillips

Field Road. The new facility was funded through a combination of Federal Transit Administration and Federal Railroad Administration dollars. The new station eliminated the need to block traffic on Phillips Field Road while loading and unloading and made turning trains easier. It also provided much better facilities for the growing cruise ship business that was regularly adding cars to the passenger consists at the time.

G0.4　**PASSENGER LOOP CONNECTION** – With the new station now located on this line, the Alaska Railroad can park trains at the station overnight. However, this means that the train is facing the wrong direction when it is ready to leave. To solve this problem, a loop has been built to turn passenger trains as they leave Fairbanks for Anchorage. This was accomplished by extending a spur around the ramp area to another industrial spur which connected to the former mainline just north of the previous station.

G0.5　**DRIVEWAY STREET** – An access road to several area industries.

G1.0　**NOYES SLOUGH** – The railroad crosses this stream using two 14' timber spans and a 123' truss bridge. The slough was known as the Chena Slough until about 1910, when the name "Noyes Slough" was accepted and adopted. Noyes Slough was named after Fred Noyes, who arrived in Dawson, Canada, via the Chilkoot Trail in 1897. Fred Noyes remained in Dawson from 1897 to 1902 and then went west to Fairbanks, Alaska. Noyes operated two sawmills off the Chena River in Fairbanks. However, Fred Noyes was best known for his riverboat, the *Idler*, that he built in 1911 and used to move logs from along the slough to his mills on the river. Noyes returned to Seattle in the mid-1920s and died an accidental death in 1928. The house of Fred Noyes still stands today on Illinois Street in Fairbanks.

Eielson Branch

G1.1 **COLLEGE ROAD** – College Road is the main highway on the north side of Fairbanks. It runs from downtown to the northwest side of Fairbanks at the University of Alaska Fairbanks campus.

G1.9 **STEESE EXPRESSWAY** – The Steese Highway, Alaska Highway 2 at this location, extends 162 miles from Fairbanks to Circle, a community on the Yukon River just 50 miles below the Arctic Circle. The Steese Highway was completed in 1927 and named for General James G. Steese, U.S. Army, former president of the Alaska Road Commission. Steese Highway runs through the richest gold mining district in the state. Just a few miles north of here, at Fox, are a number of reminders of the gold rush, including a gold dredge and the El Dorado Gold Mine.

G2.4 **D STREET** – The railroad crosses a number of local streets through this area.

G2.7 **FAREWELL STREET** – A good name as the railroad leaves Fairbanks and enters Fort Wainwright. **Please note that because the railroad passes through military property, photography is limited or not generally allowed from this point to milepost G6.0.**

G3.2 **CHENA RIVER** – The Chena River (first reported as the Indian name in 1898) forms in the hills east of Fairbanks and empties into the Tanana River near Fairbanks. The Chena River was a major factor in the founding of Fairbanks. E.T. Barnette started a trading post on the lower river when he found out miners had discovered gold in the nearby streams. While trying to move his supplies to the gold camps, the captain of the riverboat he was on refused to take him any farther up the Tanana River and left him near the junction with the Chena River. The trading post became known as Fairbanks, in honor of the senator from Indiana, Charles Fairbanks, who later became the Vice-President of the United States under Teddy Roosevelt.

The bridge that the railroad uses to cross the Chena River consists of 6 spans (4 Pratt pony truss spans, 2 deck plate girder spans) for a total of 632 feet. It is located at 447 feet above sea level. Reportedly, when it was originally built, it was decked so that highway traffic could also use it.

The Pratt Pony Truss was invented in 1844 by Thomas and Caleb Pratt. These spans were initially built as a combination wood and iron truss, but were soon constructed in iron only. This truss is practical for use with spans up to 250 feet and was a common configuration for railroad bridges as truss bridges moved from wood to iron to steel. A Pratt Pony Truss includes vertical members and diagonals that slope down towards the center, reverse of those on the Howe truss. The Pratt Pony Truss is easy to build and was a favorite of the U.S. military and other government organizations. You will see dozens of these bridges along the Alaska Railroad.

For those interested in bridges, here is an explanation of some of the terms. To start with, a truss bridge uses a structure of connected bridge parts to form triangular units to carry the load of the bridge. This is one of the oldest types of modern bridges, is easy to design, and is efficient in the use of materials. When the track is on top of the truss the bridge is called a deck truss. When the truss is above and below the track and is connected in both places, it is known as a through truss since you pass through the bridge. Some truss bridges have the truss stick above the tracks but they don't connect the tops of each truss together. This design is known as a pony truss or half-through truss.

Just railroad north of the Chena River, the railroad makes a hard turn to the right using a 10 degree curve. This turn is necessary to take the railroad around the end of the 6L runway of Ladd Army Airfield/Fort Wainwright.

Eielson Branch

G3.8 **FORT WAINWRIGHT** – Fort Wainwright started in 1939 as Ladd Field when Congress granted $4 million to construct an Army Air Corps cold weather experimental station at Fairbanks. The new base was called Ladd Field, in honor of Major Arthur K. Ladd, an Air Corps pilot killed in a plane crash in South Carolina in 1935. The Air Corps bought two homesteads near Fairbanks for a building site. Little was known then about building on permafrost, so problems quickly became evident. In addition to the airstrip, housing and office space, workers also had to build a rail spur into Fairbanks to transport equipment and supplies. The railroad was built first. Dynamite was used to blast out huge chunks of permafrost that were pushed into a big pile upon which the road bed was built. When spring came, the permafrost melted, and the rails were twisted in all directions.

The first Air Corps detachment assigned to Alaska arrived in Fairbanks in April 1940. The men stationed here tested clothing and equipment during the bitter cold winters until World War II. With the outbreak of war with Japan in late 1941 and the U.S. entrance into WWII, Ladd Field became more than a cold weather test station, it became a critical link in the Alaska-Siberia Lend-Lease route. The Lend-Lease Program enabled Russians to pick up planes from the United States and fly them west to Russia for wartime use. Ladd Field became the turnover point for large numbers of aircraft and pilots who made the arduous trip from Montana, through the Northwest Territories and into the Interior.

In August and September of 1942, the first Soviet pilots and civilians of the Soviet Purchasing Commission arrived in Fairbanks and were housed at Ladd Field. They were checked out in aircraft ranging from P-39 Air Cobras to B-25 Mitchell bombers, before the planes were transferred to them. The Russians then flew the aircraft to Siberia via Galena and Nome where they were eventually used in the Soviet war effort against Germany. The first Lend-Lease flight took place September 3, 1942, and the last in September 1945. In all, American crews delivered almost 8000 aircraft to Soviet aircrews for their war effort. Other work continued here. For example, in 1944, the first U.S. prototype jet was sent to Ladd for testing.

With the reorganization of the War Department into the Defense Department after WWII, Ladd Field became Ladd Air Force Base. By the 1950s, military personnel in Alaska were engaged in a peacetime training routine with troops from all over the Lower 48 and Canada. The troops participated in large-scale winter exercises, while at the same time guarding against the Cold War threat of Soviet aggression.

In 1960 it was announced that the installation would go back to the Army. In 1961, Wilber M. Brucker, then Secretary of the Army, dedicated the post as Fort Jonathan M. Wainwright, in honor of the World War II hero of Bataan. Ladd Field is listed in the Register of National Historic Landmarks. Today there are nearly 4600 soldiers and 6100 family members who call Fort Wainwright home.

G5.4 **BOB SMALL RUNAROUND** – This track is used to run around a cut of coal hoppers before spotting them at the Fort Wainwright coal power plant. Apparently, Bob Small was a maintenance-of-way worker from a few decades ago.

G6.0 **JUNCTION WITH FAIRBANKS AIRPORT LEAD** – Heading north, the line to North Pole makes a 90 degree turn to the left. Heading straight is a 10-mile lead to the Fairbanks airport. In 1972, a line change was made between milepost 5.4 and 6.3. The switch is powered and is controlled by the train crew using their radios on Channel 5. That is the Richardson Highway to the right. **Please note that because the railroad passes through military property, photography is limited or not generally allowed from this point to milepost G2.7.**

Eielson Branch

Details about the Fairbanks International Airport Branch are found on page 179.

G7.4 **STRYKER RAMPS** – A Stryker is a family of 4-wheel military vehicles, with many based here. These ramps are used to load and unload them from Alaska Railroad trains.

G8.6 **ARCTIC REDIE MIX** – A major cement, sand and gravel contractor in the Fairbanks area. The north boundary of Fort Wainwright is near here at the grade crossing with Badger Road.

G12.4 **GREEN CONSTRUCTION** – Look for the short spur to the right of the train as it heads toward North Pole.

G14.7 **RICHARDSON HIGHWAY** – The Richardson Highway (near Fairbanks also known as Alaska Route 2), the first major road built in Alaska, runs 368 miles from Valdez to Fairbanks. In 1898, the U.S. Army built a pack trail from the port at Valdez to Eagle (on the Yukon River), a distance of about 409 miles, to provide an "all-American" route to the Klondike gold fields. After the rush ended, the Army kept the trail open in order to connect its posts at Fort Liscum, in Valdez, and Fort Egbert, in Eagle. The Fairbanks gold rush in 1902, and the construction of a WAMCATS (Washington-Alaska Military Cable and Telegraph System) telegraph line along the trail in 1903, made the Valdez-to-Eagle trail one of the most important access routes to the Alaska Interior. In 1910, the Alaska Road Commission upgraded it to a wagon road under the supervision of U.S. Army General Wilds P. Richardson, for whom the highway was later named. The road was further upgraded in the 1920s due to an increase in motorized travel. The Alaska Highway, built during World War II, connected the rest of the continent to the Richardson Highway at Delta Junction, allowing motor access to the new military bases built in the Territory just prior to the war. The highway was paved in 1957. In the Fairbanks area, the highway has been turned into a multiple lane expressway connecting the town to many of the area industries and military facilities.

The railroad follows Old Richardson Highway into North Pole while the "new" Richardson Highway passes around town to compass north.

G15.9 SPIRIT OF NORTH POLE – Home of the special Christmas card postmark, North Pole is located 13 miles south of Fairbanks on the Richardson Highway. In 1944, Bon V. Davis homesteaded this area but sold out to the Dahl and Gaske Development Company, which subdivided it for a town. The community was first incorporated as a city in 1953. The original plan in selecting the name "North Pole" was to attract the toy industry to manufacture articles from the "North Pole." However, this idea failed but the town became the social center for the surrounding military bases.

The Alaska Railroad has a siding here measuring 1496 feet long. Look for the Alaska Railroad sign that really does say "Spirit of North Pole."

Spirit of North Pole sign. Photo by Barton Jennings.

For most people, North Pole is most famous for the Santa Claus House®. In the early 1950s, Con and Nellie

Miller, new to Alaska's interior, began a small trading business in the area. Donning an old red Santa suit, Con earned celebrity status as Santa Claus in the eyes of the village children. In 1952, the Millers began building a trading post in the new settlement of North Pole and the Santa Claus House® was born.

Santa Claus House®, North Pole, Alaska. Photo by Sarah Jennings.

Robert Norman "Bob" Ross, creator and host of *The Joy of Painting* show on PBS (yep, the "happy little trees" guy) once lived in North Pole. Ross enlisted in the U.S. Air Force at age 18 and was eventually transferred to nearby Eielson AFB. The nearby snow and mountains became the subject of much of his art. Reportedly, he developed his quick-painting technique so he could complete pieces of art during his short breaks at work.

Two oil refineries keep the community busy. The refineries produce several unit trains of product a day. For example, all aircraft fuel used at Fairbanks and Anchorage airports come from these refineries, as well as much of the motor and heating fuels consumed in the state. In 1975, the North Pole Refinery, MAPCO, began production here. Since then, a second refinery, Petro Star, has been constructed. Because of these refineries, North Pole has one of the highest assessed evaluations per capita in Alaska. Beginning in 2014, at least one of the refineries was evaluating shutting down due to the costs of operating.

Alaska Railroad: History Through the Miles

G16.0 SECTION HOUSE DRIVE – A neat name - isn't it?

G16.4 CHAPADOS – This is the location of a 5569 foot long siding.

Chapados is a unique name. Frank Chapados was appointed to the first Board of Directors of the Alaska Railroad Corporation in 1984, where he served as vice chairman. Born in Juneau in 1914, Frank worked in mining before he moved to Fairbanks in 1939 to study engineering at the University of Alaska Fairbanks. In 1942, he became a U.S. Deputy Marshal, then served in the Navy before returning to his Deputy Marshal position in Fairbanks. He later worked for the U.S. Fish and Wildlife Service, and then President Truman appointed him as U.S. Marshal for Fairbanks in 1951. After Alaska became a state, Frank served in the first and second Legislatures as a member of the House of Representatives.

G16.6 OLD RICHARDSON HIGHWAY – The original Richardson Highway was built through town. Today, it has been moved to a new bypass route on the north side of town.

G16.6 NORTH POLE REFINERY MAIN – To the south are several oil refineries which produce most of the gasoline, diesel, and jet fuel for use throughout Alaska. The refineries are connected to the Trans-Alaska Pipeline. When originally built, there was only one small refinery connected to the pipeline system, which was owned by Earth Resources Company of Alaska. This refinery was later purchased by MAPCO, then Williams Energy, and most recently by Flint Hills Refinery. In 2014, Flint Hills was considering shutting down the facility due to costs and regulatory pressures.

The Flint Hills Resources North Pole Refinery has a crude oil processing capacity of about 220,000 barrels per day. An affiliate acquired the North Pole Refinery – Alaska's largest – in 2004. It processes North

Slope crude oil and supplies gasoline, jet fuel, heating oil, diesel, gasoil and asphalt to local and international markets. About 60 percent of the refinery's production is destined for the aviation market. The company also owns and operates products terminals in Fairbanks and Anchorage that store and distribute asphalt, fuel oils, diesel, jet fuel and gasoline refined at the North Pole Refinery. The Anchorage Terminal receives products from the North Pole Refinery via Alaska Railroad tank cars, annually offloading about 35,000 rail cars. Generally one or two tank trains run daily each way between the refinery and the Anchorage terminal.

Petro Star's North Pole refinery, built in 1985, is a 17,000 barrel-per-day refinery that produces kerosene, diesel and jet fuels. The entire refinery is operated by thirteen employees. As a fully automated refinery, the plant can be run by a single operator. The North Pole refinery operates 24 hours a day, 365 days a year.

According to the City of North Pole, Flint Hills Resources and Petro Star are essential in providing fuels to Eielson AFB and Ft. Wainwright, and heating oil to Interior and rural Alaska. Flint Hills, Alaska's largest refinery, produces 16% of the gasoline used in Alaska, accounts for up to 45% of the Alaska Railroad Corporation's revenue, has historically provided up to 60% of the commercial jet fuel used at Ted Steven's International Airport in Anchorage and up to 100% of the commercial jet fuel used at Fairbanks International Airport.

G17.6 LAURANCE ROAD – Laurance Road runs east-west between Richardson Highway and the refineries at North Pole. The Alaska Railroad timetable indicates that SD70MAC locomotives are prohibited beyond G17.8. The track beyond this point is built with smaller rails and also is limited to 10mph for all trains.

G19.0 DYKE ROAD – Just east of Dyke Road, the railroad curves to the northeast for about a half mile before turning back to the southeast to cross the Moose Creek Dam and the Chena River floodway. In 1967, the Chena River flooded over its banks and put Fairbanks under many feet of water. Beginning in 1970, planning began on a major flood control project to solve this problem. The solution was the 8-mile long Moose Creek Dam which controls the water level on the Chena River and provides a floodway between the Chena River and the Tanana River to the south. As a part of this project, both the Richardson Highway and the Alaska Railroad were rerouted and moved to the north, explaining this interesting alignment.

G20.2   **MOOSE CREEK FLOODWAY TRESTLE** – This 1000-foot long trestle was built in 1977 as a part of the Chena River Flood Control Project. To the south you can see Piledriver Slough enter the floodway. Piledriver follows Highway 2 up from the south.

G20.7   **RICHARDSON HIGHWAY** – We again cross the Richardson Highway, also relocated as a part of the Chena River Flood Control Project.

G21.2   **MOOSE CREEK** – Once the site of a spur track, Moose Creek is a small rural community just outside of Eielson Air Force Base. This relatively new community is named for the nearby stream. There was once another Moose Creek station on the Alaska Railroad. It was located on the Palmer Branch about six miles east of Palmer.

G21.4   **MOOSE CREEK BRIDGE** – The railroad crosses the stream on a bridge a bit more than 110 feet long. There are dozens of Moose Creeks in Alaska.

G23.8   **MOOSE CREEK SPUR ROAD** – This was once the loop off of Richardson Highway through the business section of Moose Creek.

Eielson Branch

G24.1 BLUFF SPUR – This is the boundary between Alaska Railroad ownership (actually milepost 24.5) and military ownership of the line. The front gate to Eielson Air Force Base is located here.

G28.0 EIELSON – Eielson Air Force Base (AFB) is named for polar pilot Carl Benjamin Eielson (1897-1929). Eielson was an aviator, bush pilot and explorer who was the first person to fly from Alaska over the North Pole to Greenland. After learning to fly during WWI, Eielson eventually moved to Alaska to teach school. However, flying was his main interest and he soon became famous for his exploits.

In 1921, Eielson flew the first air mail in Alaska from Fairbanks to McGrath in 4 hours, a distance dog sleds took 20 days to cover. He is perhaps best known for flying the first airplane across the Arctic Ocean, with Australian explorer Hubert Wilkins in April 1928. In the Antarctic summer of 1928-1929, Eielson and Wilkins were the first people to make air explorations of the Antarctic, charting several islands which were previously unknown. Eielson was also responsible for establishing Alaskan Airways, a subsidiary of The Aviation Corporation of America. Eielson died alongside his mechanic Earl Borland in an air crash on November 9, 1929, in Siberia while attempting to rescue 15 passengers of the *Nanuk*, a cargo vessel trapped in the ice at North Cape (shown as Mys Schmidt on today's maps).

On June 7, 1943, the Western Defense Command ordered construction of a new airfield near present-day Fort Wainwright, then an Army airfield named after Major Arthur Ladd. Surveyor reports indicated a site a little more than twenty-five miles southeast of Ladd Army Airfield to be the best location for the new airfield due to the flat terrain. The field became known as "Mile 26" because of its proximity to a U.S. Army Signal Corps telegraph station and a Richardson Highway milepost marker using the same designation. Construction began on the initial two runways and supporting facilities on August 25, 1943, and was completed on October 17, 1944. Although more than $8 million was spent on the airfield, operational uses of Mile 26 were few throughout the rest of World War II. Mile 26 closed when the war ended.

The base reopened in September 1946, once again as a satellite of Ladd Field. The first United States Air Force (USAF) operational unit assigned to Eielson was the 57th Fighter Group, followed shortly by the 97th Bombardment Wing with their Strategic Air Command B-29 Superfortress bombers during December 1947. In 1948, Eielson moved from under the shadow of Ladd Field when the Alaskan Air Command assumed organizational control. The primary missions of Mile 26 were to support Arctic training for USAF tactical and strategic units, as well as defend the base itself. Headquarters USAF General Order 2, dated January 13, 1948, redesignated Mile 26 as Eielson AFB.

Construction boomed at Eielson AFB during the 1950s due to the Cold War. Many of the facilities still in use today were built at that time. The assignment of units here have changed over the years due to national needs. Today, Eielson is home to the 354th Fighter Wing which is part of Pacific Air Forces Eleventh Air Force.

Reportedly, Eielson AFB operates two GP40-2 locomotives to move rail traffic around on the base.

G28.3 EIELSON WYE – A wye to the north at the south end of the small yard on the base. The end of the line is at milepost 28.6.

Fairbanks International Airport Branch (FIAB) (H Branch)

Carl Ben Eielson first flew into Fairbanks in 1923 to start Alaskan Airways. Before 1951, most of the general air traffic at Fairbanks used a small landing field here. However, air carriers used Ladd Air Force Base, today referred to as Fort Wainwright. In 1948, plans were created for a new international airport which opened in 1951. The passenger terminal building finally opened in 1954. The railroad's branchline was built to haul supplies for the airport construction and to open an industrial park in the area.

Railroad directions for this line are north to the airport terminal and south to the Eielson Branch, but the line runs basically east to west. This branchline uses "H" to identify its mileposts.

H0.0   **JUNCTION WITH EIELSON BRANCH** – The line to the Fairbanks airport breaks off of the Eielson Branch at milepost 6.05.

H0.2   **RICHARDSON HIGHWAY** – The railroad crosses Alaska Highway 2 – Richardson Highway – and soon swings westward. According to the Alaska Railroad employee timetable, SD70MAC locomotives are prohibited beyond milepost H0.5.

H1.0   **FS&G SPUR** – Fairbanks Sand & Gravel, a local aggregate dealer.

H2.0   **LAKEVIEW DRIVE** – The track winds its way through a series of gravel pits.

H2.8   **NORTH STAR TERMINAL** – Another timetable location named after the local customer.

H2.9   **NORTHLAND WOOD** – Look for the lumberyard. Northland Wood started doing business in 1965 with

Alaska Railroad: History Through the Miles

a small portable sawmill off the Nenana Highway just outside Fairbanks, Alaska. After the sawmill burned down in 1966 the company moved to College Road. In 1982, Northland Wood moved to its current location on South Cushman Street.

H3.0 **WEAVER BROTHERS** – Weaver Brothers is a trucking service that covers the entire state of Alaska. According to the company's website, "Ken and Russ Weaver brought their company to Valdez by Crowley barge in 1953. For the first couple of years they hauled asphalt during the summer, then drove their trucks back down the highway. In 1954 they bought a milk transport company in Fairbanks and began running Inland Riverway Barge Lines with one tug and one barge. In 1955, the two brothers moved their main operations to Anchorage. By the mid-1970's they had terminals in North Kenai, Anchorage, Fairbanks, Valdez, and Seattle. Ownership of the company changed hands in the mid-1970's, and then once again in the fall of 1978, when the Doyle family took over the reins. Historically asphalt hauling, line haul work, and general freight drayage was provided for customers such as ARCO, Chevron, MAPCO, Sea-Land Services, SOHIO, Tesoro, Texaco, TOTE, and others. This launched a steady growth curve that continues nearly two decades later."

H3.1 **SOUTH CUSHMAN STREET** – Cushman Street heads north into downtown Fairbanks, where it serves as the main north-south street. This area has developed into an industrial zone with a very typical northern look of machinery piled everywhere around prefab office and shop buildings.

H3.7 **BRENNTAG** – Brenntag Pacific is a full line commodity and specialty chemical distribution company, serving the western portion of the United States with a wide range of products from oil and gas to food ingredients.

H4.1 **PARKER RUNAROUND** – On the north side of the tracks to the west of Lathrop Street is the old Metro Field airport facility, now closed. That is Taxiway Avenue on the north side of the long quarry pond.

H4.9 **METRO SIDING** – A 1000-foot long siding is to the south.

H5.0 **PEGER ROAD** – You can follow Peger Road to the north and arrive at the west gate of Pioneer Park.

H5.5 **OUT OF SERVICE LIMITS** – Employee Timetable No. 136 states that the track beyond this point is out of service.

H7.5 **SOUTH UNIVERSITY** – University Avenue runs south from the University of Alaska Fairbanks campus to the east side of the Fairbanks airport. A number of small air charter and tour companies have their facilities on University Avenue. The airport branch crosses South University Avenue and then curves to the southwest to loop around the south end of the airport to get to another industrial area on the west side of the airport facility. Past this location, the rail line is on airport property and is governed by airport security requirements.

H9.3 **TESORO** – This location is at West Road.

H9.6 **RUNAROUND** – Located at Airport Way, this runaround is 880 feet long.

H10.0 **FAIRBANKS INTERNATIONAL AIRPORT** – The branch ends at the Fairbanks airport. The line wraps around the south end of the airport. According to the Fairbanks Airport website, "aviation service in the Fairbanks area was initiated at an airfield known as Weeks Field, or Weeks Ball Park, in 1923. This multi-use facility gained importance in the community and throughout the Alaska aviation system from the time that Carl Ben Eielson first flew into Fairbanks in 1923 to start Alaskan Airways. A majority of the area's general aviation and commercial air traffic was accommodated there through mid-century, though air carrier aircraft used Ladd Air Force Base, today referred to as Fort Wainwright. Plans coalesced in 1948 for development of a new facility – Fairbanks International Airport. Construction was authorized by Congress that year. Operations were shifted to the new airport in 1951, though minimal facilities and no terminal building were then available. Air carriers used temporary structures until completion of the passenger terminal building in 1954."

ARR 31 approaching the Anchorage International Airport. Photo by Barton Jennings.

Anchorage International Airport Branch (AIAB) (J Branch)

Railroad directions for this line are north to the airport terminal and south to the mainline at CP1102. The branch officially starts at MP J0.00 on the south leg of the wye at CP1102 (milepost 110.13). The branch can also be accessed from the north leg of the wye at CP1107 (milepost 110.49). Charter trains for various cruise ship companies often use this line to take their customers to and from the airport. This route has been recently rebuilt and the mileposts are designated with a "J".

J0.00   **MAINLINE** – The first two miles of the branch are on a new grade, built when the West International Airport Road was rebuilt and upgraded to expressway standards. The road is where the branch used to be and the railroad is now on the north side of the right-of-way.

J0.20   **NORTH LEG OF WYE** – The highway that bridges over the wye area is Minnesota Drive, the main roadway from the airport area to downtown Anchorage. Just west (railroad-north) of here is a spur track known as

183

Alaska Railroad: History Through the Miles

Anchorage School District, shown as out of service in the 2011 Alaska Railroad timetable.

J0.68 **NORTHWOOD STREET** – After curving around and heading west, thus following the new West International Airport Road toward the airport, the railroad crosses Northwood Street.

J1.23 **JEWEL LAKE ROAD** – To the north, this road is also called Spenard Road. Jewel Lake, located several miles to the south and covering 26 acres, was named in 1912. The Alaska Department of Fish and Game has in the past stocked Jewel Lake with silver salmon and rainbow trout. There is also a swimming area and public park on its shoreline.

J1.43 **WEST INTERNATIONAL AIRPORT ROAD** – The rail line crosses to the south side of the highway.

J1.60 **AIRPORT RUNAROUND** – This 800-foot long siding can be used for locomotives to run around their passenger trains as they drop off and pick up cruise ship tour groups. It is located in an industrial area, full of warehouses and rental car garages.

J2.05 **AIRCRAFT DRIVE** – The railroad crosses this airport road on an overpass, as the railroad grade rises to the grade of the airport complex.

J2.25 **WEST INTERNATIONAL AIRPORT ROAD** – Airport Road reaches the airport, loops through the terminal area, and then circles back. We cross it on a new trestle.

J2.33 **TERMINAL TRACK** – The Anchorage International Airport Branch splits into two station tracks. The Alaska Railroad employee timetable cautions that there is close

Anchorage International Airport Branch

clearance between here and the end of track due to the terminal platform.

J2.43 **TSIA DEPOT** – TSIA is the Ted Stevens International Airport. Technically, this is the Bill Sheffield Alaska Railroad Depot at the Anchorage International Airport. This is the end of the branch, recently extended to this new train station which was built for the cruise ship trains. With the first passengers arriving on May 25, 2003, the project included an elevated track leading to a 300-foot covered passenger platform with a 3-story, 2-level passenger terminal. The building provides assembly space for 250 people and has pedestrian flow into a subterranean tunnel that leads to the main airport facility. A 1999 marketing study projected the depot, built with $28 million in federal money, could serve as many as 200,000 rail passengers annually within a year of opening. However, with no commuter rail service and declining cruise ship traffic, the airport rail station served just 20,000 rail passengers in 2009. To expand its use, the Alaska Railroad has recently begun renting the facility for special events, such as conventions and business meetings.

The station is named for former governor Bill Sheffield, who signed legislation establishing the quasi-public Alaska Railroad Corporation and its seven-member board of directors as a part of the process of Alaska acquiring the railroad from the federal government. Later, Sheffield was appointed to the Board and elected chairman.

Alaska Railroad: History Through the Miles

A train approaching the Bill Sheffield Alaska Railroad Depot at the Anchorage International Airport. Photo by Barton Jennings.

Trans-Alaska Pipeline. Photo by Barton Jennings.

Valdez Spur

Yes, at one time, the Alaska Railroad operated some track in Valdez, Alaska. This track was built to serve the construction boom of the pipeline construction between Valdez and the Alaska North Slope. Alaska Railroad Valdez operations were mainly active during the pipeline boom. Reports vary about the size of the line, but they seem to indicate that there was as much as five miles of spur and yard tracks.

After the 1964 earthquake, much of the site of "old" Valdez was taken over by the U.S. Government. With the need for a construction yard for the pipeline, some of this land was transferred to the Alaska Railroad. A rail line was built from the Valdez dock to several flat areas where multiple ramps were built to load and unload railcars. During the pipeline's construction, pipe was delivered to Valdez from Japan in 40 foot sections. Here, the pipe was welded into sections for specific locations on the route. While most of the pipe was trucked north from Valdez, pipe for the parts of the line north of Delta Junction was loaded on 40-foot flatcars with intermediate idlers and placed on barges for the trip from Valdez to Whittier. At Whittier, the pipe was moved north to Fairbanks for distribution both north and south.

The Annual Report on the Alaska Railroad, Fiscal Year 1976 stated that the "Railroad's Valdez facility was also active in the handling of pipeline freight with over 1300 carloads of 80-foot-long 48-inch diameter pipe being moved from Valdez to Fairbanks via Whittier. This was a unique movement that the pipe was loaded on rail cars in Valdez, which were then loaded on rail barges and towed 90 miles across the waters of Prince William Sound and off-loaded at the Railroad's Whittier dock facility for final movement to Fairbanks."

The railroad operation featured a four-track stub yard at the dock, and then a short mainline and siding from the dock to near Mineral Creek Road, where the route split. A short spur crossed Mineral Creek Road and formed a two-track yard with tracks 690 feet and 1119 feet long. The mainline turned to the east and connected to a three-track yard with several loading ramps. These yard tracks were all slightly more than 1200 feet long. Some of the grades are still visible to visitors.

Originally, the railroad used a small Whiting trackmobile to switch the loads, but business soon overwhelmed the operation. In 1974, the railroad acquired four U.S. Army GE 45-ton locomotives: 7249, 7324, 7331, and 7356. Locomotives 7249 and 7324 were placed into service with the other two locomotives being used for parts.

The operation was shut down soon after the pipeline was completed in 1977. Today, locomotive 7249 is on display at the Museum of Alaska Transportation and Industry in Wasilla.

Part 2

Other Information on Alaska and the ARR

The Nenana River north of Denali. Photo by Sarah Jennings.

Photo by Sarah Jennings.

Alaska – The Basics

At 3:30 in the afternoon of October 18, 1867, on the parade ground near Baranov's Castle in Sitka, an area of about 580,000 square miles (over twice the size of Texas) of Russian territory was formally transferred to the United States. Ninety-two years later this territory, Alaska, became the 49th State of the Union. The cost – $7.2 million at approximately two cents per acre. The state with the nickname of "The Last Frontier" has a name derived from the Aleut word "Aleyska" meaning "great land."

Today, the State of Alaska extends over an area one-fifth as large as that of the "Lower 48" and is unbelievably rich in landscape and other natural resources. Besides being the largest state, Alaska also contains other extremes in U.S. geography. These include the highest point (Mount McKinley, renamed Denali in 2015 – 20,320 feet), the northernmost point (Point Barrow – 71' 23" N), and relative to the Greenwich meridian, the westernmost point (Amatignak Island – 179' 10" W), and the easternmost point (Pochnoi Point – 179' 46" E) in the United States. With 670,000 people – roughly half the population of the Bronx – it's the second smallest state in population with only Wyoming having fewer people. Because of its many remote areas, Alaska has the most private airplane pilots per capita of any state. The difference in how people travel can best be shown by Juneau. Juneau is the only state capital in the continental U.S.

that is not accessible by road from the rest of the state. Ferries and airlines serve the city on a regular basis.

Of the 20 highest peaks in the United States, 17 are in Alaska. The Yukon River, almost 2000 miles long, is the third longest river in the U.S. There are more than 3000 rivers in Alaska and over 3 million lakes. The largest, Lake Iliamna, encompasses over 1000 square miles. Alaska has an estimated 100,000 glaciers, ranging from tiny cirque glaciers to huge valley glaciers. There are more active glaciers and ice fields in Alaska than in the rest of the inhabited world. The largest glacier is the Malaspina at 850 square miles, 50 percent larger than the state of Delaware. Five percent of the state, or 29,000 square miles, is covered by glaciers. Alaska has more than 10 percent of the world's volcanoes. There are more than 70 potentially active volcanoes in the state. Several have erupted in recent times. Alaska also includes America's largest national park, Wrangell-St. Elias, which covers 13.2 million acres (larger than Switzerland), stretching from one of the tallest peaks in North America (Mount St. Elias – 18,008 feet) to the ocean. Today there are more than 54 million acres preserved in Alaska's national parks, or 13 percent of the state's 375 million acres. This also makes up two-thirds of the entire U.S. National Park System. Simply put, this largest of states is big and different.

Alaska is believed by many to be the gateway to North America for the first settlers – early humans who crossed over from Asia during one of many ice ages. Some of these small groups stayed in the area, forming tribal communities. Most of these tribes occupy southeastern Alaska, where temperatures are milder and fishing and hunting are possible all year long. Here are located the Tlingit people and their matriarchal society, the Haida and their unique arts, and the Tsimshian people, who were almost exterminated in the 1860s from smallpox. The Aleutian Islands in southwest Alaska are home to the Aleut's seafaring society. The Yup'ik lived in the western and southwestern parts of the state while their cousins the Alutiiq lived in what is now Southcentral Alaska. The northern interior parts of Alaska are inhabited by the Gwich'in with their dependence on the caribou. The north coastal areas of Alaska are the home of the Inuit.

The Basics

The first modern "white" visitors are believed to have been Russians, who arrived during the 1600s. Most came for whaling and valuable skins, and traded with the natives. Within years, explorers, traders, and hunters from many countries visited the region and Russia claimed the territory to protect its fur trade. The years of Russian control include a mix of isolation, disease, starvation, and brutal slavery of the natives. However, the ventures there were seldom profitable and when Russia needed money, they were more than happy to sell.

Even after the land became a part of the United States, very little was known about the area. Dozens of major explorations over several hundred years were required to document the state, and to name many of its features. The first of these documented visits began in the late 1700s. Captain James Cook of the British Navy explored the area in 1778 looking for the famous "Northwest Passage," a sea route from the Pacific to the Atlantic. He produced some of the first maps of the coastal regions of Alaska and named many of its landmarks. Captain George Vancouver again explored the area 1792-1794 and filled in many gaps in information left by Cook. Vancouver's surveys proved that the continent extended from the Columbia River to Alaska, disproving any claim for a northwest passage within this area. Vancouver's expedition is credited with adding a great deal of new knowledge about the area, and names to the previously poorly mapped coastal areas of southeastern Alaska.

From 1799 until 1867, the Russian American Company was authorized to act as the official Russian representative in the region and worked to create trade with the natives. During the company's existence, a great deal of geographic information was also gathered and published, including the naming of many more landmarks. The company's holdings were eventually sold to the Alaska Commercial Company, a U.S. business.

The Western Union Telegraph Expedition (1865-67) was founded after several failures to construct an Atlantic telegraphic cable. The company explored routes to build an overland telegraph to Asia and Europe via the Bering Strait. For this purpose, parties worked, explored, and built some line in British Columbia, Alaska, and Siberia. The Alaska section was under the leadership of explorer and naturalist Robert Kennicott, whose name was later applied to several areas and business ventures.

In 1816 the U.S. Survey of the Coast was established. In 1878, Congress changed the name to U.S. Coast and Geodetic Survey (USC&GS). Beginning in 1867, the USC&GS conducted extensive hydrographic and topographic studies in Alaska. Among the major documents produced by the organization were coastal maps and tide books used for ocean shipping, and a survey of native names for many of the recognized features in these areas.

The U.S. Geological Survey (USGS) sent its first survey party to Alaska in 1895, making surveys of various gold and coal fields. This was followed by a systematic topographical mapping of the territory. Captain Edwin Forbes Glenn explored routes (1898-1899) between Prince William Sound and the Copper and Susitna Rivers, on west to Cook Inlet, and then north to the Tanana, naming many of the features in these areas. During the early 1900s, the USGS recorded hundreds of new topographical names, mostly given by prospectors. Mapping became more detailed in the 1930s, and again with the help of the military in the 1940s. The 1956 Brooks Range control surveys used two men to do name research, and several hundred new local names appeared on the resulting maps.

World War II brought a boom to the state as the U.S. military built bases and the Alaska Highway to help protect the territory from Japanese invasion. Population growth has historically been slow, but the number of recent television shows about the state and the increase in tourism has led to population growth. Today, the majority of Alaska's population is on a line running from Fairbanks to Anchorage and down onto the Kenai Peninsula. It basically follows the Alaska Railroad. This is also the most commonly visited part of the state due to the transportation access. Approximately 85% of these visitors arrive as part of a cruise ship tour. Most of the rest visit by air, by driving the Alaska Highway, or by taking the Alaska Marine Highway, a series of ferries that serve most coastal communities.

Hatcher Pass, site of Independence Mine State Historical Park. Photo by Barton Jennings.

Alaska Gold Rushes

What most people know about Alaska is that there were gold rushes. Maybe it was watching John Wayne in *North to Alaska*, Charlie Chaplin's classic *The Gold Rush*, or television's *Gold Rush Alaska*, but gold and Alaska seem to go together. A few of the major gold rushes were on the Russian River on the Kenai Peninsula (1850), Telegraph Creek near the former Russian settlement of Wrangell (1861), Gold Creek near Juneau (1880), Fortymile River (1886 – the first major strike in Alaska's interior), Birch Creek and Crooked Creek near Circle on the Yukon River (1893-1894), the "Three Lucky Swedes" discovery at Nome (1898-1899), Pedro Creek (today's Fairbanks in 1902), Valdez Creek (first discovered in 1903, the largest gold placer mine in North America until the 1990s), Tanana (1905), Ruby (1906), "The Last Great Rush" at Iditarod and Flat (1909), Long Creek near Ruby (1910), and finally Chisana (1913).

Notice that this list does not include the great Klondike strike (1896-1898) that created Skagway and the White Pass & Yukon Route Railroad. That is because the gold field was actually on Bonanza Creek at Dawson City in nearby Canada. This rush attracted 100,000 stampeders, although only 30-40,000 actually made it to the gold fields and only about 4000 actually found any gold. However, this massive discovery led to many of the discoveries in Alaska as unsuccessful miners spread out throughout the interiors of Yukon and Alaska.

While there have been the noted gold strikes, gold is actually found and has been mined throughout Alaska, except for the swampy areas of the Yukon Flats and along the North Slope between the Brooks Range and the Beaufort Sea. As indicated above, most of the gold has come from areas around Fairbanks, Juneau, and Nome. In 2008, there were four major hard rock gold mines operating in the state. Among the largest of these is the open pit mine of the Fort Knox Mine, located approximately 25 miles northeast of Fairbanks. The mine, operated by Fairbanks Gold Mining, a subsidiary of Kinross Gold Corporation, was originally permitted in 1994. In 2011, the mine employed more than 500 workers and operated 24-hours a day, 365 days a year. In 2012, the mine produced about 359,948 ounces of gold.

Alaska currently produces more gold (more than 725,000 troy ounces annually) than any state except Nevada. In 2007, gold accounted for 15% of the mining wealth produced in Alaska. Lead and zinc, mainly from the Red Dog mine, accounted for 73%; silver, mainly from the Greens Creek mine, accounted for 8%; while coal and aggregates accounted for nearly 2% each. Alaska produced a total of 40.3 million troy ounces of gold from 1880 through the end of 2007.

For those interested in gold mining, there are several attractions that conduct gold panning, and you get to keep what you find. Check with the state's tourism office for a list of these attractions. The Bureau of Land Management website also lists a number of locations in Alaska where gold panning can be conducted as a recreational activity.

Photo by Barton Jennings.

History of the Alaska Railroad

The Alaska Railroad is the result of three basic efforts. To the south, construction was started by the Alaska Central/Alaska Northern, private companies that attempted to build the railroad using operating revenues. To the north, the Tanana Valley was built to serve the local mining boom and to connect the mines to local rivers which had steamboat service. Connecting the two were the efforts of the federal government, built under the management of the Alaska Engineering Commission (AEC).

The **Alaska Central Railroad** began to build a rail line northward from Seward in 1903. The company built 51 miles of track by 1909 before entering receivership. This route carried passengers, freight and mail to the upper Turnagain Arm. From there, goods were taken by boat at high tide, and by dog team or pack train to Eklutna and the Matanuska-Susitna Valley. The ultimate goal of the railroad was the coal seams north of today's Anchorage, coal that could be used to resupply whaling and merchant ships sailing the northern Pacific Ocean.

The **Alaska Northern Railway Company** bought the rail line in 1909 and extended it another 21 miles northward. From the new end, goods were floated down the Turnagain Arm in small boats to reach the markets being created by several gold

Alaska Railroad: History Through the Miles

rushes in various parts of central Alaska. However, the business was insignificant and the Alaska Northern Railway went into receivership in 1914. Also in 1914, Congress passed the Enabling Act which empowered newly elected President Woodrow Wilson to locate and construct a railroad (or railroads) that would connect at least one Pacific Ocean port with a navigable river in interior Alaska and with one or more coalfields. This created an opportunity for the United States government to plan a railroad route from Seward to the interior town of Fairbanks. In 1914, the government bought the Alaska Northern Railway for $1.2 million and moved its headquarters to "Ship Creek," later called Anchorage. The government began to extend the rail line northward, with an early goal being the coal mines near Palmer and Healy. At the time, U.S. Navy ships burned coal and the availability of reliable coal supplies would extend their voyage distances across the north Pacific.

The **Tanana Valley Railroad** was a 3-foot gauge railroad in the Fairbanks area. Initial construction on the railroad near Fairbanks began in late summer of 1904 as the Tanana Mines Railway, with financing from British investors who had financed several small industrial railroads in the Dawson, Yukon Territory, Canada area and the White Pass & Yukon Route. Chena, a settlement on the Tanana River, was the original headquarters, with the construction of a sawmill, rail yard and other support structures here.

Engine #1, which had been the first steam locomotive in the Yukon Territory, became the first steam locomotive in the interior of Alaska when it arrived on the railroad on July 4, 1905. (Engine #1, the very first steam locomotive purchased for the TVRR, was eventually placed on display in Fairbanks and ended up at Alaskaland, now known as Pioneer Park. Due to the efforts of local citizens, it has been restored and returned to operation at Pioneer Park.) The Tanana mainline was completed to Fairbanks by mid-July and the golden spike was driven on July 17. Construction continued on the branch up the Goldstream valley through Fox. That branch was completed to Gilmore in September, 1905.

History of the Alaska Railroad

In 1907, the railroad was refinanced under a new name, the Tanana Valley Railroad, and on May 15, 1907, construction began on the second phase of the TVRR, an extension of the trackage to Chatanika. The route eventually went via the Fox Creek Valley to reach mining territories in Dome, Vault, Ridgetop and Olnes. However, revenues were never stable, caused by a lack of local development and the uncertainty of the mining industry. On November 1, 1917, the railroad was sold at a bankruptcy sale for $200,000. The buyer resold the TVRR to the **Alaska Engineering Commission** (AEC) for $300,000 on December 31, 1917. The government bought the Tanana Valley Railroad principally for its Fairbanks area terminal facilities. The TVRR became the Chatanika Branch of the Alaska Engineering Commission Railroad, which became the Alaska Railroad in 1923.

To complete the railroad, the AEC built an extension to Nenana to meet the track coming north from Anchorage. This new section was completed on November 7, 1919, and then widened to standard gauge as soon as the Mears bridge over the Tanana River at Nenana was completed in February 1923. The track from Happy to Fairbanks remained dual gauge to allow narrow gauge trains to reach the branch running north from Happy. The narrow-gauge Chatanika Branch was finally closed on August 1, 1930.

The Tanana River bridge in Nenana, built in 1923, was the final link in the Alaska Railroad and at the time, was the second longest single-span steel railroad bridge in the country. President Warren G. Harding drove the golden spike that completed the railroad on July 15, 1923, on the north side of the bridge.

Many improvements were made to the **Alaska Railroad** by the federal government, generally to meet military needs within the state. These improvements included new branches, the opening of coal mines, new shops, and even the port at Whittier. World War II had a major impact on the railroad. During World War II, the Alaska Railroad was used by the army to transport military personnel, supplies, and construction materials between Seward, Whittier, Anchorage, and Fairbanks. To facilitate these activities and to provide security for railroad operations, the 714th Railway Operating Battalion was assigned to operate the railroad in May of 1943 in cooperation with civilian railroad personnel. In addition to its rail activities, the Alaska Railroad also operated a river line between the railhead at Nenana and Marshall on the Lower Yukon, and modernized and operated the Eska Coal Mines north of Palmer in order to adequately supply the coal needs of the army and the railroad during the war. In addition, the 1150 men of the Battalion helped construct the Whittier Cutoff and 31 miles of branch lines from Fairbanks to nearby air bases. The army operation ended in May, 1945.

After the war, the railroad was inspected and found to be worn out, a dangerous situation since almost all freight moved on the railroad, including all coal for heating at Fairbanks and the military bases across the state. A major rehabilitation program was created to rebuild the line between Portage and Fairbanks. This included replacing the worn 70-pound rail with 115-pound rail, installing treated-fir crossties to replace the untreated native spruce ties, installing new steel bridges, eliminating line sags by raising the track as much as five feet, widening shoulders to a standard twenty feet, and placing the new track structure on twelve inches of select pit-run gravel to permit speeds as high as 60 mph. Additionally, new rolling stock and heavy construction equipment was acquired by the railroad. As this project was underway in 1954, a decision was made to rehabilitate the line from Portage to Seward.

While the railroad ran out of funds before the rehabilitation program was completed, many improvements were made. The Great Alaska Earthquake on March 27, 1964, also forced the railroad to make improvements as the lower 200 miles of track experienced damage. In some places, the railroad was completely rebuilt as the old grade was gone and rivers formed new channels.

In January 1985, the State of Alaska bought the railroad from the U.S. government for $22.3 million dollars. A number of improvements have been made since that time. New passenger cars have been acquired as an effort to promote tourism in the state. A fleet of new locomotives have arrived. New offices, shops and facilities have been acquired. Finally, major track improvements have taken place across the system with many plans for even more work.

For those who want more information on the Alaska Railroad, a great place to check out is *John's Alaska Railroad Web Page*. This website has just about everything involving the railroad, including current news, interviews with employees, history of most of the stations along the line, photography tips, maps, and tons of other information.

Permafrost

One of the major challenges of building the Alaska Railroad, and almost anything in central to northern Alaska, is dealing with permafrost. Technically, permafrost "is any soil, subsoil, or other surficial deposit that has a temperature lower than 32 degrees Fahrenheit for at least 2 years. This definition is based exclusively on temperature. Part or all of the deposit's moisture may be unfrozen, depending on the chemical composition of the water and capillary action. However, most permafrost is cemented by ice; permafrost without ice is called dry permafrost." About 20 percent of the world's land is underlain by permafrost.

A great resource on the issue of permafrost and other construction issues that the Alaska Railroad faces is *The Alaska Railroad Between Anchorage and Fairbanks – Guidebook to Permafrost and Engineering Problems* by T.C. Fuglestad. This resource is available online and gives a great description of the geological features of the land that the railroad passes through.

The report states that if undisturbed, "permafrost can form a stable foundation for a railroad embankment and other engineering structures. Unfortunately, when the Alaska Railroad was constructed, the protective vegetation cover was removed, which disturbed much of the near-surface permafrost. Also, over the years, thousands of cubic yards of gravel have been used along the railroad to fill sags and replenish shoulders. Dry gravel generally conducts heat better than silt or vegetation. Consequently, during summer, the added gravel conducts heat to the permafrost, and thawing occurs."

It is actually fairly easy to determine where there is permafrost. With the ground frozen, water often pools on the surface, and only a limited number of trees can survive. The ground surface appears very wet because a thin layer of water is trapped and unable to drain through the underlying permafrost zone. Black spruce is also often a sign of poor drainage and permafrost. This is actually a cycle. The pools of water and scattered black spruce can allow the subsoil to be heated from the sun. The melting permafrost allows the water to drain and birch and white spruce trees to germinate and mature. As these trees mature, shaded ground may allow permafrost to redevelop. Permafrost will again prevent drainage and scrubby black spruce will reappear.

On the Alaska Railroad, permafrost exists permanently between Fairbanks and Nenana, and then discontinuously on to Anchorage. Much of the railroad was originally built using the frozen material, blasted from the adjacent ditch lines. Ever since then, track gangs have worked to stabilize the roadbed. Recently, these efforts have included techniques aimed at keeping the permafrost from melting during the warmer summer periods.

Alaska Railroad 4320 passes the New Office Building of the ARR. Photo by Sarah Jennings.

Railroad Operations

Most of the railroad is operated using DTC blocks. Direct Traffic Control (DTC) is a system for authorizing track occupancy used by the Alaska Railroad, whereby the railroad's dispatcher gives track authority directly to the train crew via radio or telephone instead of via trackside signals. Watch for the begin DTC and end DTC block signs with a four-letter abbreviation for the block's name. Stretches of Centralized Traffic Control (CTC) exist between Coastal and Pittman (north of Wasilla) as well as at the siding of Hurricane. At these locations, the dispatcher authorizes train movements using the trackside signals.

During 2014, the Alaska Railroad reported that there were 468,661 passengers on various Alaska Railroad passenger trains, and 4.92 million tons of freight hauled. The railroad had 467 miles of mainline, 54 miles of branch line, and 135 miles of yards and sidings for a total of 656 miles of track. Employees are unionized, being members of the American Federation of Government Employees (269), United Transportation Union (160), International Brotherhood of Teamsters (56), Transportation Communications Union (43), and the American Train Dispatchers Association (9).

Alaska Railroad Passenger Trains

Passenger trains in Alaska have two clear and very different seasons – the heavy summer months with all of the Alaska Railroad's trains for tourists, and the basic services of winter. The real Alaska passenger train is the *Aurora*, operating from mid-September through mid-May, providing basic weekend service between Anchorage and Fairbanks, serving 7200 passengers in 2014. Saturdays see the train operate northward and Sundays see it operate southward, both on a 12-hour schedule. Also operating in winter is a once-a-month Anchorage to Hurricane train to serve local needs. In 2016, the railroad announced an expanded schedule of winter trains.

With the coming of summer and its tourists and cruise ships, the Alaska Railroad adds a number of trains to the schedule. The primary train is the *Denali Star*, running daily between Anchorage and Fairbanks on a 12-hour schedule, serving 61,000 riders in 2014. This train often has private passenger cars on the rear, owned by companies such as Celebrity Cruise, Royal Caribbean International, and Royal Celebrity Tours. When volumes are heavy, these and other cruise companies often operate their own trains, especially Princess Cruises, which uses the Woodpecker Facility at McKinley Siding south of Talkeetna. In 2014, 51% of all Alaska Railroad passengers rode in a private car operated by a cruise ship company.

Possibly the most popular summer train is the *Coastal Classic*, a train that operates through the magnificent scenery south of Anchorage along Turnagain Arm and the Kenai Peninsula before reaching Seward. This train features a long layover at Seward so its 53,000 passengers (in 2014) can go fishing, whale watching, or participate in many other tourist activities. Another train aimed at tourists is the *Glacier Discovery*, a train serving Anchorage-Whittier traffic (35,000 in 2014), along with a loop south into Chugach National Forest. In an attempt to serve the National Forest, the Chugach Whistle Stop Project was created to provide access to the spectacular backcountry. Daytrips such as rafting and glacier hikes are available from the train.

Railroad Operations

The final summer tourist train is the *Hurricane Turn*, providing rail service between Talkeetna and the Hurricane area. This train serves summer residents, fishermen and campers, and anyone looking for a daytrip through a scenic and rugged area with no road access (7800 passengers in 2014). Crews on the train keep records of what camping and fishing spots along the line are being used and when campers wish to be picked up, and often drop off supplies as they pass by. The train will stop anywhere when requested. The *Hurricane Turn* was the last home of the Alaska Railroad's RDC cars until replaced by more modern locomotive-hauled passenger cars.

Some of the Alaska Railroad passenger trains are also classrooms. As the railroad states: "Since 1981, ARRC has partnered with school districts to offer a vocational program to train high school students to serve as hosts onboard summer passenger trains." School groups also take the trains to various events across the state, and the railroad conducts numerous safety talks about rail operations.

As of 2013, the ARR had 45 passenger-related railcars, including 30 coaches, six diners, six baggage cars, two business cars (charters) and one DMU (Diesel Multiple Unit - a self-propelled car or a train that does not require a locomotive). Their history is shown in tables on the following pages.

Besides the passenger cars owned and operated by the Alaska Railroad, several cruise ship companies have their own passenger cars on the railroad. Princess, painting their cars in a blue and white paint scheme, has a fleet of Ultra Domes with 88 seats under glass upstairs, and 32 dining seats and an open platform downstairs. The coach seating is actually at tables that generally hold four adults, two facing in each direction. The newest cars (MSEX 7084-7089) were built 1992-1999 by Colorado Railcar. They also have four two-story cars (MSEX 7080-7083) built from former Southern Pacific gallery commuter cars in 1988 by Tillamook Railcar Repair. These cars seat 90 passengers each and are considered to be the largest passenger rail cars in the world.

Holland America and their McKinley Explorer railcars (painted in blue and silver with a rainbow stripe on the lower body) are also two-story cars built by Colorado Railcar. Built

2003-2005, cars HALX 1050-1059 seat 88 in coach seats upstairs and 44 downstairs in the dining area. All of the cars have local names and have a small downstairs open platform.

The third owner of private passenger cars on the Alaska Railroad is Royal Celebrity Tours, a land tour division of Royal Caribbean Cruises. Known as the Wilderness Express, the two-story cars were also built by Colorado Railcar and seat 88 in coach upstairs and 36 downstairs in the dining area. The cars also have an open platform downstairs. When built in 2001-2002, the company boasted the cars had "the most dome glass of any double-deck rail cars in the world." The cars are numbered RCIX 1001-1004 and are painted white with a bear and landscape as part of the design. It should be noted that these cars are used by both Royal Caribbean and Celebrity Cruises tours.

All three cruise companies have maintenance shops for their passenger cars just south of the Alaska Railroad shops in Anchorage.

McKinley Explorer cars heading north on the rear of the *Denali Star*.
Photo by Sarah Jennings.

Railroad Operations

ARR Gold Star seating under glass. Photo by Sarah Jennings.

Welcome aboard to Gold Star service.
Photo by Sarah Jennings.

Alaska Railroad Passenger Cars

ARR CAR NUMBER	CAR TYPE	BUILDER	YEAR BUILT	YEAR TO ARR	YEAR RE-BUILT	SEATS	NOTES
100	Baggage	ACF	1961	1971	1998	0	ex-UP 6310
101	Baggage	SLC	1962	1971	1998	0	ex-UP 6325
102	Baggage	ACF	1961	1971	----	0	ex-UP 6306, ex-ARR 6306
103	Baggage	?	?	?	?	0	ex-NP
110	Baggage	PC&F	1961	1997	1998	0	ex-SP 67XX
111	Baggage	PC&F	1961	1997	1998	0	ex-SP 6734
200	Coach	PS	1950	1971	1982	60	ex-UP 5404
201	Coach	PS	1950	1971	1982	60	ex-UP 5408
202	Coach	PS	1950	1971	1982	60	ex-UP 5413
203	Coach	PS	1950	1971	1982	60	ex-UP 5420
204	Coach	PS	1950	1971	1982	60	ex-UP 5424
205	Coach	DHI	1989	1989	----	78	
206	Coach	DHI	1989	1989	----	78	
207	Coach	DHI	1989	1989	----	78	
208	Coach	DHI	1989	1989	----	78	
209	Coach	DHI	1989	1989	----	78	
210	Coach	DHI	1989	1989	----	78	
300	Counter Café	SLC	1959	1971	1982	53	ex-UP 5012, for sale 2010
301	Counter Café	DHI	1989	1989	----	69	
351	Café Diner	PS	1958	2000	1999	49	ex-CNW 903, to Amtrak 9601 (1974), re# 9011, to Florida Fun Train Tiki railbar
352	Café Diner	PS	1958	2000	1999	39	ex-CNW 707, to Amtrak 9618 (1974), re#9013, to Florida Fun Train 50s diner
400	Diner	ACF	1949	1971	1982	48	ex-UP 4806, for sale 2010
401	Diner	DHI	1989	1989	----	56	
451	Diner	PS	1958	2000	1997	56	ex-CNW 706, to Amtrak 9617 (1974), re# 9012, to Florida Fun Train Arcade Car
452	Diner	PS	1958	2000	1997	55	ex-CNW 600, to Amtrak 9600 (1974), re# 9014, to Florida Fun Train Theater Car
500	Dome-Coach	PS	1958	1971	1998	24/36	ex-UP 7013
501	Dome-Coach	ACF	1955	1971	1998	24/36	ex-UP 7008
502	Dome-Coach	PS	1958	1971	1998	24/36	ex-UP 7014
521	Dome-Coach	Budd	1954	2000	1988	24/38	ex-SP&S 559, to BN 4626, to Amtrak 9486, re# 9408

Railroad Operations

522	Dome-Coach	Budd	1954	2000	1988	24/38	ex-NP 555, to BN 4622, to Amtrak 9482, re# 9403
523	Dome-Coach	Budd	1954	2000	1988	24/38	ex-NP 556, to BN 4623, to Amtrak 9483, re# 9404
551	Coach	CRM	1997	2000	----	76	built as Florida Fun Train 9001 using center sill of former baggage car CN 9237
552	Coach	CRM	1997	2000	----	76	built as Florida Fun Train 9002 using center sill of former baggage car CN 9269
553	Coach	CRM	1997	2000	----	76	built as Florida Fun Train 9003 using center sill of former baggage car CN 9302
554	Coach	CRM	1997	2000	----	76	built as Florida Fun Train 9004 using center sill of former baggage car CN 9297
555	Dome	CRM	2006		----	68	
556	Dome	CRM	2006		----	68	
557	Dome	CRM	2006		----	68	
651	Gold Star	CRM	2005	2005	----	72/36	
652	Gold Star	CRM	2005	2005	----	72/36	
653	Gold Star	CRM	2007	2007	----	72/36	
654	Gold Star	CRM	2007	2007	----	72/36	
655	Gold Star	CRM	2008	2008	----	72/36	
656	Gold Star	CRM	2008	2008	----	72/36	
751	Bilevel DMU	CRM	2009	2009	----	112	
"Aurora" 2000	Business Car/Conf. Room Obs.	CRM	2000	2000	----	39	built as Florida Fun Train 9005 using center sill of a Soo Line or Milwaukee Road car, never delivered
"Denali"	Business Car	Pullman	1930	1971	2006		Converted by GN shops, 1957, ARR retired 2001; restored 2006

ACF = American Car & Foundry
CRM = Colorado Railcar
DHI = Daewoo Heavy Industries
PC&F = Pacific Car & Foundry
PS = Pullman Standard
SLC = Saint Louis Car Company

BN = Burlington Northern
CNW = Chicago & NorthWestern
NP = Northern Pacific
SP = Southern Pacific
SP&S = Spokane, Portland & Seattle
UP = Union Pacific

ARR cars are designed to let light in and to allow passengers to enjoy the views. Note the extra windows. Photo by Sarah Jennings.

DHI coach interior. Note the tall windows that allow full viewing of the great scenery. Photo by Sarah Jennnings.

Railroad Operations

Alaska Railroad Freight Trains

According to the website of the Alaska Railroad, the Alaska Railroad moved more than 4.9 million tons of freight over 647 miles of track in 2014. As they state, freight is the railroad's bread-and-butter, producing 65% of the operating revenue. Many of the freight train schedules are based upon the sailing dates and times of the marine services that connect with Seattle and Prince Rupert. Unit trains moving coal and gravel generally operate based upon the customer's requirements, with gravel generally being delivered overnight for next day use.

There are normally about 1050 freight cars on the Alaska Railroad, a mix of railroad-owned and leased cars (860), as well as several hundred cars leased by customers. Cars on the railroad include more than 400 open top hoppers, 350 flat cars, almost 180 tank cars (all leased by customers except for two owned by the railroad), 40 covered hoppers, 20 air dump cars, about 15 boxcars, and 10 gondolas.

Major freight categories, and their share of freight revenue in 2011, include:

Petroleum (29.7%) – Petroleum products move from the North Pole Refinery to Anchorage. Fuel also moves from Anchorage to Fairbanks.

Barge and Interline Services (29.6%) – Alaska Rail Marine (ARM) moves railcar shipments to/from Alaska via Seattle, interchanging with railroads in the Lower 48. Containers arriving by ARM barge move from Whittier to Anchorage or Fairbanks. CN Barges move railcar shipments to/from Alaska via Prince Rupert, interchanging with Canadian National Railway.

Coal (22.1%) – Coal from Usibelli Coal Mine in Healy moves to the Fairbanks area (local, 8.9%), and to Seward, where it is shipped to overseas customers (export, 13.2%).

Gravel (6.9%) – Seasonally (April - October) aggregate products move from the Matanuska-Susitna Valley to Anchorage.

Trailers/Containers on Flat Cars (8.0%) – TOFC/COFC moves north and south between Seward, Whittier, Anchorage and Fairbanks.

Miscellaneous/In-state Local (3.7%) – Other freight includes specialty movements of very large or oddly-shaped equipment and materials, as well as in-state shipments of cement, scrap metal, military equipment and pipe.

Barge Service

The outside connection for the Alaska Railroad is regular barge service from Whittier to Prince Rupert and Seattle. The Seattle service, known as Alaska Rail Marine, operates weekly with a seven day transit time. The barges can handle approximately 50 railcars, plus numerous containers and other items on racks above the rail deck. Service from Prince Rupert connects with Canadian National, and sees about 30 voyages per year. These barges can also handle about 50 railcars on a four-day transit time, but are not built with an upper level for containers. Both barge types are pulled by ocean-going tows or lineboats, using cables hundreds of yards long. The distance allows the boats to be protected in case of high waves or winds.

Alaska Railroad Locomotives

The Alaska Railroad has 53 locomotives: 28 SD70MACs (12 equipped with head-end-power to supply electricity to passenger cars), 15 GP40s, eight GP38s and two cab/power cars. The EMD SD70MACs were acquired in several groups starting in 1999-2000 for numbers 4001-4016, and 4317-4328 in 2004 and 2007. They all have the newer style wide-nose safety cabs. The EMD GP40-2 locomotives were also built new for the Alaska Railroad (1975-1978). Numbered 3001-3015, the entire fleet is still in service. It should be noted that locomotive 3006 was originally numbered 3000, but was quickly renumbered before the locomotives delivered in 1976 arrived.

Possibly the most interesting part of the fleet are the GP38-2 and GP38u locomotives. All were originally built for other railroads and have complicated histories. GP38-2 locomotives 2001 and 2002 are former Butte, Anaconda & Pacific Railway (108 and 109), later Rarus Railway. Locomotives 2003-2007 are all rebuilt from Penn Central locomotives delivered 1968-1969. Their original PC numbers were 7812, 7773, 7752, 7754, and 7780. Locomotive 2008 was actually built as a GP40 for the New York Central. All of these were acquired by the ARR in 1986.

Locomotive fans can also look for 31 and 32. These are former Amtrak F40 locomotives, rebuilt into HEP cab control cars. One of these locomotives is often used on the *Hurricane Turn*.

Railroad Communications

The Alaska Railroad is completely covered by radio communications. Marked by signs along the railroad, the radio channels are:

Channel	Track Limits
1 / 2	Whittier to Portage
1 / 2	Seward to Indian
14	Indian to Anchorage
1 / 2	Anchorage to Houston
7 / 8	Houston to Talkeetna
1 / 2	Talkeetna to Hurricane
7 / 8	Hurricane to Healey
1 / 2	Healey to Fairbanks
5 / 6	Fairbanks to Eielson

The frequencies used by the Alaska Railroad include:

AK Rail 01   **164.6250**
  Train to Train/Alternate Dispatcher
AK Rail 02   **165.3375**
  Train to Dispatcher
AK Rail 03   **165.2650**
  Yard Operations
AK Rail 04   **164.9875**
  Gravel/Coal/Yard Operations
AK Rail 05   **161.4150**
  Yard Operations
AK Rail 06   **161.4450**
  Yard Operations
AK Rail 07   **160.3050**
  Train to Train/Alternate Dispatcher
AK Rail 08   **161.3550**
  Train to Dispatcher
AK Rail 09   **166.3125**
  Radio Telephone
AK Rail 10   **166.2250**
  Radio Telephone
AK Rail 11   **166.3750**
  Radio Telephone
AK Rail 12   **161.4750**
  Maintenance of Way
AK Rail 13   **161.5050**
  Maintenance of Way
AK Rail 14   **161.5350**
  Maintenance of Way
AK Rail 15   **161.5650**
  Maintenance of Way
AK Rail F-7   **164.9850**
  Road Channel
AK Rail Anch   **165.2650**
  Anchorage Yard Operations

Railroad Operations

Slide Zones and the Avalanche Detection System

There are a number of Slide Zones across the entire Alaska Railroad, active areas where snow and hillside material can fall down upon the tracks. A number of these are officially designated as avalanche areas with heavy snow, all between Anchorage and Seward. The Slide Zones are marked by signs alongside the track and they are numbered based upon the slide's general milepost location. Special track bulletins are released when special rules are in effect. The Slide Zone between milepost 71.2 and 71.5 has an active Avalanche Detection System which will automatically send out a radio message warning of any problems.

The railroad actually has an Avalanche Forecaster on duty to handle problems and to make recommendations about train movements during slide season. The program created uses a five color coding to alert train crews to the danger of the slide, to establish operating procedures, and to establish procedures for inspection of the area by track crews.

Automatic Whistle Warning System and Whistle Quiet Zones

Much of the area through the suburbs on the south side of Anchorage is an official quiet zone where trains only blow their horns in emergencies. One of the interesting parts of this quiet zone are the number of grade crossings that have Automatic Whistle Warning Systems (AWS). An AWS has horns installed at the crossing that blow a regular crossing alert when a train approaches. This system allows the horn noise to only be at the grade crossing and not along the track before and after the crossing. Look for them while riding the train at the crossings at mileposts 105.64 (Klatt Road), 106.42 (104th), 106.68 (100th), 108.80 (68th), 109.40 (Arctic), 110.64 (44th), 111.01 (Spenard), and 117.23 (Post Road).

Delta Junction – End of the Alaska Highway at the junction with the Richardson Highway. Photo by Barton Jennings.

Construction of the Tanana River Bridge at Salcha. Photo by Sarah Jennings.

Proposed Railroad Changes and Expansion in Alaska

Alaska is still a new and growing state, and there are many plans for railroad expansion. The two primary expansion plans include a line from near Fairbanks to Delta Junction, and the construction of a line to the new proposed port across Cook Inlet from Anchorage. Line improvements through Fairbanks and other communities have also been explored. Additionally, the railroad has studied plans for several other new lines, new passenger services, and many line improvements. There are even plans for limited steam-powered passenger excursion service.

Fairbanks to Delta Junction and Canada

What is called the Alaska Railroad Corporation's Northern Rail Extension Project is a proposal to build and operate an approximately 80 mile long rail line from the Eielson Air Force Base area to the missile defense site at Fort Greely in the Delta Junction area, also the junction of the Alaska and Richardson Highways. The project would start near North Pole at the Chena River overflow structure (milepost 20.18) on the Eielson branch rail line and would terminate in the vicinity of Delta Junction, generally following the Richardson Highway – Alaska Highway 2. Funding to build the line (estimated to be between $650 and $850 million) is coming from the Alaska state government and the United States Department of Defense.

This line is being built in four steps: [1] the Tanana River bridge at Salcha, [2] track construction from Moose Creek near North Pole to the Salcha bridge, [3] track construction from the

Salcha bridge to the Donnelly Military Training Area, and [4] track construction Donnelly to Delta Junction. Plans for the new line include military movements that are often only possible when the Tanana River is frozen, passenger service between Delta Junction and Fairbanks, and the extension of freight movements between the commercial center of Delta Junction and the ocean ports (Anchorage, Whittier and Seward) on the railroad.

Land clearing for the project began in August 2011, and construction began with a groundbreaking ceremony for the Tanana River Bridge at Salcha on September 28, 2011. During early 2013, steel girders for the bridge were trucked in from Valdez. According to John's Alaskarails website, the girders are 165 feet long, meaning the trucks moving them are about 210 feet long. Additionally, it is reported that there are more than 100 of these girders in the bridge. This bridge is unique in that it is designed to handle both rail and highway traffic with lanes for each. Construction of the Tanana River Bridge was completed in August 2014.

The Delta Junction line is considered by many to be the next step toward a line to Canada, adding Alaska to the North American rail network. Numerous routes have been examined for this connection. About 980 miles separate the end of the Alaska Railroad near Eielson Air Force Base with the northern limits of the British Columbia Railroad at Fort Nelson. This route would run through Tok and into Canada to the north end of today's Canadian National, passing through miles of rugged mountainous country. A second route that has been examined looks at connecting to the planned BC Rail/CN route through Dease Lake, a slightly longer route but one with easier grades. Traffic on this line would include Alaskan freight such as minerals, timber and oil, as well as moving tourists and visitors up from the Lower 48. Since the ports at Anchorage and Whittier are considerably nearer to Asian export centers than ports in California, some consider it possible that freight in large volumes could move on the line.

During late 2012, the First Nations and Alaskan Tribes expressed their support for a new "purpose built" railroad that

Proposed Railroad Changes and Expansion in Alaska

would link Alaska, Yukon, northern British Columbia and northern Alberta to the rest of North America.

Port MacKenzie Line

Plans for Port MacKenzie and a railroad to connect it to the Alaska Railroad have been examined for more than thirty years. The first formal efforts began on February 12, 2008, when the Surface Transportation Board (STB) began the process for an environmental impact study of the line. The proposal for the line is to construct a 33-mile rail line in the Susitna River Valley to connect Port MacKenzie to the Alaska Railroad's existing mainline track near Houston, north of Willow. On November 21, 2011, the Surface Transportation Board approved the construction of the Port MacKenzie line and construction on the first of six construction phases began in 2012.

However, work on the route was stopped on October 1, 2012, by a panel of judges from the U.S. 9th Circuit Court of Appeals. The halt was ordered at the request of Alaska Survival, Cook Inletkeeper and the Sierra Club as they tried to challenge the report and approval of the Surface Transportation Board. The court order meant the loss of about 200 jobs, the first of about 3000 construction jobs and 4000 mining jobs that the project was expected to create before its completion. A later court ruling allowed construction to resume and contracts were let in March 2013.

Construction on the Port MacKenzie Line. Photo by Barton Jennings.

Work has been slowed several times by new requirements, such as spending $1 million to move trails in the area. However, as of October 2015, most of the grading work was completed and rail at the junction just south of Houston had been installed. As of early 2017, it is reported that the project is 75% complete.

Proposed Fort Wainwright Track Realignment

Another change that could affect the route of the Alaska Railroad is a possible reroute east of Fairbanks. The Alaska Railroad has plans to reroute much of the existing rail line that passes through Fort Wainwright. The three-year project will eliminate train traffic from Fort Wainwright Army Post's populated core, eliminating a number of grade crossings on the post. The proposed $40 million project, one third of which is currently funded, aims to move track from the post's core to its northern and eastern boundaries. All train traffic moving east or west through the Fairbanks area currently traverses Army land and a residential neighborhood to the west, situations that would remain following the rerouting project.

A number of public officials and area residents have urged the railroad to focus on another prospective project, an expensive Southern Bypass that would reroute all train traffic south of Fairbanks. However, even if the new line is built, some of the rail line to Fort Wainwright will still exist as the army relies on the railroad to deliver coal to its on-post power plant and to deploy its armored Stryker vehicles.

Proposed Fairbanks Southern Bypass

The Alaska Railroad has plans to eliminate many of their problems of operating through downtown Fairbanks by building new track south of town. In particular, the desire is to eliminate the many grade crossings and slow track that is found on the east side of town. A study conducted in 1985 originally encouraged the idea but funding issues, and maintaining service to rail customers in Fairbanks, has prevented any actual construction. A number of different plans have been proposed but most have the new line cutting south just west of the University of

Alaska Fairbanks campus and looping around the south side of Fairbanks. The most popular plan sees the new line as a part of a new transportation corridor, including a new freeway bypass. Alaska Railroad officials have estimated the bypass, which under one plan would send trains down the median of a beefed-up Parks Highway, could cost as much as $450 million. Other plans include using an upgraded airport lead, a line to the north close to the original Tanana Valley Railroad narrow gauge grade, and several other routes near the Parks Highway.

Proposed New Area Passenger Services

The Alaska Railroad has commissioned a study to explore options for passenger rail service on the north end of the Alaska Railroad, between Denali National Park and Fairbanks, and between Fairbanks and North Pole. Started in 2007, the study seeks to identify potential markets, including a traditional commuter rail market between Fairbanks and bedroom communities (North Pole, University of Alaska Fairbanks and Ester), and a regional rail market that could serve intercity travel between Fairbanks and communities along the railroad south to Denali, as well as a tourist market between Denali and Fairbanks.

Proposed Steam-Powered Passenger Excursion Service

During 2011, former Alaska Railroad #557, a 2-8-0 built in 1943 by Baldwin Locomotive Works (serial number 70480), was returned to the railroad and moved to Anchorage for possible restoration, where it arrived on January 3, 2012. The steamer was later moved to its restoration facility in Wasilla. Plans for the locomotive include the operation of tourist service on the Palmer branch.

Alaska Railroad #557 was built for the United States Army Transportation Corp (USATC) as their #3523. To alleviate a major power shortage on the Alaska Railroad, twelve steamers were diverted to the railroad, arriving during December 1944. The locomotive was built as coal-fired, but was converted to oil in 1955. It last operated on the Alaska Railroad in 1964 as the final steam locomotive on the roster and was sent south, even-

Alaska Railroad: History Through the Miles

tually being sold to the Moses Lake Iron and Metal Company/House of Poverty Museum in Moses Lake, Washington. Jim and Vic Jansen bought 557 from the museum and returned it to the Alaska Railroad on the condition that it be restored to operation and put into service.

Alaska Railroad Anchorage Terminal. Photo by Barton Jennings.

Alaska Railroad Anchorage Terminal

The Alaska Railroad is based in Anchorage, using a number of buildings spread across 600 acres. Known as the Anchorage Terminal Reserve, the land includes a rail yard and other properties along Ship Creek. It is bordered by Cook Inlet to the west, Elmendorf Air Force Base to the north, the Mountain View community to the east, and downtown Anchorage to the south. The rail yard includes repair buildings, a fueling area, a steaming rack, warehouses, and offices. Activities at the rail yard have included fueling, painting, steam cleaning, freight loading, and maintenance work on locomotives and rail cars. Properties outside the rail yard, leased to tenants, have been used for many different types of activities. These include power plants, trucking and transit operations, fuel storage, auto salvage, and many others.

The building that most people notice is the Alaska Railroad Depot, completed in 1942 for $261,000 in a Moderne style, built all in concrete. The original three-story, flat roofed depot building measured 218' by 45'. In 1948, the railroad added two-story additions at the east and west ends. Structurally, the building can be described as being made up of five sections: The main building can be divided into three sections: the entrance (45 by 45 feet) and the wings on either side of the entrance (70 by 45 feet each). Then there are the additions on each end (60 by 42 feet each). The entrance, on the south side of the building, is accented by a stepped out face that rises about three feet above the building's roofline. Above the windows in the entrance section, molded into the concrete, are the words THE ALASKA RAILROAD.

The Alaska Railroad Depot. Photo by Sarah Jennings.

The station replaced a wooden shiplap building used since the early 1920s. The railroad contracted with the J.B. Warrack Company of Seattle to build the building on August 8, 1941, and it took just twelve months to build. Since then, the building has been used for offices, as a train waiting room, and as a baggage/shop area. Opened on September 15, 1942, the station was placed on the National Register of Historic Places on August 27, 1999. A fascinating story about the building states that the original plans for the station called for the exterior to be a light buff color. However, the Alaska Defense Command ordered it to be a dull gray to reduce its visibility as a defense measure.

The Anchorage Depot is at the base of a bluff, below the downtown area of Anchorage. This has been the base of railroad operations since the original construction days. About two hundred yards southwest of the depot is an area where several of the houses built by the railroad still stand, although most of the houses have been rehabilitated and converted to offices. Located at 618 Christensen Drive is A.E.C. Cottage No. 23. Listed on the National Register of Historic Places, it is described as being "an example of Anchorage's early residential structures, and is a reminder of the community's railroad roots. The Alaska Engineering Commission (A.E.C.), created by the Federal Government to build a railroad (today's Alaska Railroad – ARR) from a year-round port to interior Alaska, built a number of houses, among them Cottage No. 23, in 1915 and 1916 to provide housing for its employees in the new town of Anchorage. In 1915 the A.E.G. built thirteen houses on Government Hill (which is located across the railroad yards and Ship Creek to the north of the town site) for employees, and in 1916 it built nineteen houses on the Anchorage Townsite. Eight of the houses (called cottages) still stand on Government Hill, eight still stand on the Anchorage Townsite, and another seven exist but have been moved from their original locations. Cottage No. 23 is one of two (the other is on Government Hill) that have been minimally altered." A.E.C. Cottage No. 25 is very close by, located at 645 West Third Avenue.

Across the street from the station is Alaska Railroad #1, a 0-4-0ST built by Davenport in October, 1907. This steam locomotive was originally built as narrow gauge #802 for work on the Panama Canal. In 1917, a large amount of equipment was transferred from the canal project to the Alaska Railroad Commission, and this locomotive became #6. It was converted to standard gauge in 1930 and renumbered to #1.

Across the tracks to the north is the railroad's new administrative office building. The Alaska Railroad Headquarters Building (also known as the New Office Building or NOB) is the headquarters building for the Alaska Railroad. When built, it contained the dispatcher's office, which has since been moved. To the northeast of the NOB, located on East Whitney Road on the south side of the rail yard, is the new Alaska Railroad Operations Center, built in 2004. According to permit documents in Anchorage, this three-story building was designed with the third floor lined with glass on three sides to enable views of the railroad yard during inclement weather. The view from the third floor allows personnel to monitor train activity using binoculars. "The Operations Center consolidates operations activities into one building that are currently scattered among several facilities in the Ship Creek area. Housed within the center is a training facility, incident command center, a train dispatch center, employee lockers and changing rooms, a crew dispatch center for managing the logistics of moving railroad employees to where they are needed, and offices for monitoring freight and assembling trains."

At one time, there were warehouses located both east and west of the station. Most of these are gone today. To the east of the station is the former freight house. Built in 1941, the 349-foot wood frame building was extended in 1948. The building has been rebuilt and can be used for large groups such as cruise ship trains.

To the north of the rail yard is the shop complex. This complex includes locomotive and freight car shops, a railroad passenger car shop, and passenger car shops for the various cruise lines that operate their own cars. To the very north is the engine house, also known as the roundhouse. The three-bay engine repair shop (230' x 320'), has a very interesting history, starting near Denver, Colorado. It was originally part of the Kaiser (Remington) shell plant. After World War II, the plant was closed and the building was torn down and sold off. In 1948, the building was reassembled here as the locomotive shops. Just south of the roundhouse are the back shop, car shop, and coach shops. When trains are not on the road, this area is packed with passenger cars as just to the south are the passenger car maintenance shops of the cruise ship companies. The Princess shops are in the large blue building complex just south of the Alaska Railroad shops. The Holland America shop is a single track structure that looks like a round-top tent, with a canvas-like fabric stretched over a metal frame. Royal Celebrity Tours' Wilderness Express has its shop next to Holland America's. It is a white single track metal building.

Alaska Railroad Anchorage Terminal

Anchorage shops and rail yard. Photo by Barton Jennings.

Alaska Railroad diesel shops in Anchorage. Photo by Barton Jennings.

Freight moving in Anchorage. Photo by Barton Jennings.

Alaska Railroad Operations Center. Photo by Barton Jennings.

Passenger train ready for boarding in Anchorage. Photo by Sarah Jennings.

Railfanning Anchorage, Alaska

Rail traffic can be heavy in Anchorage, especially when all of the passenger trains are running each summer. When this is happening, three passenger trains depart each morning and arrive each evening, not counting cruise ship charters. In addition, several rock trains and fuel trains can operate through town each day, plus a few general freight trains moving intermodal and other freight cars. Finally, a few locals can spend the day serving the shippers on the south side of town and in the Port of Anchorage.

Please note that the Alaska Railroad is private property, and your purchase of a train ticket or your desire to take photos does not give you the right to trespass or to act in an unsafe manner around the trains. However, there are some great locations to safely watch and photograph trains in Anchorage. Below are some of them. Please enjoy your time in Anchorage. However, do not trespass, watch for both rail and roadway traffic, and remain safe.

Alaska Railroad: History Through the Miles

Anchorage Alaska Railroad Station is a great place to watch and photograph much of the train activity in town. The area is heavily patrolled by the railroad police – their office is across the street from the station – and private security. *Do not enter the platform or train boarding area without identifying yourself to the security officer who is generally on duty.* Just to the railroad-south (compass-west) of the station is a public road down to several industries which runs beside the tracks. The street sign actually shows an intersection of West 1st Avenue and West 1st Avenue. Just to the railroad-north (compass-east) of the station is North C Street which crosses the tracks. There is a small public park at the crossing. Further to compass-north is the freight mainline through the yards where most of the freight activity can be viewed. Stay on the sidewalks and look out for all of the heavy trucks heading to and from the port. North C Street becomes Ocean Dock Road in this area. Don't go too far north as you enter port property and security is very heavy.

East Loop Road is the large bridge across the mainlines and rail yard several blocks to the railroad-north (compass-east) of the Alaska Railroad station. While highway traffic can be heavy and fast, the wide sidewalks provide a great place to photograph the activity below.

Western Drive is the road and bridge across the tracks to the north of the Alaska Railroad station. It is good for afternoon photography, but is probably best driven to as it passes through a very active port area. When the salmon are making a run in Ship Creek, this road is lined with parked vehicles as folks come out to try to catch a few.

Ship Creek Trail starts on the north side of the Ship Creek Comfort Inn near the railroad station. Head east about a half-mile and the trail bridges over the passenger train mainline as well as Ship Creek. This is an industrial area, but nice photos can be made as trains enter and leave the city.

Railfanning Anchorage, Alaska

Tony Knowles Coastal Trail starts at the west end of 2nd Avenue and follows the railroad along the coast southward through Resolution Park, Elderberry Park, Nulbay Park and on to Margaret Egan Sullivan Park, where the tracks and trail separate. There are a number of nice locations where the train can be photographed with ocean views.

Highway 1 south of Anchorage is one of the most photographed locations on the railroad. Here, the railroad runs along the shore of Turnagain Arm. There are a number of parks and parking lots with great views, but stay off the tracks as train speeds are high and the area is patrolled by railroad security.

The Alaska Railroad moving freight in the port area. Photo by Barton Jennings.

Alaska Railroad Anchorage Terminal with the Port of Anchorage visible in the background. Photo by Sarah Jennings.

ARR 3003 near Fairbanks. Photo by Barton Jennings.

Railfanning Fairbanks, Alaska

Rail traffic in Fairbanks is not as heavy as in Anchorage. The only Alaska Railroad passenger trains at Fairbanks are the daily summer *Denali Star* and its weekly winter version. During summer, a number of cruise ship trains also arrive and depart from Fairbanks, but not as many as from Anchorage. The main freight activity in Fairbanks is the oil trains running south from the refineries at North Pole. A local is often kept busy loading and unloading intermodal equipment, serving the oil companies up on Prudhoe Bay and the North Slope. In addition, a few rock and coal trains can be seen throughout the week.

According to *John's Alaska Railroad* website, "Fairbanks gets only a freight train or two during the day. So just sitting around and waiting for one is not recommended. The train comes in from Anchorage anywhere from 7am to 9am. Usually something is heading south early to mid-afternoon. The oil train to the North Pole refinery usually heads out around 10am, returning between 1-3pm. Some days see a coal train to Eielson as well." Remember, the southbound *Denali Star* departs regularly from Fairbanks at 8:15am, so it should be easy to catch west of town (railroad south). The northbound *Denali Star* arrives around 8:00pm.

Alaska Railroad: History Through the Miles

Please note that the Alaska Railroad is private property, and your purchase of a train ticket or your desire to take photos does not give you the right to trespass or to act in an unsafe manner around the trains. There are some great locations to safely watch and photograph trains in Fairbanks. Below are some of them. Please enjoy your time in Fairbanks. However, do not trespass, watch for both rail and roadway traffic, and remain safe.

Fairbanks Alaska Railroad Station is often listed as a place to watch and photograph some of the train activity in town. Generally, the railroad parks their passenger trains here overnight, so early morning and late evening should have something to photograph. Freight trains heading toward the refineries generally pass just south of the station area. Note that the area is heavily patrolled by the railroad police. Do not enter the platform or train boarding area without identifying yourself to the security officer who is generally on duty.

Johansen Expressway Overpass is the bridge to the west (railroad-south) of the station, and it bridges over the junction through which all trains in Fairbanks pass. There is a walking and bike trail bridge on the west side of the overpass. Views are available of the main freight yard as well as the intermodal yard. Watch for the traffic as it moves through here as the road was built as a bypass for traffic to avoid the many stop signs and traffic lights on other area roads.

Richardson Highway parallels the line to North Pole and Eielson. When a train is known to be running, a chase can result in plenty of photos if you have a car.

College Road has a grade crossing on the North Pole route and there is a nice bridge just to the west. The only traffic on the route are the oil trains and trains to the military bases. Just standing around waiting on a train will likely result in a long wait and few photos.

Railfanning Fairbanks, Alaska

Charles Street has a grade crossing on the passenger train loop at Fairbanks, and most morning trains take it to turn toward Anchorage. It is a good morning photograph. However, note that much of the surrounding property is industrial, so watch for heavy truck traffic and stay off of railroad property.

Phillips Field Road runs along the south side of the Alaska Railroad shops area. It has some great views of anything sitting at the Alaska Railroad shops. However, be careful parking on the road shoulder as traffic can be busy.

Peger Road and a connecting public road that parallels the railroad access road along the main Fairbanks Yard provides some good views of freight activity. This area is west of the Johansen Expressway Overpass and can be accessed off of the Expressway.

University Avenue has some nice views from the grade crossing on the west side of Fairbanks. There is often some switching at the power plant located here. Just west of here are two overpasses with pedestrian walkways. There are some nice views as trains pass through the university grounds in this area.

Alaska Railroad: History Through the Miles

White Pass & Yukon Route Railroad #91 at Skagway. Photo by Sarah Jennings.

White Pass & Yukon #69 at Skagway. Photo by Sarah Jennings.

Other Alaska Railroads

One of the questions that many people ask about Alaska is if there were ever any other railroads. The answer is yes. Alaska has had a number of proposed railroads over the years, and many were actually built. However, almost all were built to serve specific mining or lumbering activities, and were abandoned when the business closed down. Here is a list of Alaska railroads actually built so you can research them more should you choose to do so.

Alaska Anthracite Coal & Railway Company – Organized in 1909 in Seattle, this railroad built 17 miles of standard gauge track in 1915 to access the Bering River coal fields. The major shipper was the MacDonald Mine on Bering Lake, and the coal was hauled to the terminal at Goose City, east of Katalla. The railroad operated an 0-4-0 16-ton locomotive and three 40-ton flat cars from 1917 until 1921. However, the railroad was considered to only be about 80% completed when the coal mine was closed. The railroad had actually started as the Catalla & Carbon Mountain Railway, begun in 1906 to serve the Bering River coal fields around Katalla (old spelling is Catalla).

Alaska-Gastineau Mining Company Railroad – The Alaska-Gastineau Mining Company was based in New York City and was the operating company for the Alaska Gold Mines Company. The 3-foot gauge railroad moved ore for the Alaska-Gastineau Mine/Perseverance Mine in the Silver Bow Basin, approximately 4 miles from Juneau at what was known as Thane. The narrow gauge line operated through a 2-mile tunnel to the mine 1914-1921. The Alaska-Gastineau gold crushing mill was approximately where the cruise ship docks are today in Juneau. Some of the old railroad grades and mill footings are still visible.

Alaska Home Railroad Company – At least nine railroads were proposed in 1902 to build to the new copper mines northeast of Valdez. By 1906, grading had begun on the Valdez-Yukon Railroad. However, the line failed to start service and the Alaska Home Railroad acquired the grading in 1907 in an attempt to build north. The Alaska Home Railroad was promoted to compete with the Copper River & Northwestern, and give Valdez a share of the growing copper business coming from the mountains to the northeast.

In September 1907, a locomotive arrived to operate on several miles of track. However, little was to ever be built as most of the route through Keystone Canyon, a bottleneck through which ran the only possible routing to Kennicott, was already claimed. When a survey crew entered Keystone Canyon in late September of that year, they were fired upon as trespassers, and one man was killed. Soon after, funds ran out and the operation was scrapped and the promoter jailed for fraud.

For those who are interested, you can still walk through an Alaska Home Railroad Company unfinished tunnel at Keystone Canyon, just north of Valdez. The tunnel is right next to the Richardson Highway with parking on the south end of the tunnel.

Alaska Juneau Gold Mine Railroad – Located just east of Juneau, a great deal exists of this railroad. Today, the Gastineau Channel Historical Society operates the Last Chance Mining Museum, located in the former Alaska Juneau Gold Mining

Company's historic Compressor Building. The compressor was used by the mining company from 1916 until 1944. The museum also includes the railroad's shop complex, which has numerous locomotives and rail cars that transported the gold miners to the mine.

In 1916, the Alaska-Juneau gold mine was built on the mainland near Juneau, and became the largest operation of its kind in the world. The mine closed in 1944, after producing over $80 million in gold. The railroad, powered by electricity, was seven miles long.

Alaska Marble Company – The Alaska Marble Company operated a 3200-foot tramway at its Calder Bay quarry on Prince of Wales Island. The quarry reportedly operated 1890-1910, although other sources state that the quarry opened in 1905.

Alaska Pulp Corporation – Located in Sawmill Cove about five miles east of Sitka, in southeast Alaska, this mill operated 1959-1993. The mill began when the site was sold to a newly formed company, the first Japanese investment in the United States since World War II. A barge dock allowed products to be shipped in and out by rail.

Apollo Consolidated Mining Company – This company operated a 2'-6" gauge railroad on Unga Island in Southeastern Alaska, connecting the Apollo-Sitka Mine with Delarof Harbor near Sand Point. Started in 1897, the line was abandoned about 1917. During its operation, the mine produced almost 150,000 ounces of gold. The railroad used an 0-6-0T which exists today in Corona, California.

Cliff Creek Coal Mine Railway – This small railroad was owned by the North American Trading & Transportation Company and was located 58 miles downriver from the Canadian town of Dawson City. In 1899, the 36-inch gauge line was built 1¾ miles from the Yukon River to the mine. The operation closed in 1904.

Coal Creek Coal Company Railway – This operation was located 54 miles downriver from Dawson City. The 36-inch gauge line was built 11½ miles from the Yukon River to the mine in 1903, replacing the Cliff Creek Coal Mine. From 1906 to 1909 the line was operated as the Sourdough Coal Company before becoming part of the Northern Light, Power & Coal Company. The mine closed in 1914 and the railway was abandoned in 1918.

Cook Inlet Coal Field Company Railroad – Coal was discovered in the area around Homer in the 1890s. The Cook Inlet Coal Field Company built a town, dock, and coal mine to sell coal. In 1899, the company built an 8½-mile narrow gauge (3'-6") line along the spit, connecting the docks to the coal fields along Kachemak Bay. While records show that the railroad only operated 1900-1907, and then as the Homer Mines Railroad 1907-1913, coal mining in the area continued until World War II.

Copper River & Northwestern Railway – The CR&NW celebrated its centennial in 2011, a festival attended by corporate officials of Kennecott Copper and rail enthusiasts from around the world. To get to the celebration in McCarthy and Kennicott, participants either flew in, or drove more than 60 miles of the grade of the former railroad, now the McCarthy Road.

The Kennecott mining area was named after the nearby Kennicott Glacier. Geologist Oscar Rohn named the glacier for explorer and naturalist Robert Kennicott during a U.S. Army survey in 1899. Kennicott died in Alaska on May 13, 1866, while working on the Western Union Telegraph Expedition looking for a route to build a telegraph from North America to Russia via the Bering Sea. The copper company also used the name Kennecott, but a reported "clerical error" resulted in a misspelling of the name when the company was incorporated, thus changing "Kennicott" to "Kennecott."

The Copper River & Northwestern Railway ("Can't Run and Never Will") was incorporated on May 16, 1905, and construction started the next year at Valdez. However, after some construction began, a better route was chosen from the port at

Other Alaska Railroads

Katalla, and Valdez was abandoned. The port location was soon changed again, this time to Cordova. In 1908, construction again began on the 195-mile line to the rich ore mines at Kennicott, with the line opening in 1911. As the ore grades declined and new ores were found in more accessible places, the mines, mill and railroad closed in 1939 (the last train ran on September 11, 1938). The cost of the railway was justified because the mines produced $200 million worth of copper ore during their operation.

Even after the abandonment, the tracks remained in place and the line was used by the U.S. Army and locals throughout World War II. A special railbus, built with a bus body on the frame of a 1938 Chevrolet, was used on the line for a few years. The Copper River & Northwestern Railroad "Autorailer" rail bus was saved and is currently in the Museum of Alaska Transportation and Industry at Wasilla.

Copper River & Northwestern Railway Autorailer at the Muesum of Alaska Transportation and Industry in Wasilla. Photo by Sarah Jennings.

The mill complex is located beside the Kennicott Glacier, inside Wrangell-St. Elias National Park and Preserve. The camp and mines are now a National Historic Landmark District administered by the National Park Service.

The Kennecott mill complex at the Kennecott National Historic Landmark District. Photo by Barton Jennings.

Council City & Solomon River Railroad – This railroad ended operations almost before they began. The railroad was first proposed and surveyed in 1902, with plans to build a line of 134 miles from Dickson, at the mouth of the Solomon River, to the mines at City Council, traversing the Seward Peninsula. The first 9 miles saw operation by fall 1903. In addition, a 34-mile spur from Dickson to Penny Creek was completed in 1906. During the fall of 1907, due to lack of funds and building materials, the railroad was abandoned. The tracks were destroyed in 1913 by a large storm.

Three CC&SR steamers still exist near Solomon. All three of the steamers, numbers 1, 2 and 3, were built for the New York Elevated Railroad as standard gauge 0-4-4T locomotives. They later became the property of the Western Alaska Construction Company before coming to the Council City & Solomon River Railroad. Today, they sit abandoned in the tundra, along with two passenger cars and 17 freight cars.

Golovin Bay Railroad – This 3-foot gauge railroad was built to serve the operations of the Wild Goose Mining & Trading Company in the Ophir Creek mining district, near Nome. The line was built by Charles D. Lane, who also built the Wild Goose

Railroad at Nome. Construction began in June 1902 and was completed on July 21st of the same year. The line operated between Council City and No. 15 Ophir Creek Mine, a total of eight miles. The line was abandoned in 1906 when mining in the area greatly declined.

Ketchikan Pulp Company – The Ketchikan Pulp Company built the first railroad in Southeastern Alaska and began operating it during March 1954. The line at Ward Cove (near Ketchikan), measuring two miles long, began at the entrance to the ferry slip and extended throughout the plant, providing access for the enormous quantities of chemicals and supplies required to operate a pulp mill on a year round, twenty-four hour a day schedule. According to the 1956 annual report of the company, "during 1956 more than 5000 railroad freight cars traversed this ferry slip to move some 60,000 tons of chemicals, supplies and equipment into the mill and some 130,000 tons of finished dissolving and paper pulp out on a journey by water and rail to customers in many parts of the United States and Mexico." The mill and railroad closed during the 1990s.

Rush & Brown Copper Mine Company – Located on Prince of Wales Island, this narrow gauge railroad hauled ore 2¾ miles to a deep-water harbor, known as Rush & Brown Harbor, at the head of Kasaan Bay. The Rush & Brown Mine was discovered in 1904 and ore was shipped almost continuously from 1906 to 1923 by the Alaska Copper Company. The mine closed in 1923 for lack of a convenient smelter to process the ore and due to low copper prices. According to a 1948 Bureau of Mines report, investigations to reopen the mine found that the railroad was completely deteriorated, except that about 2 miles of 16-pound rails remained. An 0-6-0 from the railroad still exists, stored at Fallon, Nevada.

Salmon Creek Railroad – Built by the Alaska-Gastineau Mining Company in 1913, this 3-foot gauge railroad extended approximately 3 miles, located just north of Juneau. Photos indicate that the railroad used a small Shay locomotive, an 0-6-0, and an

0-4-0T that still exists, stored at Fallon, Nevada. Reportedly, the railroad only lasted a few years before being abandoned.

Seward Peninsular Railroad/Wild Goose Railroad – The Seward Peninsular was part of a family of railroads in the area, all built to 3-foot gauge to serve area gold mines.

The Wild Goose Railroad was organized in 1900 to serve the Wild Goose Mining & Trading Company operations around Discovery and Anvil City. The first power was a pair of Climax locomotives. The 10-mile line, running from Nome to Anvil City, began to decline almost immediately with a reduction in area mining, and the company was sold in 1904 to the Nome Arctic Railroad. In 1906, the railroad again changed hands and became the Seward Peninsular Railroad, a project to build a railroad from Nome to the mining territory near Kougarok. Construction quickly extended the line to 87 miles long, but regular service ended in 1910. In 1922, Alaska bought the line and used it to move materials, including using dog-powered trains. The line was used by the military during World War II. During the 1950s, a tourist railroad, the Curly Q Line, operated on part of the line. Today, part of the grade is used as a road and several of the line's locomotives still exist in Chugiak, Alaska.

Treadwell Mines Railroad – The Treadwell Complex was once the largest gold mine in the world (1911-1917) and produced approximately $66 million dollars of gold. The 300 Stamp Mill was the largest in the world when it was constructed. To haul the ore to the stamp mill, a railroad was built that also connected the communities of Douglas and Treadwell. Treadwell was the community for the miners, with its own entertainment, pool, and bar. Douglas was the non-mine community and had its own businesses, school and post office.

The gold mining began when Pierre Joseph Erussard discovered gold on Douglas Island near Juneau. Later he sold his claim to John Treadwell for $400. After developing the mine, Treadwell sold his interest in the company for a reported $1.5 million in 1898. The mine and railroad operated successfully until April 21, 1917, when the mine flooded after a cave-in at sea level.

Other Alaska Railroads

White Pass & Yukon Route – Here is the short version of the history of this famous railroad. Built in 1898 during the Klondike Gold Rush, this narrow gauge railroad is an International Historic Civil Engineering Landmark, a designation shared with the Panama Canal, the Eiffel Tower and the Statue of Liberty. Originally operating between Skagway (Alaska) and Whitehorse (Yukon Territory), the 110 mile WP&YR Railroad was completed with the driving of a golden spike on July 29, 1900, in Carcross, Yukon. The company was a fully integrated transportation company operating docks, trains, stage coaches, sleighs, buses, paddlewheelers, trucks, ships, airplanes, hotels and pipelines. The WP&YR suspended operations in 1982 when Yukon's mining industry collapsed due to low mineral prices. The railway was reopened in 1988 as a seasonal tourism operation, hauling almost 400,000 passengers yearly on the first 67.5 miles (Skagway, Alaska to Carcross, Yukon) of the original 110-mile line.

White Pass and Yukon Route Railroad. Photo by Sarah Jennings.

Yakutat & Southern Railroad – The Yakutat & Southern Railroad was unique in that it didn't involve mining, instead it primarily hauled lumber and lots of salmon. On January 22, 1903, Seattle businessmen incorporated the Yakutat & Southern Railroad to construct a wharf and cannery, connected by a railroad. After being surveyed in 1904, a land grant was approved and construction started that spring. Ten miles of 40-pound rail was laid from Yakutat to a sawmill on the Situk River, with eventually 18 miles of track being built to Lost River. In 1905, the cannery had a capacity of 50,000 cases of salmon a year. The cannery went through several owners before becoming the property of Libby, McNeil and Libby (1913-1951). The Bellingham Canning Company took ownership in 1951 until selling it to the operation's final owner, Marine Foods Packing Company, which filed for bankruptcy in 1971. During the early 1940s, the U.S. Army used the railroad while building an airfield and garrison, accessible by railroad, about four miles southeast of Yakutat.

The Y&S hauled fish from the Situk Landing to the cannery in Yakutat for more than 60 years, generally operating only during fishing season, generally mid-May through October. When the train arrived at the Situk River, the fish were unloaded from the fishing boats and dumped into the gondola cars by a conveyer belt.

The first locomotive for the Y&S was a geared Heisler 0-4-2, No. 1092, reputed to have been used on the New York elevated railway prior to railway electrification. The Heisler was unsuitable, however, and was replaced in 1907 by a 2-6-2 Lima, No. 1057, built in 1907. In 1949, the Lima was retired, as it required two tons of coal to operate the round trip. The railroad then operated with a gas engine, the wheels and running gear from the Heisler, and a 1930 Packard sedan with flanged wheels. By the 1960s, the railroad operated using a 1949 Chevy truck with a large box on the back. The Y&S ceased operations before the cannery filed for bankruptcy in 1971. Much of the railroad still exists. A Yakutat park displays the Heisler diesel conversion, a Plymouth gas switcher, and Lima 2-6-2 #1057.

Photo by Barton Jennings.

Fairbanks Pioneer Park

Since many people who visit Alaska are looking for things to do, information about Pioneer Park at Fairbanks is provided. Pioneer Park is a 44-acre facility in Fairbanks that is intended to preserve the history of Interior Alaska, and Fairbanks in particular. It includes numerous museums, shops, and restaurants. Pioneer Park has no charge for admittance, although many of the individual museums do have a charge. Pioneer Park began soon after Alaska became a state when in late 1960 the Pioneers of Alaska requested public land from the State of Alaska. The plan for the land was to create a tourist attraction that showed historical Alaska exhibits. To manage the project, the Pioneers of Alaska formed the non-profit organization Pioneer Memorial Park, Inc. Almost immediately, several historic structures were moved to the property and efforts began to create a historic village explaining the history of Fairbanks. In 1965, another group known as the Alaska 67 or A-67 committee requested that the park be used for the 100th year celebration of Alaska's purchase from Russia. While seeking funding for the expanded park plans, the A-67 committee subleased the property and reopened the facility as the "Alaska 67 Centennial Exposition."

After the event, the Pioneer Memorial Park returned the property to the State of Alaska who immediately turned over the property to the City of Fairbanks. On May 1, 1968, Mayor Red Boucher of Fairbanks stated that the name for the park was now "Alaskaland." The name Alaskaland lasted more than thirty years, but there were many complaints that tourists often seemed to expect to find a theme park along the lines of Disneyland. With the theme of history and recreation, a push began in 1999 to rename the park. In October of 2001, approval was received to return the park's name to Pioneer Park and it became official in July 2002.

Today, the park is open year round, but most concessions are only open from Memorial Day to Labor Day, and generally only from noon to 8pm. Some of the major attractions in Pioneer Park include:

Harding Rail Car – This is the *Denali*, a railroad passenger car used by President Warren G. Harding when he visited the territory of Alaska in the summer of 1923. Harding was the first U.S. President to visit the territory when he came to celebrate the completion of the Alaska Railroad. President Harding arrived in Alaska by the *USS Henderson* on July 7, 1923. Harding and his presidential party started their visit in the Southeast at locations such as Metlakatla, Ketchikan, Wrangell, Juneau, Skagway and Glacier Bay. They then arrived at Seward on July 13 and boarded this car to tour the Alaska Railroad.

The Alaska Railroad supplied the presidential party a full train for their tour of Alaska. The train consisted of business cars A1 and B1; sleeper cars *Fairbanks*, *Talkeetna*, and *Anchorage*; diner car *Seward*; and compartment observation cars *Kenai* and *Denali*. Harding made a number of appearances between his arrival at Seward, his dedication of the railroad at Nenana, and his visit to Fairbanks on July 15, 1923. In poor health, Harding returned to Seward on the 17th and then returned to Portland, Oregon, via Vancouver, Canada (becoming the first president to visit Canada). At 7:35pm on August 2nd, Harding died suddenly in the middle of conversation with his wife while in San Francisco.

Pullman built this car as a Compartment Observation Car in 1905 (Lot no. 3205, Car no. 760). It contained four staterooms, one drawing room, a buffet room, card room, and observation room. The car was sold to Great Northern Railway on September 21, 1905 and it operated between Saint Paul and Seattle. GN sold the car to the Alaska Railroad in 1923 and it was renamed *Denali*. According to research on the history of the car, modifications were made to the car in 1928. It is believed that the buffet room and card room were removed to expand the observation room resulting in the change of two window configurations on the left side of the car.

In 1945, the car was converted into outfit car #003 and retired to a siding near Nenana. With the creation of Pioneer Park, the car was renovated and donated to the Pioneers of Alaska Igloo #4 in Fairbanks. The car was placed into storage, and kept there until it was damaged in a warehouse fire in August of 1966. During the 1967 Alaska Centennial Exposition in Fairbanks, it was installed at the park and received another renovation.

S.S. Nenana – This sternwheeler was launched at Nenana, Alaska, in May 1933, and operated on the Yukon and Chena Rivers as a towboat, mainly carrying cargo, but also passengers until 1952. The *Nenana* is 237 feet long, 43 feet wide, has a draw of just six inches, and once was rated at 1000 gross register tons. Like many of the Alaska riverboats, the *S.S. Nenana* was built to serve as a packet boat – carrying passengers, freight, and mail at the same time. The *Nenana* had accommodations for 48 passengers and 300 tons of freight. She also pushed as many as six barges loaded with merchandise. Reportedly, the *S.S. Nenana* is the second largest wooden vessel in the world today.

Reports state that the five-deck ship "made the 774-mile voyage from Nenana to Marshall, Alaska, every two weeks during her five-month season, traveling 24 hours a day. In the early fall or in poor weather when it was dark, a huge searchlight mounted on the steamship made forward progress possible. Her boilers were woodfired. Top speed was 17 mph downstream and 10 mph upstream. When under full steam, the boiler consumed a cord and a half of firewood every hour. About 200 cords of wood were carried on the cargo deck and 16 cords piled on the bow for ballast. In 1948, the boilers were converted to oil."

Alaska Railroad: History Through the Miles

The *Nenana* is considered to be the last and most luxurious of the paddlewheelers plying the rivers of Alaska and the Yukon. She became a museum as early as 1967 and has been under restoration since. Thanks to this work, "mahogany paneling and brass hardware gleam in the observation lounge." Today, the *S.S. Nenana* is listed as a National Historic Landmark.

S.S. Nenana in Pioneer Park. Photo by Sarah Jennings.

Chena Hotel – This two-story building has an interesting history dating to some of the earliest days of Fairbanks. The Palace Hotel originally stood near the corner of Cushman and Fourth Avenue. The name of the hotel was changed to the "Palace Hotel and Bathhouse" when bathing facilities were added and opened to serve local miners. The hotel was apparently never considered to be the best in town as it stood at the edge of the "red-light district," a row of small cabins on Fourth Avenue between Cushman and Barnette in which prostitution was tolerated behind a high protective fence. In 1906, fire destroyed most of the downtown buildings, but the hotel survived in nearly its original condition. In 1957, the hotel was renamed the Chena Hotel. With changes downtown, the building was moved to the park in 1967 and restored. It is currently used as a concession/gift shop.

Fairbanks Pioneer Park

Gold Rush Town – Since the park's founding, twenty-nine rustic cabins have been relocated and refurbished at Pioneer Park to create Gold Rush Town. Among these cabins are a few notable structures that include:

The *Kitty Hensley House* was built around the turn of the century on Eighth Avenue and moved to Pioneer Park in 1967. It resembles the small Queen Anne-style cottages of the western continental United States. Kitty Hensley was a friend of Captain Smythe of the *Florence S.* steamboat on which she and her daughter sailed for many years. Kitty died in 1931 and the local newspaper reported that her "friend" and "neighbor" Captain Smythe had been tending her fire during her brief illness. Hensley and Smythe never lived together nor legalized the union that gossips recorded for history. Even nearly three-quarters of a century after her death, Kitty is still not accepted into polite society. A hand-written sign over the staircase reads, "This cabin is not a tribute to Kitty but to the many kind and loving homemakers whose children and grandchildren are the solid citizens of today."

Judge Wickersham's House is listed on the National Register of Historic Places and was moved to Pioneer Park in 1968. On April 15, 1904, Wickersham bought the lot at the northeast corner of First and Noble Streets for $175 and built a house while he and his wife lived in a tent pitched at the front door of the house, with the first part completed by the middle of June. Leaving Fairbanks for the winter, the house was finished in June 1905. In 1906, a heating plant was installed as he and his wife planned to finally stay a winter in Fairbanks. Wickersham sold the house for $1500 in 1922. At the time the house was moved to Alaskaland in 1968, the original kitchen, woodshed, closet, porch and a north addition were believed to be too deteriorated to move. The kitchen was recreated in 1986. The original sitting room of 1904, now the dining room, and the parlor and northwest bedroom or study of 1906 have been restored.

The *First Presbyterian Church* arrived at Pioneer Park in 1966 when the church's congregation needed the original building site to build a two-story community center annex. The Presbyterian Church started when Dr. S. Hall Young arrived in Fairbanks in

1904 when only 500 people lived here. Dr. Young couldn't afford a downtown lot so he purchased one on the outskirts of town at Seventh and Cushman and gathered materials for the first church. In the 1930s, the church was moved further east on its site at Seventh Avenue and Cushman and turned to face Seventh Avenue. Sometime in those early years a front vestibule and large steeple were added. In 1931, a new building was constructed and the original building was moved to the back of the lot and used for Sunday school rooms.

Georgia Lee's House is thought to have once been an establishment of ill repute. The building started out in Nenana in the 1920s, but was moved to Fourth Avenue in Fairbanks in 1928. After its move to Pioneer Park, its interior was refinished "in the stylish manner reminiscent of its heyday." Today, the building serves as the park office and headquarters.

Doc Stearns' Cabin was built in the 1920s by the first veterinarian in Fairbanks on 6th Avenue. Doc Stearns was an avid moviegoer and also operated a small farm.

Gold Rush Town, Pioneer Park. Photo by Sarah Jennings.

Pioneer Air Museum – Housed in the Gold Dome at Pioneer Park, the organization began in 1979 and opened in 1992. The museum chronicles the development of flight in Alaska. The collection includes complete aircraft, mechanical parts, and many documents about the history of Alaska air flight.

The **Alaska Native Village Museum** takes a look at Alaska through the Athabascan culture. It houses such Native artifacts as a wolverine parka and traditional tools. A mural depicts life along the river.

Totem pole in the Alaska Native Village Museum area of Pioneer Park. Photo by Sarah Jennings.

Pioneer Museum, also known as Pioneer Hall, offers a glimpse of frontier Alaska. Pioneer Hall was built to represent the design of a fine 1900-era building and includes photos, documents and displays explaining the early days of frontier life in inner Alaska.

The **Alaska Salmon Bake** is located at the west end of Pioneer Park and is known statewide for generous portions of King salmon, steaks, and ribs grilled over an outdoor alder wood fire and rounded out with deep-fried halibut, baked beans, salad and blueberry cake. Both outdoor and indoor seating is available. The Alaska Salmon Bake is surrounded by what is known as Mining Valley, a collection of mining equipment and a working replica of a gold rush-era sluice gate.

Mining Valley at the Alaska Salmon Bake, Pioneer Park. Photo by Sarah Jennings.

Engine #1 in Pioneer Park, Fairbanks, Alaska. Photo by Barton Jennings.

Tanana Valley Railroad Museum

For rail enthusiasts, the highlight of Fairbanks' Pioneer Park is the railroad museum and their operating railroad. The Tanana Valley Railroad Museum was built and is managed by the Friends of the Tanana Valley Railroad (FTVRR). The FTVRR is a non-profit organization of volunteers. Over a period of eight years the volunteers restored and now operate Engine #1 at Pioneer Park. The $2.5 million dollar museum building was built in 2005 and opened to the public in 2006. The museum building consists of two parts: a large shop area to work on Engine #1 and other restoration projects, and a smaller area where there are displays and a short track to display #1 and other rail stock. This is a working museum where visitors can see what is going on in the shop and learn something about the engine and the Tanana Valley Railroad.

The Tanana Valley Railroad Museum shares track with a second narrow gauge railroad throughout Pioneer Park known as the Crooked Creek & Whiskey Island Railroad. The ride takes about fifteen minutes to cover two laps of the 0.6 mile route, built in 1967 as a part of the Alaska 67 Centennial Exposition. The regular boarding site is at the TVRR museum building. The museum features Tanana Valley Railroad #1, an 0-4-0 saddle tank, builder's number 1972, steam locomotive built by H. K. Porter & Co., on January 12, 1899. This steam engine was the first locomotive that operated in the Yukon and Tanana River drainages, beating the White Pass & Yukon. TVRR #1 first arrived in Fairbanks, Alaska on July 4, 1905. Currently, #1 operates on selected dates during the summertime at Pioneer Park.

When originally built, #1 operated near Dawson at various coal mines until Falcon Joslin bought it for his Tanana Mines Railway, where it ran locally from 1905 until the early 1920s. The Friends of the Tanana Valley Railroad was incorporated in 1992 to restore #1 to working order and they returned it to service on July 4, 2000. The running gear of #1 is all original, but the cab has been reconstructed and the boiler replaced, burning locally mined coal.

The early history of #1 is pretty clear; however its later history is a bit unclear. Built on January 12, 1899, by Porter, it was purchased new from company stock on May 5, 1899, by the North American Transportation and Trading Company. Its purpose was hauling coal from mines up Cliff Creek to the Yukon River (1.75 miles), about 50 miles downstream from Dawson City, Yukon Territory. It arrived in August of 1903 and stayed there until July 1903. It was sold to the nearby Coal Creek Coal Company of which Falcon Joslin was a major stockholder. The Coal Creek Coal Company mines were 12 miles by rail from the Yukon River. In early June, 1905, #1 was sold to the Tanana Mines Railway (TMR) (also a Joslin property) located at Chena, Alaska. It departed Coal Creek on June 5, arriving at Chena on July 4th, using a steam paddlewheel river boat and barge to make the move. Chena, the headquarters of the TMR, was first connected by rail to Fairbanks, ten rail miles away, when a Golden Spike was driven on July 7, 1905. By late fall 1905 (via a wye five miles from Chena) rails had reached 20 miles towards the gold mines, terminating at Gilmore. The financial backers of the TMR were the Close Brothers of London. In order to extend the railway beyond what the Close Brothers would finance, the railway was reorganized in 1907. The ownership of #1 changed to the Tanana Valley Railroad due this reorganization. The new funds enabled the TVRR to lay 25 more miles of track from Gilmore to extend the rails to Chatanika, Alaska. On November 1, 1917, TVRR was sold at a bankruptcy auction for $200,000, and then sold to the Alaska Engineering Commission (AEC) for $300,000 on December 31, 1917. In August of 1923, the AEC became the Alaska Railroad, with #1 still listed on its inventory.

TANANA VALLEY RAILROAD #1	
Class B-S, Light Four-Wheel-Connected Saddle Tank Locomotive Specifications Based Upon Porter Catalogs #9 & #12 and FTVR Website	
Track Gauge	36 inches
Cylinder Diameter	7 inches
Cylinder Length	12 inches
Boiler Pressure	150 psi
Tractive Force @ 140 psi	2915 pounds
Wheel Diameter	24 inches
Wheel Base	4 feet 8 inches
Length Over Bumpers	12 feet 9 inches
Extreme Height (includes whistle)	10 feet 11 inches
Engine Weight in Working Order	16,5000 pounds
Water Capacity of Saddle Tank	~200 gallons
Water Capacity of Boiler	~150 gallons
Fuel Capacity (in engine)	~250 pounds of coal
Minimum Rail Recommended	16 pounds/yard
Radius of Sharpest Curve, Recommended	35 feet
Radius of Sharpest Curve, Practicable	16 feet
Hauling Capacity @ 2.0% Grade	~50 tons

The actual retirement date of #1 is unclear, but there is some evidence that it was about 1924. On July 18, 1924, Alaska Railroad General Manager Lee Landis ordered the railroad to "discontinue the use of any narrow gauge equipment that has not been equipped with automatic couplers." This must have included #1 as to this day, it still has link and pin coupling. More evidence suggests a retirement date of 1924 as a letter from the railroad's Superintendent of Motive Power and Equipment to Noel Smith, Special Assistant to the Secretary of Interior, dated August 12, 1924, stated "Engine #1 – Purchased from coal road near Dawson in 1904 by the Tanana Valley Railroad. It is a small dinky and unfit for service." During FTVRR's restoration the truth of the statement "unfit for service" was confirmed.

Sometime later, but definitely by 1930, the steamer was given to the City of Fairbanks and placed on display by the old train station. It sat for almost four decades beside the downtown station before being removed in 1966, cosmetically restored, and placed on display at the Alaska 67 Centennial Exposition in 1967. Twenty-five years later, #1 was leased to the Friends of Tanana Valley Railroad for restoration, exhibition and operation. It returned to service on July 4, 2000. To haul passengers, the railroad has several small bench cars which seat approximately twenty adults each.

The Friends of the Tanana Valley Railroad shares track with the Fairbanks North Star Borough's historical park, Pioneer Park, the successor to the Alaska 67 site. Since the opening of the Alaska 67 Centennial Exposition, the historic park has operated another train, conveniently also of 3-foot gauge. This 3-foot gauge track was one inspiration to restore Engine #1. The Park today still operates Whiskey Island #67 (numbered for the centennial celebration), a Ford engine, gas-powered locomotive disguised as an 0-4-4 steam locomotive. According to data on the builder's plate, it was built in 1967 by the C.M. Lovsted Company of Seattle, Washington. C.M. Lovsted was a railroad parts supplier who also had a history of manufacturing and selling machinery and industrial elevators.

Tanana Valley Railroad Museum

Tanana Valley #1. Photo by Sarah Jennings.

The author enjoying the Tanana Valley Railroad Museum in Pioneer Park, Fairbanks. Photo by Sarah Jennings.

Engine #1500 at the Museum of Alaska Transportation and Industry in Wasilla. Photo by Barton Jennings.

Museum of Alaska Transportation and Industry

Another great place for anyone interested in the Alaska railroad industry to visit is Wasilla's Museum of Alaska Transportation and Industry (MATI). The Museum of Alaska Transportation and Industry is a non-profit organization and its mission is "the collection, conservation, preservation, display and interpretation of artifacts related to Alaska's transportation and industrial history." MATI was basically created to display and collect the machinery left over from the bursts of growth in Alaska's economy. Resources discovered meant that railroads had to be built, aircraft had to be assembled, and roads had to be cleared for the development to continue. After the resources were exhausted, the machinery used remained in the forest and tundra due to the high costs of transportation for removal of the equipment, while the workers moved out. MATI has gathered those machines left to rust and preserved them to educate the public and present an educational, historical account of the history of transportation and industry in Alaska and the people of the era.

A complete timeline of artifacts shows the progress that has been made through Alaska's history.

The museum features railroads, airplanes, boats, trucks and automobiles, as well as dog sleds and snowmobiles (known in Alaska as snow machines) – a full collection of Alaska transportation vehicles. Displays also include information on other Alaska developments such as the telephone and electrical industries. The role of the military in Alaska's development is also covered. Its aviation exhibits include aircraft from ultralights to a C-123. Several early aircraft engines are displayed, as are photographs and artifacts associated with Alaska's early flyers. Non-aviation exhibits include tractors, fire trucks, and other vehicles from the 1920s to 1960s; seven diesel locomotives and 20 pieces of railroad rolling stock; mining equipment; antique steam and gas engines; and boats. Most of this equipment is displayed across acres of museum property, while some are displayed inside the main museum building.

This museum features the original collection of the Alaska-Yukon Chapter of the National Railway Historical Society, and today includes more than 35 locomotives, passenger cars, and freight cars, plus numerous railroad displays. Included in this is the former Whitney Section House and the original "The Alaska Railroad" header from Whittier Tunnel.

Railroad equipment at MATI includes:

Locomotives

1000	Alco	RS-1	Alaska Railroad
1500	EMD	F7	Alaska Railroad
1604	GE	65-ton	US Air Force
1718	EMD	MRS1	US Air Force
1841	Baldwin	S12	US Air Force
1842	Baldwin	S12	US Air Force
7324	GE	45-ton	US Army "Alaska Railroad"

Railbuses

1205	Alaska Railroad	Used on Whittier Branch
no #	Alaska Railroad	Chrysler Fairmont Hy-Rail
no #	CR&NW	Chitina Auto Railer

Passenger Cars

5	Bureau of Mines	Mine Rescue
92	Alaska Railroad	Sleeper – 12-Sec 1-DR "Lake Minchumina"
K-603	Alaska Railroad	Troop Kitchen
S-107	Alaska Railroad	Troop Sleeper
X1305 (3)	Alaska Railroad	Rebuilt from troop car
X1701 (5)	Alaska Railroad	Troop car
X1710 (1)	Alaska Railroad	Rebuilt from troop car
X1831 (6)	Alaska Railroad	Troop Car
X1832 (2)	Alaska Railroad	Rebuilt from troop car
X1835 (4)	Alaska Railroad	Rebuilt from troop car

Other Equipment

6	Alaska Railroad	Jordan spreader
P24	Alaska Railroad	Flat car
0031	Alaska Railroad	Boom tender
0034	Alaska Railroad	Tender
0048	Alaska Railroad	Flat car
1018	Alaska Railroad	Wood caboose
1560	Alaska Railroad	Box car
X1666	Alaska Railroad	Tank car
2827	Alaska Railroad	Flat car
8019	Alaska Railroad	Box car
60432	Alaska Railroad	Hopper
no #	CR&NW	Wood box car
4027	NRC	Wood bunk car
7505	USA	Brownhoist crane
7508	USA	Brownhoist crane

Whitney Depot at the Museum of Alaska Transportation and Industry in Wasilla. Photo by Barton Jennings.

Motorcar #G757 at the Museum of Alaska Transportation and Industry in Wasilla. Photo by Sarah Jennings.

Photo by Barton Jennings.

Engine 557 Restoration Company

Another unique opportunity for the rail enthusiast is a tour of the restoration shops of the Engine 557 Restoration Company in Wasilla, Alaska. Locomotive 557 was one of 2120 S-160 class Consolidation 2-8-0 locomotives built for the U.S. Army Transportation Corp (USATC) between 1942 and 1945 for use in Europe and Africa during World War II. The S-160 was designed by U.S. Army Corps of Engineers Major J.W. Marsh, and the locomotives were manufactured by Baldwin Locomotive Works, American Locomotive Company and Lima Locomotive Works. The S-160 carried the nicknames of GI Consolidations or Gypsy Rose Lee locomotives (stripped down for action). During the war, a dozen S-160 locomotives were sent to Alaska to help handle the huge increase in freight movements over the Alaska Railroad. USATC 3523 arrived in December 1944 and quickly became Alaska Railroad 557. With the significant weather differences between Alaska and its intended European destination, 557 was modified with larger compound air compressors mounted on the front pilot; steam coils installed to heat the cabs; and a snow plow fashioned for seasonal use. Alaska Railroad 557 burned coal until it was converted to oil in 1954.

Alaska Railroad 557 was the last steam locomotive in regular service on the railroad. The primary reason for its survival was to help during highwater conditions in Nenana, where the

Tanana and Nenana Rivers regularly flooded the entire town and railyard. The 557 also continued in occasional service for special events such as the annual fair trains and excursions. When the locomotive was finally officially retired in 1964, Washington scrap dealer and museum owner Monte Holm purchased the 557. On June 14, 1965, the locomotive left Alaska from Whittier, where it was loaded onto the *Train Ship Alaska* bound for Everett, WA. Instead of scrapping the 557, Holm preserved it for school groups to witness steam engine history in action. Starting in the 1970s and running through most of the 1990s, Engine 557 was kept in running condition and parked at Holm's House of Poverty Museum in Moses Lake, Washington.

In 2011, Jim and Vic Jansen, owners of several Alaska-based transportation companies, purchased the locomotive from the Holm estate to ensure its return to Alaska. The Jansens donated the locomotive to the Alaska Railroad with the condition that it be relocated to Anchorage, rehabilitated and eventually put back into service. The Alaska Railroad arranged for ARR 557 to be moved back to Alaska via rail/barge service between Seattle and Whittier. The engine arrived in Whittier January 3, 2012, and was then moved to Anchorage on a railroad flat car later that day.

In June, the non-profit Engine 557 Restoration Company was formed to raise funds for, and to coordinate and oversee, the locomotive's rehabilitation. On August 15, 2012, ARR 557 was moved by an Alaska West Express truck and lowboy trailer from the Alaska Railroad Anchorage yard to the project facility in south Wasilla. Since the original oil tender was scrapped, it was replaced by an oil tender donated by the Alaska Transportation Museum. The bulk of the restoration work will be accomplished at the Wasilla-based project facility, formerly known as the Kenai Supply Building. Owned by the Alaska Railroad, the facility is located at 1400 E. Wasilla Shops Circle.

The goal is to re-establish the 557's full classic appearance as well as bring it into compliance with today's passenger rail regulatory requirements. Major costs include initial tooling, asbestos removal and abatement, replacing galvanized steel cladding, new insulation, boiler and tubing replacement and repair, gear

Engine 557 Restoration Company

inspection and repair, painting and positive train control (PTC) electronics. The cost estimate for restoration is $1.2 million. When the work is complete, ARR 557 will pull a few refurbished railcars on the Palmer Branch as an excursion or dinner train operation. When complications dealing with federal laws such as PTC signaling requirements are overcome, service could be expanded with charters on the ARR mainline..

Restoration of Engine 557. Photo by Barton Jennings.

Alaska Railroad: History Through the Miles

Steam engine drive rods being restored for Engine 557 in Wasilla.
Photo by Sarah Jennings.

Wild grizzly bear fishing for salmon near Valdez, Alaska. Photo by Barton Jennings – using a long telephoto lens!

The Wildlife of Alaska

As you ride the Alaska Railroad, you will probably see a large amount of wildlife – wildlife that is probably very different from what you are used to seeing. Diverse and abundant wildlife are central to Alaska's economy and people. Over 1000 vertebrate species are found in the state, sometimes in huge numbers. More than 900,000 caribou roam in 32 herds across vast tundra landscapes. On the Copper River Delta alone, five to eight million shorebirds stop to forage and rest each spring on their way to arctic breeding grounds. Alaska has 32 species of carnivores, more than any other state. Most of Alaska's fish and wildlife populations are considered healthy. In the rest of the nation, more than 400 species are listed as threatened or endangered. In Alaska, only 20 species are listed this way.

If you are interested in the birds of Alaska, the University of Alaska Museum has a list on their website which identifies 493 native birds. There are also several books available that provide information on these birds, including *Guide to the Birds of Alaska* by Armstrong, *Alaska Birds - An Introduction to Familiar Species* by Kavanagh, and *Native Birds Of Alaska* by Books LLC.

Just a few of the birds that are often seen include the Trumpeter Swan, Tundra Swan, Arctic Tern, and of course, the Bald Eagle.

You are very likely to see some of the larger mammals while riding on the train. These can include bear, moose, fox, Dall sheep, and beaver. A brief discussion of the major mammals is below, but for those wanting more details, check out the books *Mammals of Alaska* (Alaska Geographic Guides) by Doogan and *Recent Mammals of Alaska* by MacDonald and Cook.

Arctic Ground Squirrels are considered to be the largest and most northern of North America's ground squirrels. They generally live in colonies and create underground communities. They survive the long, cold winters by hibernating as much as 7 to 8 months. While cute, they are considered to be the "staff of life" for much of Alaska as almost everything eats them, including eagles, foxes, and grizzly bears.

Arctic Ground Squirrel. Photo by Barton Jennings.

Beaver are North America's largest rodent and live throughout all of Alaska's forests. Their dams and lodges can be seen in almost every stream. Beavers in the wild live about 10 to 12 years, and very old, fat beavers can weigh as much as 100 pounds. To survive, beavers must be assured of 2 or 3 feet of water year-round, providing a refuge from enemies and a way

The Wildlife of Alaska

to float and transport heavy objects such as branches and logs for food and construction. Food for winter use must be stored in underwater food caches during autumn. A beaver may work alone or with family members to build a dam, using piled logs and trees secured with mud, masses of plants, rocks, and sticks.

Black bears are the most abundant and widely distributed of the three species of North American bears. An estimated 100,000 black bears inhabit Alaska. The black bear is the smallest of the North American bears. Adults stand about 29 inches at the shoulders and are about 60 inches from nose to tail. Black bears can vary in color from jet black to white. Black is the color encountered most frequently across the state, but brown or cinnamon-colored black bears are sometimes seen in Southcentral Alaska and on the Southeastern mainland. Cinnamon-colored black bears are also common in Alaska's Interior. Some bluish-colored bears called glacier bears may be found in the Yakutat area and in other parts of Southeast Alaska.

Three black bear cubs follow their mother. Photo by Sarah Jennings.

Brown and grizzly bears are classified as the same species even though there are notable differences between them. Kodiak bears (brown bears from the Kodiak Archipelago) are classified as a distinct subspecies from those on the mainland because they have been isolated from other bears since the last ice age about 12,000 years ago.

Brown bears typically live along the southern coast of the state where they have access to seasonally abundant spawning salmon, which allows them to grow larger and live in higher densities than their grizzly cousins in the northern and interior parts of the state. Brown bears are usually larger than black bears, have a more prominent shoulder hump, less prominent ears, and longer, straighter claws. Brown bear colors range from dark brown through very light blond. Brown bears are the largest living omnivorous land mammals in the world.

Adult grizzly bear. Photo by Barton Jennings.

Caribou may be mistaken for some sort of deer by those seeing them for the first time, and they are in fact a unique type of deer. Caribou are the only member of the deer family in which both sexes grow antlers. In Europe, caribou are called reindeer, but in Alaska and Canada only the domestic forms carry the reindeer name. Technically, all caribou around the world are the same species, but there are seven subspecies. Alaska has only the barren-ground subspecies, but in Canada the barren-ground, woodland, and Peary subspecies are found. Caribou are herd animals, although lone individuals can be found, and keep moving to find adequate food. In summer, caribou eat the leaves of willows, sedges, flowering tundra plants, and mushrooms. They switch to lichens, dried sedges, and small shrubs (like blueberry) in September. Caribou have large, concave hoofs that spread widely to support the animal in snow and soft tundra. The feet also function as paddles when caribou swim. When they walk, their feet make a clicking sound.

Collared pikas are the only species of pika found in Alaska. The word pika is derived from the Siberian name for this animal: *puka*. In North America, they also are often called "rock rabbits." This is interesting since they are actually closely related to hares and rabbits. Pikas have stocky bodies, short legs, large round ears, and are almost tailless – and are actually very small, weighing less than half a pound. They generally live in colonies in mountainous terrain, often in old rock slides or around large boulders where protection is provided, usually with a meadow or patches of vegetation in the vicinity. They are generally out during the morning and late afternoon – listen for their short, shrill bark.

Coyotes are newcomers to Alaska. Coyotes were first noted in the state shortly after the turn of the 20th century, first reported on the mainland of Southeast Alaska and then slowly expanded northward into the upper Tanana Valley. The population peaked around 1940. Portions of the state with the highest densities of coyotes are the Kenai Peninsula, the Matanuska and Susitna valleys and the Copper River Valley. The coyote, like the wolf, is a member of the dog family and resembles a medium-sized shepherd-collie type dog. Distinctive features of the coyote are its sharp pointed ears that never droop, a sharp pointed nose, and long bushy tail. The legs of the coyote are generally slimmer and the feet smaller than those of a dog of comparable size. Coyotes average 22 to 33 pounds or about one-third the size of wolves.

Dall Sheep inhabit the mountain ranges of Alaska. These white creatures are most notable for the males' massive curled horns. Females (known as ewes) also carry horns, but theirs are shorter and more slender, and only slightly curved. Until rams reach the age of 3 years, they tend to resemble the ewes quite a bit. Dall sheep are common along Turnagain Arm just south of Anchorage, and in the Denali area.

Dall Sheep seen from a train near Turnagain Arm south of Anchorage. Photo by Sarah Jennings.

Foxes are found throughout all of Alaska, and consist of two types. The familiar **red fox** is found throughout Alaska, except for some of the islands of Southeast Alaska and the western Aleutians and is rare in Prince William Sound. It is native to Kodiak Island but is an introduced animal on many islands in the state as a result of fox farming operations in the early 1900s. The **arctic fox** is found in treeless coastal areas of Alaska from the Aleutian Islands north to Point Barrow and east to the Canada border. Both blue and white color phases occur, with the blue phase more common on the Aleutian and Pribilof Islands. The white color phase is more common in northern populations. Weighing less than ten pounds, their short legs and body, short ears, and dense winter fur give them a stocky appearance compared to the red fox. Arctic foxes shed their long winter fur in early April and are soon covered with short, brown summer fur. The change to winter white begins in September and is complete by November.

Hares are like giant rabbits, and there are two species in Alaska, both of which turn white in the winter. The **snowshoe**, or **varying hare**, is the most common and widespread of these. It is distributed over the state except for the lower Kuskokwim Delta, the Alaska Peninsula, and the area north of the Brooks Range. The **Alaskan hare**, also called the tundra hare, populates much of the western coast of Alaska, including the Alaska Peninsula, but has a spotty distribution along the Arctic coast and the north slope of the Brooks Range. Snowshoe hares are found in mixed spruce forests, wooded swamps, and brushy areas while the Alaskan hare is generally found on windswept, rocky slopes and upland tundra, often in groups. These big hares usually avoid lowlands and wooded areas. Snowshoe hares are somewhat larger than cottontail rabbits and average around 18 to 20 inches in total length and weigh 3 to 4 pounds. The ears are dark at the tips. The large hind feet are well-furred, adapting these animals for the deep snows of the boreal forests – thus the name "snowshoe." The Alaskan hare is larger at 22 to 28 inches in length and 6 to 12 pounds in weight. Hares are often called rabbits, and both are members of the family Leporidae. However, hares are born fully furred and with eyes open, while newborn rabbits are blind and hairless.

Lynx are the only cats native to Alaska, roaming throughout most of Alaska except for many of the major island chains. The lynx is a large, short-tailed cat, similar to the bobcat, but distinguished by its long legs, furry feet, the long tufts on the tip of each ear, and a black-tipped tail. The large broad feet function as snowshoes to aid the lynx in winter hunting and traveling. Their populations shrink and grow in direct proportion to the hare populations, their major food source.

Marmots are the largest members of the squirrel family in North America. Three species of marmots live in Alaska: the **hoary marmot**, the **Alaska marmot**, and the **woodchuck**. The hoary marmot can be found in talus slopes, boulder fields, and rock outcrops in alpine areas of Alaska, south of the Yukon River. The Alaska marmot lives in similar habitat throughout much of the Brooks Range, the Ray Mountains, and the Kokrines Hills (north of the Yukon River). The woodchuck digs its den in loess (wind-deposited soils) along river valleys in the dry lowlands of east central Alaska. The hoary and Alaska marmots can weigh 10 pounds and exceed 30 inches in total length while the woodchuck weighs between 2 and 9 pounds and may grow to be 26 inches long. The hoary marmot has a white patch above its nose while the Alaska marmot does not.

Moose are the largest member of the deer family, and are known as elk in Europe. The Alaska-Yukon race is the largest of all moose. An adult moose can range in size from 800 pounds (small adult female) to1600 pounds (large adult male), and they can be almost 6 feet tall. They can range in color from golden brown to almost black, depending upon the season and the age of the animal. Newborn calves have a red-brown coat that fades to a light rust color within a few weeks.

Young moose twins near Denali National Park. Photo by Barton Jennings.

Moose are easily recognized by their antlers, carried only by the males. Trophy class bulls are found throughout Alaska, but the largest come from the western portion of the state. The largest sized antlers are usually produced when bulls are 10 - 12 years old, but bulls can reach trophy size as young as 6 years of age. In the wild, moose rarely live more than 16 years. They are especially abundant on timberline plateaus, along the major rivers of south-central and Interior Alaska, and in recently burned areas that have generated dense stands of willow, aspen, and birch shrubs.

Mountain goats are sometimes confused with Dall sheep, but sheep prefer drier country. Dall sheep are not found in Southeast Alaska while mountain goats are. Mountain goats are easily distinguishable from Dall sheep by their black horns. Mountain goats can be seen south and east of Anchorage. The appearance of both sexes is much alike except that males are about 40% larger than females and have differently shaped horns.

Muskrats are one of Alaska's most visible and numerous furbearers. Often mistaken for a beaver at first glance, the muskrat's small size (less than a foot long and weighing less than five pounds) and rat-like tail are the most immediate identification marks. The highest populations of muskrat are in the broad floodplains and deltas of major rivers and in marshy areas dotted with small lakes, but are located throughout most of Alaska's mainland.

Porcupines are found throughout all of Alaska except the Alaska Peninsula and a few of its islands. Porcupines are second in size only to the beaver among rodents of Alaska. They are easy to identify due to their long quills. Porcupines are vegetarians, living off the inner bark of spruce, birch and hemlock and spruce needles in winter and buds and young green leaves of birch, aspen, cottonwood and willow trees during the spring and summer. They also feed on shed antlers and the bones of dead animals to obtain sodium and calcium, as well as things like plywood and tool handles.

Sitka black-tailed deer are smaller, stockier, and have a shorter face than other members of the black-tailed group. The average October weight of adults is about 80 pounds for females (does) and 120 pounds for males (bucks), although bucks of over 200 pounds have been reported. A Sitka black-tail buck's antlers are dark brown with typical black-tailed branching. Sitka deer are sometimes seen along the railroad south of Anchorage.

Sitka black-tailed deer. Photo by Barton Jennings.

Squirrels can be found in Alaska. The two types include the **northern flying squirrel**, a small nocturnal animal which can be found in interior Alaska, the northern and western limit of the species' range. The **red squirrel** can be found in spruce forests over most of Alaska.

Wolverine reside throughout mainland Alaska and some of the islands of Southeast Alaska. A relative of the mink and weasel, its scientific name means "glutton." Wolverines have long dense fur that is generally dark brown to black with a creamy white to gold stripe running from each shoulder along the flanks to the base of the tail. A white hair patch on the neck and chest is common. A wolverine will eat almost anything to survive and has no trouble hunting or traveling in Alaska's deep snows.

Wolves are pretty common in Alaska. Early taxonomists recognized about 24 New World and eight Old World subspecies of Canis lupus, with four subspecies thought to occur in Alaska. Only two Alaska subspecies are now recognized. The pelt color of Alaskan wolves ranges from black to nearly white, including every shade of gray and tan. Gray or black wolves are most common. Wolves in Southeast Alaska tend to be darker and some-

The Wildlife of Alaska

what smaller than those in northern parts of the state. In Southeast Alaska, wolves prey on the plentiful Sitka black-tailed deer, while in mainland Alaska wolves hunt moose and caribou. Adult male wolves in Interior Alaska generally weigh between 85 and 115 pounds, but will occasionally reach 145 pounds. Wolves reach adult size by their first birthday.

Many Alaska Railroad train crews will announce an animal sighting, and will sometimes slow or even stop so that passengers can view the animal. This is especially true for wolves, bear, moose, and Dall sheep. Don't hesitate to let the crew know if you see something interesting.

The Alaska Wildlife Conservation Center, located south of Anchorage at Portage, is a great place to see and photograph wildlife. Most of the animals are located in large pens where the animals can be easily photographed. The new bear enclosure features an overhead walkway, and a number of special events happen every day. More information is included in the explanation and history of Portage River at milepost 63.0 on the route from Anchorage to Seward.

Alaska Railroad: History Through the Miles

Fishing near Chena Hot Springs. Photo by Sarah Jennings.

Photo by Sarah Jennings.

View of Fireweed Mountain near McCarthy. Photo by Sarah Jennings.

For More Information

There are a number of sources of information about the Alaska Railroad, the communities that it serves, and the many attractions that the state offers. Many of these have very detailed websites which can help visitors, and those planning or dreaming of a visit. These include:

Alaska Railroad has everything from tickets to merchandise for sale, as well as tons of schedule information. The website also has some basic route descriptions and information about the future plans of the railroad. The Alaska Railroad Giftshop has branches at their Anchorage, Denali, and Fairbanks train stations. Each shop features apparel of all kinds from pajamas to jackets to T-shirts to hats, books and DVDs, model trains, posters, and collectibles of all kinds. You can also buy "authentic Alaska Railroad Souvenirs" through their website.

John's Alaska Railroad Web Page is THE source on what is happening with the Alaska Railroad, as well as the history of railroads in the state. This web page is updated almost daily with news items and as historical information is unearthed. Any research on Alaska's railroads should start here.

Travel Alaska is the official State of Alaska travel and vacation information site. They have information on just about every place that you could think of going in the state.

Visit Anchorage has lots of information about the various tourist attractions, lodging, and restaurants found in the Anchorage area.

Explore Fairbanks has lots of information about the various tourist attractions, restaurants, and lodging found in the Fairbanks area.

The Milepost describes itself as the "legendary Alaska trip planner and Alaska travel guide," and that may be understating its importance. Updated and printed each year, this huge book (800 pages) provides details about pretty much every mile of roadway in the state as well as most of the communities, and also includes route information for those driving from the "Lower 48."

Fairbanks Pioneer Park website has information about all of the attractions, shops and restaurants found in the park.

The Tanana Valley Railroad Museum operates the Tanana Valley Railroad Museum in Pioneer Park at Fairbanks. This website has all sorts of historic information on the Tanana Valley Railroad and the operating museum in Fairbanks. There is also lots of information on their steamer – Tanana Valley Railroad #1.

Museum of Alaska Transportation & Industry website has basic details about the museum's collection and events. The museum is located at Wasilla, about an hour north of Anchorage, and includes railroad equipment displays, as well as information about other modes of transportation and the industries they supported.

Alaska Wildlife Conservation Center is a nonprofit organization dedicated to preserving Alaska's wildlife through public education. Check out their website for photos of their animals and information about their future plans, including the release into the wild of their wood bison herd. For those wanting a guaranteed animal sighting, this is the place to go.

White Pass & Yukon Route Railroad has information on all of their passenger trains and every type of souvenir possible. While not a part of the Alaska Railroad, the WP&Y is an Alaska favorite and a part of many visitor's railroad experience.

About the Author

For almost three decades, Barton Jennings has been organizing charter passenger trains and writing the route descriptions, both for planning purposes and for the enjoyment of the passengers. These trips have been from coast to coast, often covering operations that haven't seen a passenger train in decades. In addition, he has written a number of articles about various railroads for rail hobby magazines. In 2013, Bart coordinated the rail operations of the convention of the National Railway Historical Society, which included a week of charter trains over the Alaska Railroad, and wrote the text for the convention guide book using pre-existing research and materials.

Bart has visited Alaska numerous times and has ridden the Alaska Railroad from end to end, taking detailed notes about the operation and what can be seen from the trains. He has been fortunate to get to know many of those who have known and researched the railroad. His basement has several rooms full of books, timetables and other documents about this and other railroads – important research items from a time long before today's internet. Today, Bart Jennings, after years working in the railroad industry, is a professor of supply chain management and teaches transportation operations. He also still teaches regulatory issues for the railroad industry, a way to stay in touch with the industry he loves.

This book is an outgrowth of all of these experiences and previous writings about the Alaska Railroad. Much of the information comes from internal railroad records, government and public records, railroad workers, and conversations with old and new friends. It is hoped that you enjoy your adventure with the railroad and that this book is of assistance in some ways – Alaska Railroad: History Through the Miles.

The author waiting for a train at Potter, Alaska.
Photo by Sarah Jennings.

www.ingramcontent.com/pod-product-compliance
Lightning Source LLC
Chambersburg PA
CBHW050626300426
44112CB00012B/1680